HARDPRESS.NET
HOME OF HARD-TO-FIND BOOKS

The Divine Authority and Perpetual Obligation of the Lord's Day
by Daniel Wilson

Address:
HardPress
8345 NW 66TH ST #2561
MIAMI FL 33166-2626
USA
Email: info@hardpress.net

THE

DIVINE AUTHORITY AND PERPETUAL OBLIGATION

OF THE

LORD'S DAY,

ASSERTED IN

SEVEN SERMONS,

DELIVERED AT THE PARISH CHURCH OF ST.
MARY, ISLINGTON,

IN THE MONTHS OF JULY AND AUGUST, 1830.

AND NOW PUBLISHED

AT THE REQUEST OF THE PARISHIONERS.

BY DANIEL WILSON, M.A. VICAR.

LONDON:

G. WILSON, ESSEX STREET, STRAND.

1831.

LONDON
IBOTSON AND PALMER, PRINTERS, SAVOY STREET, STRAND.

TO THE

RIGHT HONOURABLE AND RIGHT REVEREND

CHARLES JAMES,

LORD BISHOP OF LONDON,

THIS VOLUME,

COMPOSED IN CONSEQUENCE OF HIS LORDSHIP'S EXERTIONS
IN THE SAME GREAT CAUSE,

IS,

WITH EVERY SENTIMENT OF RESPECT AND DUTY,

DEDICATED,

BY

THE AUTHOR.

CONTENTS.

SERMON IV.

Revelations i. 10.—*Page* 84.

THE SABBATH TRANSFERRED BY DIVINE AUTHORITY, FROM THE SEVENTH TO THE FIRST DAY OF THE WEEK, OR LORD'S DAY.

SERMON V.

Ezekiel xx. 12.—*Page* 119.

THE PRACTICAL DUTIES OF THE CHRISTIAN SABBATH.

SERMON VI.

Isaiah lviii. 1, 2.—*Page* 147.

THE UNSPEAKABLE IMPORTANCE OF THE RIGHT OB-SERVATION OF THE SABBATH WITH THE EVILS OF THE OPPOSITE ABUSE.

a 5

SERMON VII.—*Page* 172.

Nehemiah xiii. 17. 18.

THE GUILT WHICH IS CONTRACTED BY CHRISTIAN NATIONS IN PROPORTION AS THE LORD'S DAY IS OPENLY PROFANED.

APPENDIX.

PASTORAL ADDRESS

TO THE INHABITANTS OF

THE PARISH OF ISLINGTON,

ON

NEW YEAR'S DAY, 1831.

My dear Friends,

Allow me to offer you the following Discourses, as a
new year's token of my sincere regard for your welfare.
It is with no feigned language that I wish you all the
blessings of the season of Christmas.   From the bottom
of my heart do I desire and pray, that the Nativity of
our Lord may be the source of joy to every one of you
all.   The incarnation and sacrifice of Jesus Christ is
the foundation of the Christian religion; and I trust it
is, and will be, the main object of my life and labours
amongst you, to bring you, by the grace and blessing of
God, to a practical obedience to this divine Saviour.   I
seize therefore, with eagerness, every fit opportunity of
addressing you both in public, and by the more familiar
means of a pastoral letter.   If I had health and time, I
should rejoice to visit you more than I do, in the retire-
ment of your families, and to enlarge that personal and
friendly acquaintance, which an experience of your
kindness for nearly seven years, has encouraged me to
improve.   But I must resign myself to the will of my

heavenly Master, who gives strength and opportunity to his servants as he deems meet. It is a consolation to me to reflect, that my labours are now divided amongst so many able and devoted clergymen, who delight to minister to you in the gospel. And I desire to be grateful for that measure of health, which enables me in general to take a share in the public duties of the church, and to devote myself still in various ways to your service.

The subject to which I now would request your attention is, as you are aware, the divine origin and perpetual obligation of the Lord's day—a topic so important in itself, and standing connected so intimately with the application of all the doctrines and precepts of Christianity, to ourselves and our families, that I trust you will permit me, after I have explained the occasion and plan of the work, to suggest some thoughts on THE AUTHORITY OF REVEALED TRUTH, as involved in it.

The substance of these sermons was delivered in the autumn of 1827. They were then three in number; and, when I was requested to print them, I was compelled to decline the invitation, from the full occupation which the " Lectures on the Evidences of Christianity," as you know, gave me. A new and more favourable occasion of treating the question occurred last spring. The Lord Bishop of London addressed a most able and impressive letter on the neglect of the Lord's day, to the clergy and inhabitants of the diocese. Public attention was instantly awakened. I lost no time in bringing this communication before you. The authority of the divine institution was urged, as you will remember, on the same Sunday, from all our pulpits; and you speedily formed an association for the better observance of the Christian Sabbath. The rules and regulations, after having received the Lord Bishop's approval, were signed by nearly four hundred of the most respectable inhabitant housekeepers ; and the committee and officers are now carrying into effect, in every kind and prudent method, consistent with the laws of our country, the great design. Encouraged by the prospect of these effective measures, I was induced to examine the whole subject more thoroughly than I had previously done. It grew upon my mind. I discerned more and more its immense importance, if we would honour God, preserve religion in the world, or save our own souls, and those of our family and neigbbourhood. I discovered also, as I thought, the sources of the more current objections; and at the same time their fallacy, when once the whole bearing of the argument from Scripture was understood. Thus I was led on to treat the question in detail. I delivered seven discourses in the months of last July and August. I was then so earnestly entreated to commit them to the press, that I have given almost all my retired time to this duty since. I have consulted our chief writers; have weighed again and again the difficulties which are alleged: and I hope I have succeeded in showing that, from the creation of man through all succeeding periods, one day in seven was appointed by Almighty God, as the season of special religious repose, and of public and private worship. I hope I have succeeded in showing that this appointment is essentially moral and immutable in its obligation, though, from the nature of the case, with so much of a positive character, as the determining of the exact proportion of time demanded. I hope I have succeeded in showing, that our Lord never relaxed, nor meant to relax, the law of creation or of the fourth commandment, but only to vindicate it from the false comments of the Jewish doctors, and leave it in more than its original dignity and force. I hope I have succeeded in showing, that the day of the observation of the Sabbath, under the gospel, was authoritatively changed by our Lord and his apostles, to honour the resurrection; and was in entire consistence with the original bearing of the institution, and the subsequent manifestation of the divine will concerning it.[1]

I was for some time doubtful, whether the argumentative air of the first four sermons, in which these points

---

[1] The result of this further study has produced considerable changes in the course of the sermons; and in one or two instances I have placed more appropriate texts at the head of them.

are established, was likely to be generally useful to you.
I thought that perhaps the objections had not spread far
in our neighbourhood'; and that the devout inculcation
of the practical duties of the Lord's day was the safer
course.   And indeed, in general, this is our best wisdom : not one in a thousand of our population ever heard
of Paley's objections.   Creation—the fourth commandment—the exhortation of the prophets—the custom and
doctrine of our Saviour and his apostles—the practice of
the whole Christian church—their own sense of gratitude for the spiritual blessings conveyed—the obvious
state and wants of man—the prospect of an eternal Sabbath in heaven,—are plain, common-sense arguments to
every pious mind ; or rather, matters of fact, which no
plausible theories can overthrow.

But on further reflection, I conceived that a discussion
of the main objections might not be unimportant to you.
We live in a reading age : we adjoin an immense metropolis.   The temper of the times inclines rather to intellectual pride, than to the sober exercise of the understanding in the obedience of faith.   Men catch at any thing to
escape from the sacred obligations of a day devoted to
spiritual religion, and the care of the soul.   The name
of Paley, and his just reputation in matters of his own
province, is seized with avidity.   Some late pamphlets
have detailed his statements with unwonted levity, and
yet confidence of manner.   The deplorable ignorance of
theology manifest in these publications, to all who are
versed in the inspired Scriptures, and who submit really
to their authority, forms no hindrance to the diffusion of
the poison amongst the young and uninformed.   The
youth in our universities, our tutors, our junior clergy,
are not altogether free from the contagion.   Open infidelity, semi-scepticism, profaneness, worldly-minded-
ness, unconcern for the soul, and a readiness to follow
what is new and daring, all lean the same way.   It
seemed to me, therefore, to be the duty of those who
adhered to the doctrine of the Bible, and the universal faith of the church, to come forward and enter their
protest against the gigantic evil.   This I have endea-

voured to do. I have interwoven, however, with the argumentative sermons, practical exhortations; and I have treated, in the last three discourses, the specific duties of the Christian Sabbath at length.

With regard to the authors to whom I have been indebted for aid, you will find most of them referred to, as I have had occasion to cite their authority. But the fact is, that the whole church of Christ, in the proper sense of that term, has maintained this fundamental point, in every age. Subordinate matters have, of course, been disputed: but the commanding truth of a day of religious exercise and holy rest, after six days' work, has through all the periods of our ecclesiastical annals, been acknowledged as of divine obligation.

Perhaps, the best single sermons, in a practical point of view, are those of Dean Milner, Archdeacon Pott, and Dr. Chalmers—the last is in the most powerful and awakening manner of its author, and of itself settles the question. Some essays of the late Mr. Hey of Leeds, seem to me the clearest upon the controversy—he confutes Paley in a masterly and conclusive style. The most elaborate work on the whole argument, as handled in his day, is perhaps, The Exercitations of Owen. The change from the last to the first day of the week is thoroughly defended, in his lucid and convincing way, by J. Edwards—to whom J. Mede's sermon should, by all means, be adjoined. Bishop Andrews on the fourth commandment, is an incomparable discussion—full of learning, the soundest judgment, and rich knowledge of the materials of his argument. Mr. Holden has, in a recent work, arranged most of the reasonings and conclusions of preceding writers. He gives a list of nearly one hundred and fifty. He has furnished a valuable compendium. The chief authors of any popularity, that have fallen in my way, who impugn the divine authority of the Lord's day, are Bishop J. Taylor, —whose mistakes are not confined to this topic, mighty and various as were his powers, and sound in many views his theology—and Dr. Ogden and Dr. Paley, whose names will not weigh greatly with those

who are acquainted with many other of their opinions.
The primary error of supposing the narrative in Genesis, to be by prolepsis or anticipation, is maintained by
Archbishop Bramhall—who, in part, redeems the fault,
by a bold and uncompromising defence of the divine authority of the Christian Sabbath.   Baxter confines himself to the argument from the example of our Lord
and the inspired authority of the apostles, which he
enforces in one of his very best treatises—omitting, but
in no way questioning, the proofs from the Old Testament. The judicious Hooker, Bishop Hall, Archbishops
Usher and Sharpe, Bishops Stillingfleet and Pearson,
Archbishop Secker and others, defend the generally
received doctrine, in their own profound and impressive
manner, though some of them treat it only incidentally.
The learned Horsley has three noble sermons on the
subject, in which he powerfully maintains the same
view.   I think he errs in considering the Sabbath an
appointment more of a positive than moral character.
Indeed, if I am not deceived in my judgment, this error
pervades almost all our writers, to the treatises of J. Edwards, and Hey. They too much concede, that the fourth
commandment is of a positive nature. That there is, as
I have said, something positive in it, may be granted—
from the nature of the case it could not well be otherwise
—but the positive part is as little as possible—so little,
that the grand duty of devoting some portion of time to
the immediate service of God is its main purport—the
commandment is moral *per se*—arises from the fitness of
things, and rests, like the other precepts, on the primary relation in which man stands to his Creator. The
opinion of the reformers is uniformly in favour of the
divine obligation of the Lord's day—Cranmer, Latimer,
Luther, Melanchthon, Calvin, Beza, maintain it with
one voice, though sometimes, especially at the early
period of the reformation, they support certain festival
days in common with it.

To refer to the authors where references to the question, or brief discussions occur, would be endless.
Lightfoot, Watts, Doddridge, Walker of Truro, Scott,

and most practical writers, have something valuable. I have found interesting papers in the 8th volume of the British Review, in the Encyclopædia Britannica, and the Eclectic Review of the last year. . The Bishop of Down and Connor has also recently published an excellent pamphlet on the subject, chiefly in refutation of the idea of an anticipated narrative, which he has treated with more force of argument than Hey or Dr. Dwight. This last name deserves especial notice — Dr. Dwight, as well as his illustrious countryman, Edwards, has honoured the American School of Theology—rapidly rising into importance—with a most convincing and able discussion of the question in all its branches, both theoretical and practical—this perhaps forms the best of our modern treatises ; though it would be unjust to Dr. Humphrey of Amherst College, to withhold a tribute of applause from his excellent Essays. I spare a direct reference to one or two publications in our own country of a late date, because I trust maturer reflection will lead the writers to withdraw statements which are alike insulting to revelation and injurious to the youthful student.

But I will not proceed. I have said so much, to show you that I have not been inattentive to the opinions of others—and likewise to suggest a course of reading to any of you who may have time for such an inquiry. The points upon which I hope I may have thrown new light, are the direct moral character of the fourth commandment—the importance and dignity given to the Sabbath even during the vigor of the Mosaic economy —the real bearing of our Lord's conduct and doctrine —and the way in which the change of the day was introduced by Christ and his apostles. These are not, however, essential to the main argument—whether I am right or wrong in my particular suggestions, the glory and obligation of the day of God remain the same.

And this leads me to notice the authority of revealed truth as connected with this subject, and forming its only true support. For it is on this footing I place the doctrine of the Lord's day—it is a part of God's mer-

ciful revelation of his will to man. You will perceive
that I make no compromise in the course of these sermons. I trust I am cautious on topics not essential to
the great truth itself: but on the main duty I dare not,
cannot, do not hesitate to speak my mind. I know it
is the opinion of many most excellent persons, that
whilst we yield not a moment the question of the divine
obligation in point of argument, we may yet better urge
its practical duties on the ground of expediency. In a
public letter addressed to the mixed inhabitants of an
immense metropolis, with the single view of exposing
the neglect of the Sabbath, it may be prudent to waive
this point, and proceed to the details of the deplorable
violations which abound on all hands—in this I bow
most implicitly to the sounder judgment of my Diocesan
—an address of that nature was undoubtedly not the
place for a theological discussion; and if I understand
his lordship aright, he fully maintains the divine authority of the institution. At all events my own case
was very different. I am assured that you will
agree with me that in the pulpit, and in the measures pursued in our several parishes, we can have no
hope of success, unless we place the duty on its only firm
footing, the express command of Almighty God. Expediency may obtain a decent compliance with custom,
but will never subject the affections. Expediency may
carry a man once to church, but it will not carry him
there twice, it will not regulate his family duties, it will
not suppress the Sunday recreations, the Sunday Newspapers, the Sunday parties, the Sunday dinners, the
Sunday journies, the general Sunday secularities. Expediency may conceal or controul some outward enormities, it cannot implant principles of religion, it cannot
inspire love to God, it cannot check weariness and inat-
tention, it cannot animate to prayer, it cannot change
the human heart.

To do this we must invoke the power of the supreme
Potentate, and all those aids and operations of grace
which he has promised as the accompaniments of his
own truth. That is, we must ascend from human to

divine agency. And here we see the importance of admitting duly THE AUTHORITY OF REVEALED TRUTH. Let me pause and take advantage of the occasion to urge on you this great topic generally, and not merely as it refers to the point before us.

The authority of religious truth as revealed in the Bible, rests on the infinite perfections of God who communicates it, on the relations in which man, his accountable and fallen creature, stands to him, and on the implicit obedience which his Creator and Judge demands. Revealed truth comprehends every thing needful for us to know in order to glorify God and attain salvation—it is inspired and dictated by the Holy Spirit—it is the remedy for the disorders of a ruined world—it is a system of infinite grace, in the person and incarnation of Jesus Christ offering himself a sacrifice for sins, and in the gift of the Holy Ghost as the source of life and holiness—it is a scheme of redemption formed " before the ages," and gradually developed in successive dispensations, according to the good pleasure of God.

Revealed truth therefore is not so much many doctrines, as ONE STUPENDOUS DOCTRINE OR FACT, branching off into various parts. It is identical, indivisible, immutable, eternal—and has been acknowledged in all its essential characters by the whole spiritual church. Like the various prismatic colours, though divided off into its several rays, it yet constitutes one splendid, pure, and unmixed effulgence. Receive this divine truth on the authority of God and by the grace of his Holy Spirit, and it works as the sovereign remedy of human woe. It illuminates, sanctifies, consoles, blesses the heart. It unites to Christ and to God in and through him, by the communion of the Holy Ghost. But if it be taken only upon the authority of man, it is weak, disjointed, incomplete, inefficient.

View this grand discovery in its different branches, and you will see how they constitute only one doctrine, founded on one stupendous fact.

The fall and condemnation of man, his accountableness, his impotency to any thing spiritually good, the deep, and, in a proper sense, total corruption of his nature, the misery and blindness, the disorder and enmity of the world, the propensity of the human heart to flesh, and self, and earthly pursuits, and its inability to recover itself to God and holiness—this is one part of essential truth—this is the case which redemption has to meet.

The person, glory, incarnation, sufferings and propitiation of the Son of God; his supreme divinity, pardon and justification by faith only, in his obedience unto death; acceptance and adoption through him: his mediatorial kingdom; his intercession at the right hand of the Father; union with him as the head of his church; love to him, gratitude, dependance, endeavours to honour him and imitate his example—these are another division—the centre of religious truth, that on which all redemption rests—salvation itself.

The personality and proper deity of the Holy Spirit, in the awful and mysterious union of the Father and the Son—his operations in the human heart—regeneration and conversion by his grace—sanctification in and through him as the author and giver of spiritual life—his offices as the Comforter, Teacher, Guide, Conductor of the church—this is another branch of the same series.

The Christian morals—obedience to God—the ten commandments, the rule of conduct—prayer—the church of Christ—the sacraments—and the ministry of the word—communion with God—a life of penitence, mortification of sin, watchfulness, growth in grace—support and consolation under the trials and afflictions of this life—the ascription of every thing effective in our salvation to the merciful will of God, and a humble dependance upon him to accomplish his work in our final redemption—these conclude the sketch of the scheme of revelation—these are the consequences and fruits of justification. All these truths are one—one remedy—one declaration of the infinite mercy of God—one scheme of salvation provided for man.

In connexion with this revealed truth, and the platform,

as it were, on which the machinery is erected, is the Holy Sabbath—coeval with man—the example of the Almighty proposing it to him—creation so distributed as to lay a foundation for it—the powers and faculties of rational and irrational creatures formed upon the supposition of it—the proportion of one day's rest to six of labour infixed in the order of this beautiful world by the Almighty artificer—this institution goes along with redemption—marks the season of religious worship, affords the leisure, sets to work the ministrations, collects all the materials for the diffusion of this truth and the celebration of the praises of its author—maintains the front and bearing of religion in the world—is the visible representation of Christianity, and the pledge of its heavenly reward.

Such is truth—such it has been held in every age—such it was held substantially and in a darker form from the period of the fall—such it was held by the martyrs and reformers of the sixteenth century—such it will be held to the consummation of all things.

What then, my dear friends, is the AUTHORITY of truth—of such truth—of truth so new, so harmonious, so sublime, so important—what its CLAIMS UPON THE CONSCIENCE? Is it to derive its force from secondary considerations? Is it to borrow its strength from human expediency? Doubtless the highest measures of expediency are found to attend our obedience to this revelation: and we fail not to urge in a subordinate view this motive. We tell men that Christianity has "the promise of the life which now is, and of that which is to come." But then we place not truth on this footing. We build nothing on the shifting foundation of expediency, where the corrupt passions of men are the casuists, and the corrupt example of the world the judge. We appeal to the consciences of men upon the sure and immoveable authority of the Eternal God. We cite the inspired word. Then we have a blessing; then God honours his own truth; then the Holy Spirit vouchsafes effective grace; then the human heart responds to the call; then the gospel brings forgiveness, peace, holiness, joy, salvation; then it becomes the instrument of conveying all the blessings of redemption to man. Its efficacy is derived from God its author; the Bible is the inspired record where He has placed it; and the Holy Spirit the blessed source of grace which he opens to the heart. And thus the doctrine of the Sabbath, in common with all the essential branches of truth with which God has connected it, becomes a spring of salvation to man. There is no revealed truth without a Sabbath for the meditation of it; and there is no Sabbath without the authority and command of God for its observance.

And do not imagine, my dear parishioners, that because revealed truth has been controverted, it is less binding upon the conscience. We clear it from misrepresentation—we answer objections—we silence vain reasonings—truth shines conspicuous through the intervening cloud, on every eye which is not wilfully closed to its beams. If we cannot remove every obscurity, its main features are distinct and refulgent still. There is enough of what is perspicuous in the Bible on all capital points, to outweigh difficulties on attendant questions.

The deity of Christ has been controverted, I admit—the doctrine of justification by faith has been controverted—the personality of the Holy Spirit, regeneration, the nature of the spiritual life, the influence of the love of Christ, the virtue of the sacraments, the blessed joys of communion with God, the hope of everlasting life—every thing has been controverted—even the truth of Christianity itself—and therefore the obligation of the Lord's day—has been controverted. But what then? Is truth less certain—less obligatory upon man? Ask only two questions, In what sense, and By whom has it been controverted, and all difficulty is removed.

For IN WHAT SENSE have these points been controverted? This divides off one half of the disputants. As to subordinate details, there is a wide field for variety of judgment. And it is in these respects, and no other, that truth has been disputed by real Christians. The order of the divine purposes—the union of man's responsibility and free agency with the operations of grace—the entrance and permission of moral evil—the mystery of the divine subsistencies, in the tri-unity of the Godhead—the narrow limits of the actual benefits of Christianity—the small apparent number of the elect—the apostacies of the east and the west—the condition of the heathen world—the disorders and scandals of the visible church—these and similar topics have ever been matters of dispute. But what is all this? It does not affect any one of the substantial verities of revelation. It is only saying that man is ignorant—that God has given us a revelation not complete in itself, but complete for the purposes he had in view—that this world is a probationary state—that an eternal judgment will rectify the temporary irregularities of the divine proceedings here—that truth is so revealed in the Scriptures, as to be a trial of our submission of heart to God—that all is clear as to practice and our application of it, though much is obscure as to theory and the supposed combination of things in the divine mind.

To keep, indeed, upon broad and acknowledged ground, is the dictate of wisdom, and the just inference from the perplexities of dispute. It is when we refine, that we differ. And this the Bible never does. There is nothing abstract, nothing little, nothing rigid and systematic, nothing recondite and metaphysical in the Scriptures. Truth meets us there in her simple majesty—enjoins on us implicit obedience—and promises peace and joy. And thus it is that the humblest Christian has most tranquillity of heart. Truth is the medicine of his soul; he feels, as he receives the doctrines of Christ Jesus the Lord, that he has found "the hidden treasure," that he has obtained the "pearl of great price," that he has discovered the source of life and felicity, that he has reached the true end of his being.

But when controversies relate to fundamental truth, then, I ask, BY WHOM are they raised? This is the

second question. Is it not by the heretic bringing into
the church the spirit of unbelief? Is it not by the Socinian, the Neologian, the Semi-sceptic, the proud as-
sertor of intellectual might? Is it not the insidious
opponent of the grace of God, the Pelagian or Semi-
pelagian controversialist, the secular theologian, the
disputer of this world? Do we not perceive in the
whole spirit of the opposition, that there is no due subjection of heart to revealed truth, that the authority of
God does not weigh, that it is man's opinions, not divine
revelation, which sway the judgment? See the hazard-
ous criticism, see the irreverent language, see the unholy tone of scorn, see the rash and sweeping conclusions, see the enmity to established sentiments, see the
absence of spiritual affections, see the love of ambition
and fame and the reliance on merely human lea rn ig
which betray the state of the heart.

The authority of revealed truth, in its commanding features, is, therefore, so far from being lessened by these
considerations, that it is greatly aug nted. Amidst
the wanderings of human opinion, the Bible is th nly
safe guide—amidst the follies of human conjecture, it
is the only authoritative wisdom—amidst the conflic-
tions of human reasonings, it is the only decisive jue   —
amidst the miseries and errors of human ignorance, it is
the only light that shines—amidst the doubts and mis-
givings of the human conscience, it is the only effectual
friend and counsellor.

And thus the plain and commanding doctrine of salvation by Christ Jesus, stands aloft and eminent above
the doubtful opinions of men ; thus the dignity and
obligation of truth is elevated above the region of doubt
and hesitation; thus the conscience of man is bound
to all the main particulars of that revelation which God
has made to his fallible and sinful creatures. The fall
of man, and his redemption in Christ Jesus, are thus
left with all their claims upon our faith ; and the Sabbath, as subservient to this great remedy, remains as
the distinguishing rite of revealed religion.

My dear friends, let me intreat you to examine

yourselves whether you have received the gospel in its paramount authority, and its salutary effects, as THE TRUTH OF ALMIGHTY GOD ?   With respect to the knowledge of your fallen and ruined state ; have you felt it, and are you feeling it more and more---as a sick person feels a painful and oppressive disease ?   Do you long for deliverance ?   Are you, in penitence and contrition, acknowledging your guilt and depravity, and imploring pardon and reconciliation with God ?

And as to the death and passion of our Lord Christ ; are you relying upon it with a lively and penitential faith ? Do you look for pardon and everlasting life only to the merits and sufferings of the divine Surety ?   Do you renounce heartily, and from a conviction of its worthlessness, your " own righteousness which is of the law," and do you trust simply to that Saviour who has become, by his obedience unto death, " the end of the law for righteousness to every one that believeth ?"   Do you desire with St. Paul, " to count all things but loss for the excellency of the knowledge of Christ Jesus the Lord ?"

And with regard to the work of the Holy Spirit ; are you imploring his secret and gentle, but effective and saving influences to impart spiritual life and feeling ; to " give you a right judgment in all things ;" and to infuse holy habits into the will and affections ?   Are you " renewed in the spirit of your minds ;" " quickened from the death of sin ;" " born from above ;" " delivered," not visibly merely, and sacramentally, but really and practically, " from the power of darkness, and translated into the kingdom of God's dear Son ?"

If you have any knowledge of these things, revealed truth in its majesty and authority has produced its genuine effects.   You bow with all the powers of your soul to the will of God in the Holy Bible.   The opinions and controversies of men weigh nothing against the infallible word of inspiration.   The Christian Sabbath becomes spontaneously your delight.   Faith receives implicitly the account of its institution—conscience responds to the command.   The Lord who appointed it,

b

has now prepared you to use it aright. There is a correspondence, a harmony between all the parts of truth and your own mind, which springs from the operations of grace there. The same God which indited the Bible has taught and sanctified your heart. Truth in the record of Scripture, and truth in your judgment and feelings, is written by the same hand.

If, however, this happy change—this conversion has not yet fully taken place in you—I mean if real religion is not yet seated in your hearts—then let me intreat you no longer to delay this great, this first duty of an accountable being, the care of the soul. I intreat you to remember the authority of truth—it claims your attention, it lays before you the most powerful body of evidences as to its divine origin—it promises you every aid in making your inquiries. The Bible is given to save your soul. Consider, I beseech you, the danger of trifling with conscience. Employ the interruption to worldly affairs which the weekly Sabbath affords, for studying your Bible, for examining your heart, for attending the public worship of God with greater devotion and more fixed attention. Be in earnest. Pray. Act as a reasonable being under a dispensation of mercy.

Above all, avoid that most perilous state of mind WHICH COMES TO NO CONCLUSION—which "halts"—and continues to "halt"—and at last "halts" systematically "between two opinions,"—which goes on for years with no opinion formed—no religion governing the soul—with unprofitable intentions of future penitence and faith—and a most insidious and fatal vacillation between God and the world.

I conceive there are too many in all large parishes, and therefore amongst my own beloved flock, in this state—the most opposed imaginable to the authority of revealed truth. They profess generally the Christian religion—they attend the means of grace—they respect their ministers—they admire the national church—they join in certain benevolent objects. In all this they do well. But they are not truly converted from the love

and service of sin and sensible objects, to the supreme
love and service of God in Christ Jesus. Truth has
not its just sovereignty in their hearts.

And how does this come about? There is a fallacy at work. They say of some parts of truth,
"I think them doubtful, they are controverted;" they
say of other parts, "I dread being a party man, I
fear going too far, I receive the general doctrines of the
church as they are commonly understood—I mean the
same—there is no difference; we all believe the gospel:" they say of certain duties, "I admit the expediency
of thus acting, but the time will not allow of it, my circumstances and connexions forbid; I am a man of
peace." Thus they strike a balance, as it were, between God and the world. They come to a compromise. They deny no article of the Christian faith ex-
plicitly; but all the spiritual, humiliating parts, they
evade—all the peculiar grace of Christ Jesus they
evade, all the glory and efficacy of the work of the Holy
Ghost they evade—all the real mortification of heart
to sensible objects and worldly pursuits they evade—
all the reproach of the cross, and the shame following
the humiliating doctrine of the gospel they evade!
Miserable subterfuges these—snares of the great adversary. What! are the opinions of men, or the fear
of a party-spirit, or the fashion of the day, or the standard of piety which happens to be reputable in a rebel
world, any sufficient arguments against the authority
of revealed truth? You are bound to yield to the call
and demand of your Creator and Redeemer, whatever
may be the consequences. It is this commanding claim
which I am most anxious to urge upon you. It is not
man, it is not this or that writer, it is not the church, it
is not ministers; it is GOD HIMSELF who speaks. Faith
is the submission of the soul to all he declares—and
therefore it is that faith is not an intellectual effort, or
a cold assent, but the cordial acquiescence and repose of
the understanding and will of man upon the Bible as the
word of the living God. It is the work of the Holy
Spirit in the human heart. To seek this blessing, I

most affectionately invite you, that you may know the things which belong unto your peace, and attain the blessings of salvation.

Nor is it upon the general body of my friends and parishioners merely, that I would press the authority of religious truth; I would turn to those who do admit this authority, and are endeavouring to act uprightly in obeying it, both as it regards the great scheme of salvation, and as it respects the holy season of the Lord's day, which is appointed to accompany it.

Let me guard you against the prevalent invasions of the authority of revealed truth which abound in the present day. I need not say any thing to put you on your watch against the neologism, the daring criticism, the love of novelty, the impatience of old-received truth, the pride of a false philosophy, the pretence that knowledge can sanctify and bless mankind, the questioning the plenary and unerring inspiration under which the Scriptures were written, and the rage for bold interpretations of their sacred contents, which are the spurious progeny of a time like the present.

I would rather caution you, with great tenderness, against more covert attacks on the authority of truth, by excess of statement—by over earnestness respecting the unfulfilled, and therefore inscrutable scheme of prophecy—by disproportionate attention to matters doubtful at the very best and not essential to salvation—by vehement assertions of our own particular sentiments on these points, and the public inculcation of them upon others. These are dangers to which I believe you are at present very little exposed. I rejoice to think of the simplicity of your faith, and your unfeigned subjection to the whole Bible in all its holy instructions. But I would caution you. The tendency of all such misplaced vehemence is to sap the authority of truth. It eats out the life and grace of religion. It occupies the time, distracts the thoughts, takes off the attention from God and Christ, and pardon and justification, and the Holy Spirit, and growth in holiness, and watchfulness and humility—and it gradually and unconsciously draws off the mind towards minute and subordinate points, which can never be settled, and if they could, would not change one duty nor one motive of the Christian life. My dear friends, I only suggest a hint. I speak to my younger parishioners and fellow Christians, as a father to his children. I do not say, " Study not the prophecies"—for I study them myself with increasing delight. I do not say, " Indulge not the most glowing hopes of the future millennial triumph of the church"— I indulge them myself. I do not say, " Expect not. the second coming, the second personal advent of our Lord"—I expect it myself—I watch or endeavour to watch with my " loins girded and my lamp burning." On all these points there is no difference of opinion. The danger is, when particular explications of the unfulfilled prophecies with respect to them, possess the mind— the danger is, when the imagination dwells, till it is inflamed, upon minute and secondary details on the time and manner of our Lord's approach—the danger is, when an hypothesis is first admitted into the mind, then admired, then defended, then made an article, or almost an article of faith—the danger is, when repentance, faith, love, obedience, communion with God, watchfulness, growth in grace, the discharge of social and personal duties, are insensibly jostled out of the mind ; and these new and subordinate matters thrust into their place. You do not mean this—you are not convinced it is possible. But let me beseech you to be on your guard. The human mind is a narrow place. The time we have for religious exercises is short. The corruption of man leans always towards theory rather than practice. Novelty, when it once gains the imagination, soon gets possession of the time and heart.

Unnumbered examples in ecclesiastical annals testify how the effects of a similar course (unconsciously admitted by the most pious persons) have exposed the church to the wiles of our great adversary. Three times in the course of thirty years, have I witnessed such a process myself. Whatever takes us off from holy repenting, holy believing, holy walking, holy

b 3

loving, holy watching, holy dying, is an artifice of that arch-deceiver. It is thus, in every period when they have arisen, that the church has been divided, that claims to miraculous powers have been made, that an inflation of mind has been produced, that the idea of a special inspiration has been imbibed, that all argument and expostulation have proved fruitless, that the Holy Spirit has been grieved, that scandals of the most fearful description have at length arisen, and the honour of Christianity been tarnished.

The wisdom, my dear friends, of the humble servant of God, is to take warning betimes ; to avoid the first steps—the succeeding may be beyond his power—but THE FIRST STEPS he may shun—and at the same time he must take care, that in doing so, he is not betrayed into any opposite extreme, equally dangerous though of another character.

The remedy is, THE AUTHORITY OF TRUTH—the soul subjected to God—the reason and conscience taking the simple, unsophisticated declarations of the Bible—stopping where God stops—and not first imposing human notions on this sacred book, and then calling those notions the Bible. To help us to walk safely in all these respects, we must pray much for the Holy Spirit, take counsel with friends, be willing to be ignorant of many things, mark the first admonitions of conscience, shun novelties, and fly before we are entangled in the net of the subtle foe.

But I have detained you too long. I hasten to return for a moment to the immediate subject before us.

As to the practical duties of the Holy Sabbath, I would only urge you and myself, my dear friends, to be continually on our watch against the growth of unfavourable habits. The more holy it is kept, the better. Let it be set apart for spiritual duties. Give it up exclusively to God. Obey the fourth commandment. Carry its injunctions into effect in your hours, your arrangements, your spirit, your influence, your example, your whole conduct.

Endeavour to make the duties of the day pleasant

and interesting to children and servants. Imbibe the Christian spirit of love, of tenderness, of the compassionate example of our Lord. Young persons cannot enter as you do, into all the reasons of the institution; but they can be attracted, led on, encouraged by degrees.

Do not open your minds to objections, when you have once been relieved from doubts—which I trust the following sermons may assist in effecting—Do not again admit them. Let the question be considered as settled—dismiss the controversy, close the debate; and give yourselves to the practical authority of truth. To listen to cavils, after you have come to a calm determination, is to tempt God. To dispute again, is to grieve the Holy Ghost. Life is too short for interminable bickerings.

With regard to public measures for observing the Lord's day, I need scarcely invite my kind neighbours to aid the new Association to which I have already adverted. I am sure I may rely on the heads of families, and persons in station and influence, to give effective directions that tradesmen bring home to them no articles of food, or other merchandise, on the Lord's day.

I am sure I need not entreat them to attend with their families, twice on the Sunday, the public worship of God.

I am sure I need not beg of them to avoid the reading of secular books and public newspapers, the writing of letters of business, the paying and receiving of ordinary visits, the indulging in worldly and vain conversation on the sacred day.

Nor is it necessary for me to say much to those of my parishioners who are engaged in the affairs of trade, to induce them to close their shops, their counting-houses, their offices, their books of account, on this blessed day. The divine favour will never prosper those who violate the divine command. The Lord's day is the tradesman's time of repose, of refreshment, of spiritual improvement.

But I conclude, Accept, my dear friends, my best

thanks for all your kindness. Pardon the unnumbered defects which have attended my honest efforts. Bear with me both as to the manner and matter of this address. It comes from my heart. Let mutual prayer bind us together more and more. We have seen things go forward now for nearly seven years with gratifying success. The division of the parochial districts has just been completed, and the ministers have recently read themselves, as incumbents, into their perpetual curacies. The schools for the poor, in the several districts, are nearly finished; and I trust the funds for paying for the buildings and discharging the ordinary expenses will not be long wanting. The District Visiting Societies and the Sunday Observation Society have been formed this year; as the Irish Education was during the last. The great national schools, the dispensary, and the maternal societies are pursuing their beneficial course. The Savings' Bank continues to receive the deposits of the frugal poor. The Mutual Assurance Society, from whatever cause, has failed in our particular neighbourhood. I trust some similar institution may soon succeed it, and be allowed to employ the sums contributed. We have also Bible and Church Missionary Associations in activity.

The Islington Proprietary School for the education of the upper classes in our neighbourhood, under the patronage of the Bishop of the diocese, has consummated our plans for the instruction of all orders in our parish, in sound religion.[1]

Now is the season, then, for supplication to Almighty God, to animate, to quicken, to aid with his blessing these introductory measures. All depends on his grace and mercy in the first place, and then upon

---

[1] I would remind my respectable parishioners of the duty of attending the meetings of the vestry—commonly not more than three in the year—if they would preserve the peace of the parish, or testify their gratitude to the noble-minded officers and trustees, who devote their time, their influence, and often their health, without fee or reward, for the high end of honouring God, and benefiting their fellow-countrymen.

the spirit of union and love amongst ourselves; upon the simplicity of the gospel being preserved; upon the humility in which we teach and preach, and in which you hear and obey, the truth; upon the real conversion of souls which is carried on; upon the fruits of charity and holiness which we produce, upon the patience with which we sustain the trials, and the perseverance with which we discharge the duties of life; and upon the ascriptions of praise and glory which we offer to our God and Saviour, for every thing good in ourselves and others.

For these and all similar ends let me entreat you to preserve the unity of the Church of which we are members. Experience, antiquity, and the history of former ages, are not to be indiscriminately rejected. Whilst we abhor the tyranny, the exclusive claims, the pretended infallibility, the impious reliance on human traditions, the superstitions and idolatry of the church of Rome, let us remember there is such a thing as "a church;" there is such a thing as "the keys of "the kingdom of heaven;" there is such a thing as "doing all things decently and in order;" there is such a thing "as submitting ourselves to those who have the rule over us;" there is such a thing as "rejecting a heretic, after the first or second admonition;" there is such a thing as "a false apostle." Man wants aid— he wants something to fall back upon. The right of private judgment, and the capacity of judging wisely, are very different matters.

If our own Protestant reformed Communion, then, is a branch of Christ's true universal church—with whatever subordinate defects, for there is nothing perfect in this world—to preserve the unity of it, is, I am persuaded, conducive to the glory of God and the edification of our souls. Liberality, in the proper sense of the word, I love; but indifference, disorder, negligence of Scripture discipline, I would shun and avoid. I merely say this, my dear friends, to caution you against any who would sow divisions. Conscientious dissentients I reverence. I give them the full freedom which I claim myself. I have acted with them most cordially in all matters of common concern, ever since I came amongst you. In the Bible, the Mutual Assurance, and the Sunday Observation Societies, I rejoice in their co-operation. I aim at no proselytism; and I heartily wish them, this new year, a return of every temporal and spiritual blessing. But I am anxious to discharge my vows to the church of which, from conviction, I am a member. I believe it to be in the main most scriptural. I believe it to be one great instrument of upholding pure religion in this country. I believe it to tend to sanctify and elevate the state with which it is allied. I believe it to be calculated, if the more abundant dew of the divine grace rest upon it, to be more than ever the source of blessings to our own people, and amongst the nations of mankind. I am persuaded much error prevails as to the importance of its mild and paternal order and discipline, in the propagation and maintenance of Christianity. A church referring every thing meekly to Scripture as its standard—and a church thrusting itself into the place of Scripture, and blasphemously assuming the authority of God—are as distinct as two things can well be. The one is a principal means of upholding the faith of Christ in the world, and tends to the glory of God—the other overthrows Christianity and tends to a base superstition.

But I will not proceed. I bid you farewell. I entreat your prayers on my behalf. We stand on the margin of eternity. I cannot long hope to have strength for any considerable efforts for your welfare. Whilst we have time, may we labour with all diligence; and may each Lord's day, as it revolves, be spent better than the preceding, and prepare us more for that "rest," that celebrating of a Sabbath—" which remaineth for the people of God."

I am,

Your most affectionate Minister and Friend,

D. WILSON.

SERMONS.

SERMON I.

THE INSTITUTION OF A WEEKLY SABBATH IN PARADISE, AND ITS CONTINUED AUTHORITY UNTIL THE DELIVERY OF THE MORAL LAW.

GENESIS II. 1—3.

Thus the heavens and the earth were finished, and all the host of them.

And on the seventh day God ended his work which he had made; and he rested on the seventh day from all his work which he had made.

And God blessed the seventh day and sanctified it; because that in it he had rested from all his work which God created and made.

THE glory of God is peculiarly connected with 'the due observance of the day which he is pleased to call his own, and on which he has suspended, in every period of the church, almost all the practical effects of that mighty salvation which he has provided for man. The Christian sabbath is one main distinction of the gospel dispensation, as the Jewish was of the Mosaical, and the patriarchal of the first revelation of the divine will to Adam. The profanation of that day goes to annihilate all the blessings of reve-

B

lation.   It leaves the world without any visible token
of the authority of Christianity, and strips the church
of the best means of openly testifying its faith and
obedience.   If the sabbath be taken away from the
mass of mankind, no time is left for religious duties,
for the worship of Almighty God, domestic piety,
the instruction of children, the visiting the sick and
needy, the reading and hearing of the gospel, the celebration of the sacraments, the preparation for that
rest of heaven of which it is the pledge and foretaste.
Without it, the remaining classes of society would
never, in fact, allot a time for those duties, which
being left open, would not be obligatory; nor could
they sustain with effect the honour of religion in their
families or the world.

Christianity is indeed abridged and summed up in
the weekly return of the day, when its solemn services
and duties are performed.   As real piety declines in
any country, this symbol of it is forgotten or contemned ; as it revives in its doctrines and spirit, men
awake again to the value of those means of grace, of
which the Sabbath is the first in importance and
dignity.   .

The divine authority of a weekly religious rest has
ever been one of those primary truths in which the
universal church has most generally agreed.   Its institution in paradise and its insertion in the moral law,
have given it an authority on the consciences of men
which nothing has been able to shake. Christian states
have hitherto, without exception, recognized it, and pro-
tected their subjects in the peaceable enjoyment of its
repose.   The disputes of controversialists have chiefly
affected subordinate questions, and have left the divine
authority undisturbed as an article of the general faith
of Christendom.   The neglect of its practical duties
has, indeed, from the corruption of man, been but
too common in every age ; but open assaults upon the
origin and continued obligation of the day itself, have
been rare till of late years.

Now, however, the spirit of covert scepticism or

lukewarm Christianity, has not spared this most ancient of institutions. Not content with impugning the
separate doctrines and mysteries of Revelation, it
makes bold to call in question that sacred season when
all those doctrines and mysteries are inculcated. The
platform and arena of religion is taken from under
our feet—the great external distinction of the Christian
faith is annihilated—and man, erring sinful man, is
deprived of his day of repose and recollection, and
turned adrift to learn his Christianity and celebrate
its rites, as chance may dictate and expediency persuade. And though most of the opponents of the
divine authority of the Sabbath are ready at present to
allow its importance, and are loud in their admiration
of those public services which custom and the laws of
our country enjoin, yet the tendency of their writings
is to sap the principle on which all this rests, to take
men off from the firm footing of conscience and the
command of God, and transfer them to the sandy
ground of human recommendation and casual example.

The duty of the minister of the gospel, under such
circumstances, is plain. He is bound to instruct the
young with more care than usual in the doctrine of the
Holy Scriptures on this great question. He is bound
to examine the more popular and mischievous objections. He is bound to state what real difficulties rest
on the subordinate points of the inquiry. He is bound
to assure the poor and simple in his flock, that they
may rely on the grounds of their former faith. He is
bound to recall the intelligent and elevated classes
from the fatal course on which they are seduced to
enter.

And in honestly attempting this, he may look for
the blessing of Almighty God, who only permits his
truth to be assailed in different ages, by different classes
of error, in order to prove and try our faithfulness,—
in order to carry on, in fact, that system of moral pro-
bation and discipline which he has been pleased to establish in this world, and which is apparent, not in

this question only, but in every other connected with the evidences, the doctrines and the precépts of Christianity. God has indeed left things so in the Bible, says Bishop Butler, that his will is plain to the humble inquirer, but obscure and difficult to the proud—that there is darkness enough on secondary matters and points not connected with our immediate duty, to be the occasion of excuse to the unwilling; whilst there is sufficient light to guide the sincere and docile.

For it is to practice that the doctrine of revelation on this subject, as well as every other, tends. The day of rest, not in its theory, or even its divine obligation, but in its holy duties and in its peculiar blessings, is the object which it has in view. And to this we shall direct all our attention, as soon as we have cleared our way through those arguments which are necessary as an introduction to practical exhortation. In this respect it is that the theory and doctrine of the Sabbath, its divine authority and perpetual obligation, are so important. They are wanted as a ground-work. When this is firmly laid, we raise our superstructure with safety.

The whole subject, then, of the Christian Sabbath divides itself into two parts—THE DIVINE AUTHORITY of a day of weekly rest—and THE MANNER in which that day should be observed under the Christian dispensation. The former question will occupy the first four sermons; the latter, the last three of the present series.

In the first division we shall have to examine the foundation on which the duty rests, that is, the grounds we have for believing that a seventh portion of our time, now termed the Lord's Day, and formerly called the Sabbath, is required by Almighty God to be dedicated to his immediate service; and the nature of the objections raised by our opponents. In the second division we shall point out the practical duties of the Christian Sabbath, the unspeakable importance of observing them, the evils of the opposite neglect, and the necessity of personal and national repentance, if we would avert the Divine displeasure.

We enter, then, now on the first general branch of the whole question.   Here the points which most decidedly establish the divine authority and perpetual force of a weekly day of rest, are—the institution of it in Paradise, its solemn insertion in the decalogue, the position it holds under the Mosaic law, the energy with which the prophets insist upon it as one of the primary and universal obligations of religion, and the observance of it by the apostles, divinely directed to found the Christian faith, and by all the primitive Christian churches, immediately instructed by them.

The chief difficulties which our adversaries oppose to these arguments are, that there are no vestiges, as they assert, of the observance of a Sabbath in the patriarchal ages—that therefore the narrative of its institution in the book of Genesis, is by anticipation; that it was not established, in fact, till the time of the ceremonial law, and then merely formed a part of that preparatory economy; that we have no express command for the observation of it, or of any day in lieu of it, in the New Testament; that our Lord repealed it by his doctrine and conduct, of which the change of the time of its celebration is, as they maintain, a sufficient proof; and that, finally, the example of the apostles and the primitive Christians, gives it only the force of a moral expediency, subject to the regulations of each Christian church, in each following age.

Such is the state of the question.   Our opponents proceed on the silence of Scripture during the patriarchal ages : this we shall show to be an unsound argument; and shall prove that it was instituted in Paradise and revived and re-established in the wilderness. [1]   Our opponents insist that it is a ceremonial appointment appended to the Mosaic dispensation : we shall show that it was inserted in the immutable law of the ten commandments before that dispensation ; that it was exalted during the course of the Mosaic economy above all merely typical institutions, and was enforced by the prophets as of universal obli-

[1] Sermon 1.

gation. [1]   Our adversaries say there is no express command for it under the New Testament, whilst the doctrine and conduct of our Lord virtually repealed it : we shall show that no new statute was to have been expected ; and that our Saviour honoured it on all occasions, and only vindicated it from uncommanded austerities. [2]   Our opponents consider the change of the day as a proof of its abrogation : we shall maintain, that this was in itself a subordinate point ; and was altered upon the authority of the Lord of the Sabbath.   Finally, the example of the apostles is reduced by our adversaries to a mere commendation of the observance : we shall show it to have a divine obligation derived from the inspiration under which they acted. [3]

These topics will occupy four sermons.   We shall in the present one confine ourselves to THE ORIGINAL INSTITUTION OF A WEEKLY SABBATH IN PARADISE, AND ITS CONTINUED AUTHORITY, TILL THE DELIVERY OF THE MORAL LAW.

Our text contains the history of "the first Sabbath." [4]   No sooner were the heavens and the earth finished, and Adam placed in the garden of Eden, than God blessed and set apart, as our text asserts, one day in seven for his own immediate service.   He " who knew what was in man," and who had a right to all his obedience and love, was pleased to appoint that six portions of his time should be allowed him for his ordinary labour, and the seventh exclusively devoted to religious repose, and the exalted duties of communion with his Maker.

Every circumstance connected with this first institution is calculated to give us the highest idea of its essential and moral character.   The whole controversy hinges here.   The universal obligation of the Sabbath is not disputed, if it be proved that it had its origin

[1] Sermon 2.   [2] Sermon 3.   [3] Sermon 4.
[4] The opinion of the venerable translators of the English Bible is manifest, by the above title being given in the contents of the second chapter of Genesis.

in paradise.   And how men of gravity could ever persuade themselves that a narrative so express was merely inserted in the chapter from which our text is taken, by a figure of speech, whilst the Sabbath was never in fact heard of till two thousand five hundred years afterwards; is one of those startling positions for which the perverseness of man's fallen nature can alone account.   The notion of an anticipated history seems first to have been broached by the Jewish doctors, in their zeal to magnify the Mosaical ritual. [1] Their folers in modern times, especially one popular writer, [2] have failed to establish any satisfactory case.

The absence of any vestiges of the observance of a Sabbath during the brief history of the patriarchal ages, is a species of argument which, if it were ever so well sustained by the supposition on which it proceeds, is wholly without force, as we shall presently show.   It will be proper, however, to proceed in order. Let us state,

I. THE DIRECT REASONS why we believe the Sabbath to have been instituted at the time when the sacred narrative begins.

The transactions of the seventh-day immediately follow those of the sixth, precisely as those of the sixth follow the fifth—the history is chronological, unbroken, complete. This is the reason, Each day's work comes in order. As on the first day the chaotic mass and the light were called into being; and on the second the firmament was created; and on the third dry land was made to appear; and on the fourth the sun and moon were ordained to shine; and on the fifth the fishes and winged fowl filled their several elements; and on the sixth the terrestrial animals, and man, the Lord of the lower creation, were made; so on the seventh God " ended his work "—" rested from all his work "—and " blessed and sanctified the seventh day, because on it he had rested

[1] Owen. Exercitations.
[2] Dr. Paley.   Archbishop Bramhall was the chief supporter of this notion in the century before last.

from all his work which God created and made." These were the transactions of the seventh day, which come as directly in succession after the preceding, as any of the other days. And can we, then, be at liberty, merely because we think subsequent notices of its observation should occur in the history of the patriarchs, to transfer an event thus recorded in a regular series of transactions, to a period two thousand five hundred years distant? We might as well break asunder the links of the history of the creation, at any other period, as at this. We might as well suppose that the heavens and the earth were not created, or that man was not formed on the days which the sacred history records. We might as well imagine that the sun and moon did not begin to shine as soon as they were made, as that the Sabbath was not granted to man at the time which is assigned to it.

The whole foundation of faith is overturned by such a process. If in a plain historical narrative, and especially a series of successive actions, we are not to believe that the events really occurred as they were affirmed to have occurred, the Bible is no longer a clear and safe guide, but an enigma and a riddle. The plain literal common-sense interpretation of the history of the Scripture is indispensable to faith.

But in the present case we have yet further reasons. The distribution of the work of creation into its parts would be deprived of its object and end, if the institution of the Sabbath is expunged. For why this distribution, but to mark to man the proportion of time allotted him for his usual labour, and the proportion to be assigned to religious exercises? As the narrative stands in the Scripture, all is consistent. The six days' creation, the seventh day's rest, have their relative place. They teach man a great moral and religious lesson. Take away the first Sabbath, and all is left incomplete and detruncated—the object in which it terminates is wanting.

Again, where is the example in Scripture of any instituted commemoration not beginning from the time

of its appointment? Did the passover wait two thousand years before it was celebrated, after the deliverance which it was designed to commemorate? Did
circumcision under the Old Testament, or baptism and
the Lord's Supper under the New, remain in abeyance
for centuries before they were acted upon? And shall
the commemoration of the glories of creation be
thought to be suspended for more than two thousand
years after the occasion on which it was appointed had
taken place? And especially as the reason for the
celebration existed from the beginning; related to the
whole race of mankind more than to the Jews;
and was indeed most cogent immediately after the
creation—for in the following ages sin had marred
the Almighty's work.

One is ashamed to urge more arguments in such a case
—but what meaning, I ask, had Moses in his reference
to six days' labour and a seventh day's Sabbath, as matters familiarly known, at the time of the miraculous
fall of manna before the giving of the law, if there had
not been a preceding institution? Or what is intended
by the citation of the very language of my text in the
fourth commandment, if the reason there assigned had
not really reposed on facts—" For in six days the
Lord made heaven and earth, the sea and all that in
them is, and rested the seventh day; wherefore the
Lord blessed the Sabbath day, and hallowed it"—
where it is to be noted, that the words are not, " the
Lord blesses and hallows;" or, " will bless and hallow;" but, " wherefore the Lord BLESSED the Sabbath
day, and HALLOWED it," at the time that " he rested"
from his creative work. Add to this the language of the
apostle in his Epistle to the Hebrews, where he takes
for granted that the original rest of the Sabbath began
when " the works were finished from the creation of the
world;"[1] and we have the strongest moral certainty that
the narrative of the institution of the Sabbath in paradise[2] is and must be literally interpreted.

[1] Heb. iv. iii.
[2] The opinion of the Reformers on this subject is uniform.

But it is further objected, that, allowing this account to be in its natural place, it contains no enactment of a Sabbath—it states merely that God blessed and hallowed the seventh day, but for what purposes it does not affirm.

But we ask in reply, for whose use then did the Almighty bless and hallow the seventh day—what is the meaning of God's condescending to say that he "rested and was refreshed after the six days' work"—what instruction do we derive from the division of creation into six portions, followed by a seventh of repose? Were not all these done for the sake of man, the reasonable, intelligent creature of the great artificer? Did the Almighty rest for his own sake, or bless and hallow the seventh day, that he within himself might observe it? Unreasonable, if not impious, are such suppositions. God's working six days and resting the seventh, were doubtless designed to be of general and universal use in determining the proportion of time to be severally devoted to human and divine duties—by them the conduct of mankind was to be regulated—by them God intended to teach us that we should, after his example, work six days, and then rest and hallow the next following—that we should sanctify every seventh day—that the space between rest and rest, between one hallowed time and another, among his creatures here upon earth, should be six days. [1] And indeed there is no other sense in which the word "sanctified" is used in the Old Testament, when employed with respect to inanimate things, or to persons fulfilling an office or function. Thus the priests, the tabernacle and all its furniture, days of fasting and penitence, &c. were declared to be sanctified, when

---

Luther says, If Adam had continued in innocency, yet he would have had a sacred seventh day. Beza says, that the day of the Sabbath continued from the creation of the world to the resurrection of our Lord, when it was at length changed by the apostles into the Lord's day. I need not go on.

[1] J. Edwards.

they were separated from common employments, and set apart for the especial service of God. This is the uniform import of the terms : when it is said, therefore, that God blessed and sanctified the seventh day, it means that he set it apart and consecrated it for religious rest, and annexed the promise of his special blessing to the discharge of its duties.

And this meaning, which common sense requires, is rendered certain by the exposition of its terms in the fourth commandment, where the minute injunctions with regard to the Sabbath expressly repose upon the words of our text, which it cites and explains.

The objections to the received faith of the church on the institution of the Sabbath in paradise, you see, are weak and nugatory. They have not even a shadow of proof. Not one person in a million of those who read the sacred narrative, would ever dream that it was an anticipated history, or that it did not imply a most decisive command to keep holy the day of rest.

Here, then, we fix our foot. Now let us turn from facts to

II. THE JUST INFERENCES to be drawn from them as to the glory and dignity of the Sabbath.

We learn from them, first, its ESSENTIAL NECESSITY to man as man. Though Adam was in a state of innocence, his all-wise Creator saw it necessary to call him off from even the moderate and gentle labour of dressing and keeping the garden, to the immediate contemplations and exercises of religion. Adam loved God " with all his heart and soul and mind and strength"—he required no season of repose to withdraw his mind from the eagerness of worldly pursuits, in the sense in which we require it, nor to recreate his body from excessive toil—and yet the Sabbath was necessary for him. Judge from this of its essential moral character. Judge from this how indispensable it is to fallen man, with that propensity to earthly things which now weighs down his soul, and that aversion and enmity to communion with a holy God which sin has superinduced.

Consider, further, that it was the FIRST COMMAND given by God to Adam, as soon as ever the work of creation was finished. Man never was without a Sabbath. The moment there was a creature formed capable of knowing and serving God, a special time was assigned for that end. The Sabbath is coëval with the human race. It takes precedence of the prohibition of the tree of knowledge. It rests on the essential relation of a creature with his glorious Creator.

Observe, further, that this command was not merely made known to man, in some of those ways in which his Maker afterwards communicated his will, but it WAS PLACED, AS IT WERE, ON THE FOOTING OF CREATION ITSELF. By the Almighty hand all nature might have been called into being in an instant. The distribution of the work over six days, followed by the repose on the seventh, was to infix this grand principle in the mind of every human being, that after six days labour, one day of religious rest should follow. God worked in a certain order, that man might work in the same; God rested at a certain time, that man might rest likewise. In this glorious manner is the law of the Sabbath graphically set forth; this is the distinction which crowns the brow of the Queen of days. We have already noticed the proof this furnishes of the Sabbath having been instituted at the time assigned in the sacred story; but we now deduce from it the importance and dignity of the appointment itself. It is an appointment not written merely by inspired men, not graven on tables of stone, not indented in lead on the rock for ever, not uttered in the first instance from the summit of the mount by the voice of the Almighty and amidst the thunders and terrors of Sinai—but infixed in the creative order of the universe, inscribed on the heavens and earth, exhibited in the radiant character of the six days' work, associated with every commemoration of the wisdom and glory of God, promulgated with the majesty and example of the great Lord of all

—and therefore requiring no subsequent enactments, except to incorporate it with the various dispensations of religion, and revive it when forgotten, that it may go on and accompany man so long as he continues upon earth.

We learn also, from this order of creation, that man was made, not for constant and unrelieved employment, or for earthly pursuits chiefly, but FOR LABOUR WITH INTERVALS OF REPOSE, and IN SUBORDINATION TO THE GLORY OF HIS GOD: man was formed not for seven days' toil, but for six—man was formed not for secular and terrestrial pursuits merely, but for the high purpose of honouring God, meditating on his works, and preparing for the enjoyment of him for ever. The essential nature of the institution obviously lies in the proportion of time fixed by his beneficent and all-wise Creator—for his body six days' labour, for his soul one day of religious rest; and this corresponds with his compound nature —his intellectual and moral part calling him up to the exalted and delightful offices of religion, and his bodily and animal part requiring recreation and repose. The Sabbath is the spiritual badge and charter of man.

What a dignity, then—what an importance—what an obligation attaches to this sacred day! Well may it be admitted by our chief opponent, that if " the divine command was actually delivered at the creation, it was no doubt addressed to the whole human species alike, and continues, unless repealed by some subsequent revelation, binding upon all who come to the knowledge of it."[1]

III. Let us next show that, THERE ARE TRACES OF THE OBSERVATION OF A WEEKLY REST DURING THE PATRIARCHAL AGES. For it is upon this assumption, as we have stated, that the idea of an anticipated narrative is founded. " There are no vestiges,

[1] Paley.

not a single allusion," say our opponents, " of the
knowledge of a sabbatical rest, till the Mosaical law;
and therefore the account in the book of Genesis is
by prolepsis."

We allow that there are no express notices of a
weekly Sabbath as observed by the patriarchs.   We
allow that the detailed scenes in the lives of Abraham
and Jacob are without any direct declaration on the
subject.   That there are allusions and vestiges we
shall presently show.   But we admit the difficulty
so far as the objection is founded.   But what does
it amount to, even supposing it be conceded in all its
extent?   Would the loss of. the original law of the
Sabbath for two thousand five hundred years, amidst
the corruption flowing from the fall, prove that no
such law had been enacted at the creation?   The original law of marriage was lost during a much longer
period, but was it the less re-asserted by our Saviour,
as the primary and binding appointment of the Almighty?   But we admit not that the observation of
the Sabbath was wholly forgotten during this period.
The objection can only pretend to rest on the silence
of Scripture.   Now to argue from that silence, is
most unfair and most injurious to the interests of revelation.   An objection derived from things not being
expressly mentioned so often as we might please to
expect, is wholly inconclusive.   No mention is made
of sacrifices from the time of Abel till the deluge, a
period of fifteen hundred years, nor from the arrival
of Jacob at Beersheba[1] till the deliverance from
Egypt, a space of two or three hundred more; but
does this prove that sacrifices were not offered?   We
read nothing about circumcision from the death of
Moses to the days of Jeremiah, an interval of eight
centuries; but does any one imagine that circumcision
was not performed?   No mention of the Sabbath occurs in the histories of the books of Joshua, Ruth,
first and second of Samuel, and first of Kings, which

---

[1] Gen. xlvi. 1.

are so much more detailed than those of Genesis; and yet this was during the Mosaical law, when the institution was confessedly in its fullest vigour. The ordinance of the red heifer, again, is never once noticed from the period of the Pentateuch, till the close of the Old Testament; but the apostle refers to it, and argues from it in the New, as a rite well known, and in constant use. Even in the book of Psalms and in the Prophets, the Sabbath is seldom expressly mentioned, except when the neglect of it provoked the indignation of the Almighty.

So little force is there in the objection, even allowing it all it demands. It is not for us to prescribe to the Almighty how often, or under what circumstances, any of his commands should be repeated. It is enough for us to know with regard to the Sabbath, that it was instituted in the most solemn and resplendent manner. From this we may justly infer, that the observation of it was never wholly lost amongst the descendants of Seth, and in the line of Abraham, and the other patriarchs; though the celebration of it is not expressly recorded. It is thus we deduce from the continual offering of sacrifices, that that institution was divinely appointed, though we have no express mention of that appointment. The cases, indeed, of sacrifice and of the Sabbath are in one respect similar. The record is not complete : but we infer what is wanting from what is expressly stated. Of sacrifice, the celebration by the patriarchs after the deluge is perpetually recorded, though we have no direct account of its institution. Of the Sabbath, the original law is distinctly given, though the continued observance by the patriarchs is not expressly mentioned. If objections are urged on the ground of these omissions, it is surely permitted to us to reply, that from the celebration of sacrifices by Abel and the patriarchs, we justly infer its divine appointment : and from the glorious and singular institution of the Sabbath, its subsequent observance by the holy seed.[1]

[1] Owen.

But we are proceeding too long upon the concession that there are no traces in Scripture of a weekly
rest, from the creation to the time of Moses.   For in
truth there are traces, faint, perhaps, if taken by themselves and separated from the first record of the institution in paradise, but sufficiently discernible in
that connexion, for the purpose of rebutting a mere
objection.

The very first act of divine worship after the fall
affords indications of a day of religion.   Cain and
Abel brought their offerings " in process of time," as
the common reading has it, but literally, and as it is
in the margin, " at the end of the days."   Thus we have
in the sacred narrative, the priest, altar, matter of
sacrifice, motive, atonement made and accepted, and
appointed time—indications these entirely consistent
with the supposition of a previous sabbatical institution, and indeed proceeding upon it—for that is the
meaning of the expression, " at the end of the days."
But one division of days had been yet mentioned, and
that was of the days of the week, the Sabbath being
the last or seventh day—we may, therefore, reasonably suppose that holy season to be here termed, " the
end of the days."

Again, we read that "men," in the days of Seth,
(two hundred years, perhaps, after Abel's sacrifice,)
" began to call upon the name of the Lord," or, " to
call themselves by the name of the Lord;" and four
hundred years later, " that Enoch walked with God"
—terms of large import, and which, when illustrated
by the eleventh chapter of the Hebrews, where the
faith of the patriarchs in the divine order of creation
is so highly extolled, are, to say the least, entirely
consistent with the observation of a day of religious
worship.

We come to the flood.   Sixteen centuries have
elapsed since the institution of the weekly rest.   And
now we find the reckoning by weeks familiarly referred to as the ordinary division of time.   The Lord
said unto Noah, " Yet seven days, and I will cause it

to rain upon the earth." And again, " It came to pass after seven days, that the waters of the flood were upon the earth." These passages occur in the seventh chapter. Then in the next, when the flood is decreasing, Noah sent out a dove, which returned; he then stayed " yet other seven days," and again sent it forth. And again in the same terms, " And he stayed yet other seven days," and "sent forth the dove out of the ark for the third time, which returned not again to him any more."[1] Surely here are vestiges by no means doubtful, not only that days were reckoned by portions of seven, but that the use of that method of calculation was familiar in the line of the patriarchs. Nothing can be more certain than that the return of seven days brought something peculiar with it; and we judge it probable, from the institution of the Sabbath, that that peculiarity was the day of sacred rest.

Accordingly after the flood, the tradition of that division of time spread over all the eastern world— Assyrians, Egyptians, Indians, Arabians, Persians, unite with the Israelites in retaining vestiges of it. In the earliest remains of the heathen writers, Hesiod, Homer, Callimachus—the sanctity of the seventh day is referred to as a matter of notoriety. Philo, the Jew, declares that there was no nation under heaven where the opinion had not reached. The days of festival solemnities among the heathen had in all probability this source. Indeed, as the obscure notices of the original state of man, of the fall, of sacrifices, of the deluge, were scattered amongst the remotest nations, so also faint traces of a weekly religious rest are discernible. The very number seven, in Hebrew and the kindred languages, is expressed by a word which primarily signifies fulness, completion, sufficiency; and was probably applied to a week because that was the space occupied in fully completing the work of creation.

[1] Gen. vii. 4, 10; viii. 10, 12.

But we come to the history of Abraham. Here it is deserving notice, as we pass, that the rite of circumcision was to be performed after the lapse of seven days from the birth ; but the commendation of Abraham's example, " That he commanded his children and his household after him, to keep the way of the Lord, to do justice and judgment," implies that there was a way prescribed by the Almighty, and certain observances in which consisted justice and judgment, amongst which the Sabbath was probably the chief. But in the more full declaration afterwards made concerning him to Isaac ; " That Abraham obeyed his voice, and kept his charge, his commandments, his statutes, and his laws ;" the terms employed are so various, as to be by no means naturally interpreted of the ordinances of circumcision and sacrifice only, [1] but to include, as much as if it were named, the charge and law of the Sabbath.

We come to Jacob ; and few, I think, can doubt, that when he uttered the devout exclamation, " This is none other than the house of God, this is the gate of heaven ;" and then vowed, that the " stone should be God's house"—he alluded to what was customary with the pious patriarchs, the worship of God in a stated place, and on a stated time—the Sabbath ; without which, a house of God would be a term of little meaning ; but with which it would indeed be the pledge and anticipation of heaven. Even Laban seems to have had the notion of a weekly division of time ; " Fulfil her week, and we will give thee this also." [2] But I will not dwell on more particulars. The numerous, the almost perpetual notices of places, of altars, of sacrifices, of the worship of God, of solemn titles given to particular spots, all confirm the supposition, which is the only reasonable one, that the sabbatical institution was not unknown to the patriarchs. We may notice the case of holy Job, as confirming this, who, remote as was the place of his

---

[1] Gen. xvii. 12 ; xviii. 19 ; xxvi. 5.   [2] Gen. xxix. 27.

abode, more than once reminds us of " a day, when the sons of God came to present themselves before the Lord." [1]

So utterly gratuitous is the assumption that the observation of a day of religious worship was unknown to the patriarchs. Probably the very notoriety of the institution might be one cause why the sacred historian judged it unnecessary to dwell on particular recurrences of its observance. At all events, the mere silence of Scripture afterwards, can never be fairly alleged against the previous institution of the Sabbath in paradise, when even the admission that the patriarchs had actually lost the traces, or neglected the celebration of it, would have had no such consequence.

Doubtless, as time rolled on, and particularly during centuries of bondage in Egypt, the memory of this primæval ordinance became faint, and the observation of it by the enslaved people almost impracticable. But it does not appear to have been even then wholly forgotten. For we observe, that,

IV. THE MANNER IN WHICH THE SABBATH WAS REVIVED AND RE-ESTABLISHED BEFORE THE COMMENCEMENT OF THE MOSAICAL ECONOMY, proves that it was a previous institution, which had never been entirely lost; and therefore confirms all we stated of its origin in paradise and its continuance during the patriarchal ages. An interval of two thousand five hundred years had elapsed since the fall, eight or nine hundred years had passed since the flood, and more than four hundred since the call of Abraham. Two centuries of captivity in Egypt had also reduced the religious knowledge of the people of Israel to the lowest ebb. If, therefore, the authority of the Sabbath survived this last state of bondage, we may fairly conclude that it had not perished in any of the preceding periods. Mark the history. The manna is announced; a double portion is promised on a certain day. But in what

[1] Job i. 10; ii. 11.

terms ? " It shall come to pass that on the next day
they shall prepare that which they bring in, and it shall
be twice as much as they gather daily." [1]   Here is no
express mention of the Sabbath, nor any reason assigned why they should find a double portion on the sixth
day.   But the reason was known—the reference was
intelligible.   The language is not that of one delivering
a new precept, but restoring an old and well-known,
though neglected one.   Accordingly, Moses, in explaining the fact, speaks of the Sabbath as not effaced
from the memory of the people.   " This is that which
the Lord hath said, To-morrow is the rest of the
holy Sabbath unto the Lord your God."   What had
the Lord said ?—nothing directly about the Sabbath;
but the allusion to the division of time into six working
days was enough—the Sabbath was known to follow
them.   If similar terms were employed in any modern
act of parliament, every one would understand that it
referred to some previously existing statute or custom,
of which the knowledge was not altogether lost.

And thus the restoration of the Sabbath before the
Mosaical law, seems designed to link the patriarchal
with the Jewish day of rest ; it proves that the first had
not been altogether obliterated, and it shows that the
second was founded on a law of primæval and universal obligation; whilst the threefold miracle of the
manna on each Sabbath, clearly points out the importance attached by Almighty God to the institution.

On what particular day of the seven this renewed
rest was first celebrated we cannot determine. The stress
of the commandment lies on the proportion of time in
the order of creation. The exact computation of weeks
from the first institution, had in all probability been
lost ; and the new calculation, we may conjecture,
dated from the day of the deliverance from Egypt, as
the commencement of the year undoubtedly did. Thus
the redemption of Israel may have fixed the particular
day for reckoning the series of Sabbaths then ; as a

---

[1] Exodus xvi.

greater redemption did at the introduction of a more glorious era.

But we pause. Our inquiries have hitherto been successful. All is consistent. The grandeur of creation gave an impulse and projection to the law of the Sabbath, which human corruption was unable to efface, even before Moses arose to recall men to the purity of religion, and the hope of future redemption. In the line of the patriarchs faint traces of it are discernible. The intervening re-enactment, before the ceremonial economy unites the patriarchal and Jewish day of rest; and confirms us, by its reference, in the faith of the positive fact of a previous institution, to which that reference points.

I. Let us then, first, in applying this part of our subject, observe, THE EXTREME VIOLENCE WHICH IS DONE TO THE CHRISTIAN FAITH, when any important fact in the Scriptures, such as the institution of the Sabbath in paradise, is attempted to be explained away by the fancy of man. The authors of such novelties think little of the consequences of what they are about. The thought is suggested to them by another. It is strange, it is hardy.—This commends it. They are ingenious men—they can write—they can defend the monstrous supposition. The great body of the church disregard and despise the perversion; but the young are injured. In an inquisitive age, half-knowledge prevails. The human heart is too much disinclined to spiritual religion, not to catch at any plea for neglecting the day of divine worship. Thus the evil spreads. The original author was not deeply penetrated with that reverence for revelation as the communication of the will of God, which forbids rash innovation—was not, perhaps, conscious that the foundation of all faith is overturned, if the plain, strait-forward interpretation of historical passages is exchanged for conjecture, hypothesis, inventions of an anticipated narrative. But what can be so mischievous? Such daring criticism, like a magic wand, can make every truth and

every fact of the Bible change their places and import.
Indeed, this same kind of ingenuity denies the fact of the
fall of man, calls in question the existence of evil spirits, doubts the temptation of our Lord, and goes on to
question the truth of the Mosaic or Christian miracles.
Thus all faith soon disappears; for it is but another
step in the same process to deny the corruption of our
nature by the fall, the divinity and atonement of Christ,
the doctrine of the Holy Spirit, the truth of our regeneration by that blessed Spirit, and of spiritual religion
altogether.   Thus the peculiar revelation of the Bible
is gone, and yet we call ourselves Christians.

We must resist this fatal poison.   To say that the
narrative of the institution of the Sabbath in Paradise
is put out of its place, is a violence to faith.   This is
enough. When the idea is first started, the mind of the
Christian trembles—he supposes he cannot demonstrate
that the assertion is groundless.   But he can demonstrate it.   TO CHANGE A SERIES OF EVENTS IN A
SCRIPTURAL NARRATIVE IS A VIOLENCE TO THE
FIRST PRINCIPLES OF ALL BELIEF IN REVELATION.
This is a moral demonstration against any mere hypothesis.

And more especially should we act with this decision
in respect to so fundamental a fact as the entire scheme
and glory of creation, the whole design and proportion
of divine wisdom in the order of the six days' work,
the primary distribution of time into its proportions for
the use of man;—that first prodigious act on which the
subsequent parts of revelation hang for their consistency and force.   And this disposed of by a mere assumption—the fact transposed from the period of creation, to a distance of two or three thousand years, without an intimation in the narrative itself, against all the
laws of interpretation, and to supply a necessity which,
after all, is found not to exist.   Such a conduct is portentous.

Let us cleave, then, to the foundation of all faith in
the various other facts of revelation, by adhering to
this; and let us cultivate more and more that humility,

that submission of heart to God, that restraint of human curiosity and presumption, in which the essence of faith so much consists. It is the wrong state of heart which is the hot-bed where these pernicious notions are generated. Let the heart delight in the divine worship ; let the heart meditate on the divine perfections in Christ Jesus with holy complacency ; let the heart rejoice in God as its happiness, and such errors will not readily find entertainment. I vindicate the first Sabbath, that I may lead you to celebrate with more devotion every other. I resist with indignation the attempt to sap the institution of it in paradise, that I may lead you to due contemplations on the glories of creation, as often as the day of grace returns.

II. Yes, come with me, before we close this discourse, and LET US ADORE AND PRAISE THE ALMIGHTY FATHER OF ALL, FOR THE DISTINCT GLORIES SHED UPON the day of religious repose. Come and praise him for condescending to imprint its first enactment, and the reasons on which it is grounded, on the six days' creative wonders. I am persuaded, that the first Sabbath is not enough magnified. We are familiar with the tenor of the simple and sublime narrative from our infancy. Our hearts are cold to devotion ; objections poison our first feelings. Enter more into the dignity of that day, for the institution of which all days were formed. Imbibe the exalted spirit of that portion of time, to encircle and ennoble which all other portions took their place, as courtiers around the queen and mistress of days. No other command of God has the peculiarity of this ; no other institution, no other service, no other ordinance of religion has, or can have, the majesty blazing around it, which illuminates the day of God. Come, glorify your God and Father. He bids you rest, but it is after his own example. He bids you labour, but it is after his pattern. Imitate the supreme Architect. Work in the order in which he worked, cease when he was pleased to cease. Let the day of religion, after each six days' toil, be to you a blessed and a sanctified season. Plead the promise attached to the Sabbath : it is blessed of God, it is sanctified of God, it is hallowed of God. Implore forgiveness of your past neglect.   Let no Sabbath henceforth leave you, without having sought the blessing promised, and performed the duties to which it is dedicated.   Let your devout meditation on the glories of creation swell the choir of your Maker's praise.   Join " the sons of God " in their joys and songs at the birth of the universe. [1]   Adore the kindness and benevolence of the Almighty, in interposing one day's repose after every six, between the toil, and confusion, and passions, and secularity of this world's duties.   Bless your Redeemer and Saviour for preserving some traces of this most ancient of institutions amidst the patriarchal ages, to remind us of our greater privileges, (as we shall see in the subsequent discourses,) now that we have had the ten commandments again promulgating its divine obligation ; the prophets enforcing its observance ; the blessed Jesus vindicating its gracious simplicity ; the Apostles and the universal church handing down to us its sacred obligations.   Yes, let the brighter day of the gospel guide our feet to that sacred temple and that sacred season, which were first erected and consecrated in paradise, which were then surrounded with the garb of ceremonies ; then left in the beautiful and merciful mantle of the Saviour ; and, lastly, committed to us as a pledge and foretaste of the heavenly state.   Yes, the Sabbath stretches through all ages ; affects all men in every period of time ; distinguishes the true servants of God from the wicked more than any other ordinance ; upholds the visible profession of religion before the eyes of mankind ; keeps up the face and aspect of Christianity in the world ; is the most direct honour that a man can pay to the name and will of the ever-blessed God ; and will never cease in its authority here till our Sabbaths on earth give place to that eternal Sabbath of which they are the pledge, the preparation, the end.

[1] Prov. viii. 23—31.

SERMON II.

THE AUTHORITY AND DIGNITY OF THE SABBATH UNDER THE LAW OF MOSES.

———

EXODUS xx. 8—11.

Remember the Sabbath day, to keep it holy. Six days shalt thou labour and do all thy work : but the seventh day is the Sabbath of the Lord thy God : in it thou shalt not do any work, thou, nor thy son, nor thy daughter, thy man-servant, nor thy maid-servant, nor thy cattle, nor thy stranger that is within thy gates : For in six days the Lord made heaven and earth, the sea and all that in them is, and rested the seventh day ; wherefore the Lord blessed the Sabbath day, and hallowed it.

HAVING proved that the Sabbath was instituted in paradise by adhering simply to the inspired record, and having silenced the objection raised on the supposed absence of any vestiges of its observance till the time of Moses; we come now to consider the position which it held under the ceremonial dispensation. And here the objection to its divine authority and obligation rests on its being merely a ceremonial and temporary appointment, which lost its force with the economy which gave it birth. This difficulty has already been virtually removed. For if the narration in the book of Genesis is correctly given ; if the patri-

C

archs cannot be proved to have neglected the divine command ; and if at the deliverance from Egypt, Moses clearly referred to it as not effaced from the memory of the people; then the Sabbath did not owe its birth to the ceremonial law, and cannot have ceased by the abrogation of it. But this is little. As we not only answered the objection advanced against the patriarchal Sabbath, but triumphantly established its essential dignity and perpetuity from the glory cast upon it by the order of creation ; so we hope, not merely to refute the present objection, but to draw from the law of Moses copious materials for confirming all our preceding arguments, and for placing in a yet stronger light the immutable obligation of the day of weekly rest.

We assert, then, that from the very commencement of the Mosaical economy, the fourth command was incorporated in the moral law—that when the ceremonial usages were in their greatest vigour, the Sabbath appeared high and distinct above them— and that in the latter ages of the Jewish church it was insisted on by the prophets as of essential moral obligation, and as about to form a part of the gospel dispensation.

I. The insertion of the law of the Sabbath into the decalogue confirms all we have already advanced, and affords the most decisive proof of its perpetual force. If there were nothing else in the whole Bible, this would be enough to satisfy the humble Christian. The fourth commandment is just as binding as any of the remaining nine. There it is, a part of the moral law of God! If the attempt to feign an anticipated history was proved to be an invasion on the first principles of faith ; the endeavour to displace the fourth commandment is AN OPEN INVASION OF THE FIRST PRINCIPLES BOTH OF FAITH AND OBEDIENCE. For every thing conspires to cast an importance around the ten commandments peculiar to themselves.

Consider the BROAD LINE OF DEMARCATION between them and the ceremonial usages. The decalogue is a summary of all those dictates of the love of God and man, which were written upon the heart of Adam before the fall. These commands were kept, in substance, by the patriarchs before they were reduced into a code. They are the eternal rules of right and wrong, resting on the authoritative will of God, and arising from the essential relations in which man stands to his Creator, and his fellow-creatures. They are the standard of human obedience, the transcript of the divine holiness. The unchanging authority of these precepts is the foundation of the Christian religion, the rule of domestic life, the bond of civil government, the grand tie and security of all human society. Between these and the ceremonial usages there is a vast interval. The judicial and ceremonial law was temporary, of positive enactment, for a time and for certain purposes only; had no existence before its express appointment; derived all its force from something substantial and glorious, of which it was the shadow; and was swept away and abrogated when the more perfect dispensation appeared. All its enactments were without the boundary of the moral law. Within that boundary nothing was abolished when Christ came; without it, every thing. Within the boundary all was eternal and immutable; without it, all was temporary and changeable. No confusion was ever made by any considerate Christian on this subject. The conscience of man, when duly informed, responds to every one of the moral commands. The additional motives appended to some of them, arising from the circumstances of the Jews, affect not their universal authority. The particular redemption from Egypt, the length of days attached to filial obedience, the punishment of idolatry visited on the third and fourth generation, and the mercies to thousands promised to the keepers of the divine law,[1] in no respect change the

---

[1] Even these are, in their comprehensive and typical import, of perpetual force—in the redemption of Christ, the spiritual blessing on filial obedience, &c.

main, grand, distinctive foundations of moral obligation
on which the commandments repose.   These constitute
a code, a book, which stands distinct and separate
from all others, which is divided into two tables, and
has been known in all ages as the " Ten Commandments," or " The Decalogue ;" just as the books of
Scripture are distinguished from other books by the
name of " The Bible."

Now, of these ten commands THE LAW OF THE SAB-
BATH IS ONE.   Whatever authority any have, that
authority is possessed by this.   Whatever obligation
the first, the second, the third, or any others carry with
them, that same obligation carries with it the fourth.
If men are bound in every age and under all dispensations to acknowledge one only God,[2] to worship him,
not with graven images, but in spirit and in truth,[3] to
reverence the divine name,[4] to obey their parents,[5] to
abstain from murder,[6] adultery,[7] theft,[8] false witness,[9] concupiscence,[10] they are equally bound to consecrate a Sabbath to their Maker's service, after six days of ordinary
labour and toil.[11]   This proportion of time had been
made known to man in paradise, and published in the
very order of creation.   The natural and essential
duty, therefore, of devoting some time to the worship
of God, being thus expounded by a revelation of what
that time should be, the whole stands a moral and unchanging rule of man's obedience.   As the first command fixes THE OBJECT of worship, and the second
the MEANS, and the third THE REVERENTIAL MANNER,
so the fourth determines THE TIME.   And as the preceding commands are founded in the real relations of
things, and made clear to us by the authoritative will
of God, so the fourth is founded on the real relation
of things, and made clear to us by the authoritative

[2] 1st commandment.   [3] 2nd.   [4] 3rd.   [5] 5th.
   [6] 6th.   [7] 7th.   [8] 8th.   [9] 9th.
     [10] 10th.   [11] 4th.

will of God. The only difference is, that the other commands, requiring no limitation of time, were more obvious in all their parts to the consciences of men, whilst this depended, from the very nature of the case, upon the revelation of God's will as to the exact proportion of time to be consecrated to his service. The authority of that appointment, however, when once made known, is as inviolable as any of the others. The fourth commandment is an integral part of the moral law.

And now let us advert to THE TENOR of this fourth precept. It is unlike the rest, it is more detailed, more explicit, extended to more classes of persons, sustained by more reasons. Its introduction also is different. Instead of a mere injunction or prohibition, it refers to a preceding enactment, "Remember the Sabbath day to keep it holy;" as if on purpose to connect the law of the Sabbath in paradise with its republication at the solemn establishment of the Mosaical dispensation—a design which is made yet more apparent at the close of the commandment, by the citation of the reason given, and of the blessing and sanctification attached to the institution by the Almighty, when he first granted a day of rest to man at his creation.

Nor is THE PLACE which this fourth precept occupies in the decalogue to be overlooked. It is the last of the first table of the law, and prepares for the second. It is the keeper and guardian of the preceding commands, and the preparation for the following. It makes the three first precepts practicable. For after faith in one God, worship to him, and reverence for his name, it prescribes the time in which this pure worship of the only true God is to be celebrated, the persons who are to unite in it, and the interruption to all ordinary labours without which it cannot be performed. So that as the tenth commandment shuts up the second table, and reduces, as it were, its injunctions to practice, by forbidding that concupiscence which would infallibly lead to their violation; so the fourth

accomplishes the first table by assigning the time and
season when its injunctions may be fulfilled.

We must not pass unnoticed, also, that the whole
moral law, held together, as it were, by the fourth of
its precepts, WAS PUBLISHED BEFORE THE CEREMO-
NIAL ENACTMENTS of Moses. It stands, not in the
midst of the ceremonies, but distinct and separate from
them. The Mosaical law did not, properly speaking,
begin till after these primary rules of obedience, which
man had almost lost through the corruption of his
nature and the lapse of time, were restored by a solemn
republication.

Nor can it be said with truth, that the law of the
Sabbath is merely of a ceremonial nature, because
THE STRICTNESS OF ITS OBSERVATION WAS RE-
LAXED UNDER THE NEW TESTAMENT. For even
allowing the fact; a change in the tone and spirit of
a commandment, springing from a more benignant
dispensation, affects not its fundamental moral authority. But we deny the fact. The ceremonial and
judicial enactments which were afterwards connected
with it, form no part of the fourth commandment, the
tenor of which was always intended to be interpreted
according to the merciful construction which our Saviour put upon it, against the uncommanded comments
of the Jewish doctors. The prohibition of doing any
work never included, nor was intended to include,
acts of real necessity and mercy. The whole moral
bearing of this command is just as entire now, as the
whole moral bearing of any other of the divine code.
" I will have mercy and not sacrifice," was an axiom
of the Mosaic, as well as the Christian economy, as
will be seen in our next discourse.

It is painful to have occasion to say so much on so
plain a case; and nothing but the great importance
of the subject would warrant such detail. The fourth
command, then, is not displaced from its station, nor
weakened in its authority by the objection we have
been considering. On the contrary, every aspect in
which it is viewed, heightens our conception of the

dignity which it derives, equally with the rest, from the broad line of demarcation which separates it from the merely ceremonial observances.

And now we must go on to consider THE SOLEMNITIES WHICH ATTENDED THE PROMULGATION OF THE MORAL LAW, of which the fourth command is so distinguished a part. These differed from the majesty which accompanied the first institution of the day of rest in Eden. Then it was enregistered in the bold and legible characters of the six days' order of creation; whilst the written record was brief and general. Now it is surrounded, in common with the remaining elementary branches of duty, with those traits of visible glory, that awful voice of words, that detailed record, that reference to a preceding enactment, those reasons of universal application, which, after a lapse of two thousand five hundred years, were best adapted to explain its import, and ensure human obedience in all future periods of time. The moral law stands singular and alone, amidst the revelations made to Moses. The other communications were by more ordinary and usual means; the ten commandments by the immediate voice of God. The other parts of the Jewish economy were conveyed by calm impressions; this by thunderings and lightnings, and attendant angels, and the trembling mount, and the darkness, and all the terrors at which Moses "exceedingly feared and quaked." Recall to mind the solemn scene, that you may imbibe the full dignity of all the precepts of the moral law, and of the sabbatical amongst the number. Hear; the trump sounds, and the voice of words are uttered. See; no one but the holy prophet may approach—"if so much as a beast touch the mountain, it is stoned, or thrust through with a dart." Behold; two tables of stone are prepared by the Almighty himself. Upon these the finger of God inscribes "The Ten Commandments," and ADDETH NO MORE. The tables are broken by Moses as he descends from the mount—and, lo, the law is rewritten on second tables with the same hand; and is finally deposited, not with the rest of the Mosaic statutes, but separate and alone, within the ark of the covenant. Can any circumstances impress us with a more awful sense of the singular importance of every precept? Can any thing more distinguish and elevate the moral and perpetual, above the temporary and ceremonial law—and separate and single out the decalogue in point of dignity and prominence from all other enactments? The whole Bible contains nothing so peculiar and majestic, as this introduction to this new dispensation. Where is the man that will venture to lessen the number of the commandments? Where is the man that from ten will presume to reduce them to nine? Where is the Protestant that will expunge, with the Church of Rome, the command which happens most to militate against his corrupt practices?[1] Where is the man that will obliterate that precept especially, which so immediately respects the honour of God and the glory offered to his name, which, standing in the very heart of the code, binds its injunctions together, and gives strength and consistence to the whole?

I conceive it is impossible for simple-minded Christians to consider these things, and not to see at once the marked distinction between the shadow and types of a particular dispensation, and the eternal rules of right and wrong. Their prayer, I am persuaded, will continue to be, as to each particular commandment, and as to the fourth no less than the others, " Lord, have mercy upon us, and incline our hearts to keep this law;" and as to the entire series, without exception or difference, " Lord, write all these thy laws on our hearts, we beseech thee."

II. But we proceed to show, that even when the CEREMONIAL USAGES WERE IN THEIR GREATEST VIGOUR, THE SABBATH APPEARED HIGH AND DISTINCT ABOVE THEM.

[1] The Popish catechisms have frequently omitted the second commandment; the practice may now be discontinued perhaps.

For the law of the weekly rest passes through the Mosaical dispensation. It will be important, then, to show its position during this part of its course. It entered this economy, or rather preceded it, by the promulgation of the moral law, of whose majesty and perpetuity it partakes. It now, however, receives additional rules and appendages, which attend it during the continuance of the Mosaic dispensation. But it is remarkable that these ceremonial enactments are no part of the essential law of the Sabbath as inserted in the decalogue; and that even during the greatest vigour and first observance of them, the moral obligation of the day of weekly rest lifts up its head high and distinct above them. These are the points which we are now to prove.

For the Sabbath is now a part of that preparatory dispensation, and is attired with robes of state and ceremony during that period. Two lambs are offered on its weekly return, beside the usual burnt-offering; the shew-bread is renewed on the golden table; the ministers of the temple enter on their courses; other times of holy solemnity are instituted and included under the general name of Sabbaths; its external rest is enforced with temporal sanctions; the presumptuous violator of it is subjected to the punishment of death; it is constituted a sign of the national covenant, and is enjoined as a public protest against idolatry; finally, the spirit of bondage and condemnation lowers over this part, as over every other, of the introductory economy of Moses.

Here, then, for the first time, we recognize the features of a ceremonial Sabbath. Many commandments of the decalogue, and the fourth amongst the number, are now invested with temporary statutes, as " shadows of good things to come," or parts of the peculiar theocracy of the Jews.

But the essential moral character of each precept of the decalogue loses none of its force by its ceremonial and judicial observances. The sin of worshipping any but the one true God, remains just as

great, after all the numerous statutes peculiar to the
Jews.   The sin of making graven images, of taking
God's name in vain, of disobeying parents, of committing murder, adultery, theft,   of bearing false-
witness, of coveting the goods of our neighbour, are
precisely the same violations of the immutable rules of
right and wrong, as before the temporary enactments
which affected the chosen people.   In like manner,
the fourth commandment is unaltered in its essential
injunction of a weekly religious rest for the service of
God, though it is associated with many temporary and
figurative appendages.   Nothing can be clearer than
this.   The principle is admitted with regard to nine
of the commandments, and can never be fairly refused
as to the tenth.

And accordingly not one of these ceremonial and
civil statutes is incorporated in the ten commandments
themselves—not one is written with the finger of God—
not one is found on the consecrated tables—not one
is deposited within the ark of the covenant.   They
are all delivered afterwards, in another form, with
other views, and to occupy another station.

But let us go on and follow the Sabbath as it passes
through the ceremonial dispensation.   It might, indeed, have pleased God, that it should have been
entirely shrouded by this dispensation during its continuance.   It would then have lost none of its original
force, and we should merely have had to resume our
consideration of it, after it had been disembarrassed
from the emblematical ceremonies.   But this is not
the state of the case.   The Sabbath lifts up its head
high above all the ceremonial usages, even in the Pentateuch itself, and during the full vigor of the introductory economy.

For first, after the record of the promulgation of
the decalogue, three chapters of judicial statutes
follow; but in the midst of these, the people are re-
minded of the essential importance of the Sabbath, in
a manner quite distinct and peculiar.   It is associated
with the primary duty of worshipping the one true

God, as of equal obligation, and indeed as necessary
to it. "Six days shalt thou do thy work, and on the
seventh thou shalt rest, . . in all things that I have
said unto thee, be circumspect, and make no mention
of the name of other gods, neither let it be heard out
of thy mouth."[1] This is sufficiently remarkable.

Again, after six chapters more concerning the tabernacle and its various services and sacrifices, the whole
communication of the forty days' abode on the mount
is concluded with a re-inculcation of the Sabbath-
rest, in a manner the most solemn and affecting.
"And the Lord spake unto Moses, saying, Verily my
Sabbaths ye shall keep; for it is a sign between me
and you throughout your generations, THAT YE MAY
KNOW THAT I AM THE LORD THAT DOTH SANC-
TIFY YOU. Ye shall keep the Sabbath, therefore,
for it is holy unto you; every one that defileth it shall
surely be put to death; for whosoever doeth any work
therein, that soul shall be cut off from among his people. Six days may work be done; but in the seventh
is the Sabbath of rest, holy to the Lord; whosoever
doeth any work in the Sabbath-day, he shall surely
be put to death. Wherefore the children of Israel
shall keep the Sabbath, to observe the Sabbath
throughout their generations, for a perpetual covenant.
It is a sign between me and the children of Israel for
ever, for in six days the Lord made heaven and earth,
and on the seventh day he rested and was refreshed."[2]
Can any thing give dignity to the sacred day as founded
in the essential relation of man to his Maker and
Redeemer, if this sublime language does not? Every
idea of sanctification, every sense of importance from
a sign of a covenant between God and man, every
sanction derived from the awful punishment of death,
unite to impress upon us the duty; whilst the proportion noted between the working days and the day
of rest, and the reason drawn from the order of creation, extend the obligation to every human being.

[1] Exod. xxiii. 12, 13.   [2] Exod. xxxi. 12—17.

In the following two chapters we have as many additional recapitulations, with fresh cautions. The book of Exodus closes. The enactments concerning sacrifices and purifications are, however, no sooner despatched in the following book, than we meet with a passage in which one commandment of the second table of the moral law, and two of the first, are united with the fourth commandment as of equal obligation, and this as a matter well known and requiring no explanation; " Ye shall be holy, for I the Lord your God am holy. Ye shall fear every man his mother and his father, and keep my Sabbaths; I am the Lord your God. Turn ye not unto idols, nor make to yourselves molten images; I am the Lord your God." [1]

I will not dwell on other passages in this book. I hasten to fix your attention on the punishment of death inflicted on the Sabbath-breaker, as recorded in the next. Few persons consider how deeply this case is designed to impress us with the essential obligation of the fourth commandment, and of the immediate honour of God involved in a presumptuous violation of it. This last point is not to be overlooked. The man was not condemned merely for gathering sticks on the Sabbath; but for doing this in the face of the divine prohibition. Accordingly he was put in ward, till the will of God should be distinctly known. The whole proceeding was marked with a calm solemnity which makes the warning more pointed and decisive. The "soul that doeth aught presumptuously, whether he be born in the land or a stranger, the same reproacheth the Lord; and that soul shall be cut off from among his people; because he hath despised the word of the Lord and hath broken his commandment, that soul shall be utterly cut off, his iniquity shall be upon him. And while the children of Israel were in the wilderness, they found a man that gathered sticks upon the Sabbath-day. And they that found him gathering sticks, brought him unto

---

[1] Lev. xix. 1—4.

Moses and Aaron, and unto all the congregation. And they put him in ward, because it was not declared what should be done to him. And the Lord said unto Moses, The man shall be surely put to death."[1]

I add only the striking passage, in which, at the close of life, Moses re-inculcates, as a preacher, the commandments which he had delivered before as a legislator. In this recapitulation, the other nine precepts of the decalogue stand as they were first promulgated from Mount Sinai—at least, the variations are extremely slight, but the fourth is amplified and enforced with many additional motives, as if it claimed more regard than any other. " Keep the Sabbath-day to sanctify it, as the Lord thy God commanded thee : six days thou shalt labour and do all thy work ; but the seventh day is the Sabbath of the Lord thy God ; in it thou shalt not do any work, thou, nor thy son, nor thy daughter, nor thy man-servant, nor thy maid-servant, nor thine ox, nor thine ass, nor any of thy cattle, nor thy stranger that is within thy gates ; that thy man-servant and thy maid-servant may rest as well as thou. And remember thou wast a servant in the land of Egypt, and that the Lord thy God brought thee out thence through a mighty hand and a stretched-out arm; therefore the Lord thy God commanded thee to keep the Sabbath-day."[2] What a distinction does this amplitude of detail confer on the law of the Sabbath ! And how does this and the passages before cited, take out this commandment from the mere ceremonial and positive institutions with which for a time it is mingled, and lift up its head in the midst of the temporary and fugitive elements of the Jewish polity ! How evidently does even the Pentateuch exhibit it as a moral precept, directed to the highest ends, beyond what was peculiar to the Mosaical dispensation, and losing nothing of its permanent and essential force from the combination !

[1] Numb. xv. 30—35.   [2] Deut. v. 12—15.

III. But proceed we to show that, in the latter ages
of the Jewish church, the weekly Sabbath was insisted
upon BY THE PROPHETS AS OF ESSENTIAL MORAL
OBLIGATION, AND AS DESTINED TO FORM A PART
OF THE GOSPEL DISPENSATION.

Hitherto the objection raised against the perpetuity
of the Sabbath on the ground of its being a merely
ceremonial enactment, has not only been silenced, but
refuted.   It is a constituent part of the moral law:
to call it a mere ceremony, is to sap all the foundations of faith and obedience.   During the vigour of
the ceremonial usages, it lifts up its head above them,
and is enforced as of moral obligation: to call it a
mere ceremony, is to be ignorant of the very first facts of
the case.

But we now go on to the prophets, the reformers of
the degenerate people, the preachers of the divine will,
the seers of the gospel age, the assertors of the moral
and eternal rule of duty, the bold proclaimers of the
law of conscience and the bonds of a covenant relation with God.   If they are found to urge the spiritual
observance of the day of rest, as designed to form a
part of the evangelical economy; and if they do this
at the very time that they cast contempt on the mere
outward ceremonies of the Jewish law—if they are
found to denounce the divine indignation on no transgression, except idolatry, with so much vehemence—and
if they appear anxious to reform the manners of the
people in this capital point more than in any other,—
then our argument gains strength at every step, and
the divine institution will stand at the margin of the
Christian dispensation, ready to enter it, in common
with the other branches of essential religion.

Consider then, in the first place, the language of the
BOOK OF PSALMS, and observe how little allusion is
made to the ceremonial rites connected with the Sabbath, and how completely the stress is laid on the permanent and spiritual duties of that holy season.   The
Jewish Sabbath was indeed now in force.   But it is

upon the praises of God generally—his glory, his majesty, his compassion, his providence, his redemption, that the Psalmist dwells. "One thing have I desired of the Lord, that will I seek after, that I may dwell in the house of the Lord all the days of my life, to behold the beauty of the Lord and to inquire in his temple ... How amiable are thy tabernacles, O Lord of hosts, my soul longeth, yea, even fainteth for the courts of the Lord, my heart and my flesh crieth out for the living God ... I was glad when they said unto me, Let us go unto the house of the Lord."[1]

These are detached passages. In the 92nd Psalm we have an express hymn or song for the Sabbath-day, the topics of which are spiritual, and not ceremonial. First, the praises of God are enjoined, which are the proper business of the Sabbath;[2] then the wonders of God in creation, the very reason for the institution;[3] next, the dealings of the divine providence in the overthrow of the wicked;[4] and lastly, the operations of grace in the fruitfulness, even to old age, of those who " are planted in the house of the Lord."[5]

Contrast with this the language of the 50th Psalm, in which a marked disregard is shown for mere ceremonies : " I will not reprove thee for thy sacrifices or thy burnt-offerings to have been continually before me. I will take no bullock out of thy house, nor he goats out of thy folds. For every beast of the forest is mine, and the cattle upon a thousand hills. I know all the fowls of the mountains and the wild beasts of the field are mine. If I were hungry, I would not tell thee, for the world is mine and the fullness thereof. Will I eat the flesh of bulls or drink the blood of goats, &c. ?" In this denunciation, you will observe that nothing is included which in the least belongs to the essential matters extolled in the former Psalms.

In like manner, with what holy indignation does the prophet Isaiah REJECT THE MERE OUTWARD OB-

---

[1] Psalm xxvii. 84, 120.   [2] ver. 1—3.   [3] ver. 4, 5.
          [4] ver. 6—11.   [5] ver. 12—15.

SERVANCES of the Jewish law : "To what purpose is
the multitude of your sacrifices unto me? saith the
Lord : I am full of the burnt-offerings of rams, and
the fat of fed beasts ; and I delight not in the blood of
bullocks, or of lambs, or of he-goats.   Bring no more
vain oblations ; incense is an abomination unto me ;
the new moons and Sabbaths, the calling of assemblies,
I cannot away with ; it is iniquity, even the solemn
meeting.   Your new moons and your appointed feasts
my soul hateth, they are a trouble to me, I am weary
to bear them."[1]   In this vehement expostulation the
Sabbaths, including that of the weekly rest, are swept
away, when superstitiously relied on, in one common
reprobation.

But with what earnestness, on the contrary, is THE
DUE CELEBRATION OF THE SABBATH EXTOLLED in
the subsequent chapter—how is it placed on a level
with the PLAINEST MORAL PRECEPTS—how is the not
polluting of it made the principal thing that pleases
God—and how are THE LARGEST PROMISES OF THE
EVANGELICAL DISPENSATION connected with such a
spiritual consecration of the holy day! " Blessed is the
man that doeth this, and the son of man that layeth
hold on it ; that keepeth the Sabbath from polluting
it, and keepeth his hand from doing any evil."   Here
the observation of the weekly day of rest is spoken of
as a great part of holiness of life, and is placed among
moral duties.   The prophet proceeds, " Neither let
the son of the stranger that hath joined himself to the
Lord, speak, saying, The Lord hath utterly separated
me from his people ; neither let the eunuch say, Behold, I am a dry tree.   For thus saith the Lord unto
the eunuchs that keep my Sabbaths and do the things
that please me, and take hold of my covenant.   Even
unto them will I give in mine house and within my
walls, a name better than of sons and of daughters.
I will give them an everlasting name, that shall not be
cut off."   The prophet is here speaking of the gospel

[1] Isaiah i. 11—14.

age, when the ceremonial law which prohibited eunuchs from coming into the congregation of the Lord, shall be abolished; yet the eunuchs, when thus at liberty from the law of ceremonies, are described as being still under an obligation to keep the Sabbath. Nay, they are directed to use this very method of obtaining a share in the blessings of Messiah's kingdom. And so with regard to the Gentiles generally, here called strangers; "Also the sons of the stranger that join themselves to the Lord, to serve him and to love the name of the Lord, to be his servants, every one that keepeth the Sabbath from polluting it, and taketh hold of my covenant;" where we notice again, that the sanctification of the Sabbath is put on the same footing with the laying hold of God's covenant, the serving the Lord, the loving the name of the Lord, the being his servants—and is indeed described as the main proof of all those parts of essential piety. The prophet then adds this evangelical promise, which by our Lord's own citation is predictive of the gospel-state— "Even them will I bring to my holy mountain, and make them joyful in my house of prayer; their burnt offerings and their sacrifices shall be accepted upon mine altar; for mine house shall be called an house of prayer for all people." The Gentiles, then, who shall be called in the times of the gospel, will be under the same duty of keeping the Sabbath; and shall thus be made "joyful in that house of prayer" which is destined for all people. All this falls in exactly with another prediction of the same inspired writer, the language being still in the terms of the dispensation then prevailing. "It shall come to pass that from one new moon to another, and from one Sabbath to another, shall all flesh come to worship before me, saith the Lord;" which has constantly been fulfilling in the Christian church, when ALL FLESH have worshipped before the Lord in that weekly day of religious rest into which the Jewish new moons and sabbatical periods have subsided. Add to this the description which the same divine author gives of the duties of the Sabbath.   They have so clearly a moral obligation and universal force, and involve a tone of devotion so elevated, that we may truly say, If the Sabbath be a ceremony, we have lost under the gospel one of the brightest glories of revelation.   "If thou turn away thy foot from the Sabbath, from doing thy pleasure on my holy day, and call the Sabbath a delight, holy of the Lord, honourable, and shalt honour him, not doing thine own ways, nor finding thine own pleasure, nor speaking thine own words; then shalt thou delight thyself in the Lord, &c."[1]

But we pass from this class of passages, to notice those DENUNCIATIONS OF THE SIN OF VIOLATING THE SABBATH, which are only surpassed by the anger of the Almighty against idolatry itself, with which, indeed, it seems ever to have had a close affinity.   We have already noticed the sentence executed early in the history of the sacred people on the presumptuous sabbath-breaker.   But hear the prophet Jeremiah : "Thus saith the Lord, Take heed to yourselves and bear no burden on the Sabbath-day, nor bring it in by the gates of Jerusalem : neither carry forth a burden out of your houses on the Sabbath-day, neither do ye any work, but hallow ye the Sabbath-day, as I commanded your fathers.   But they obeyed not, neither inclined their ear, but made their neck stiff that they might not hear nor receive instruction.   But if ye will not hearken unto me—then will I kindle a fire in the gates thereof, and it shall devour the palaces of Jerusalem, and it shall not be quenched."[2]   All the prosperity of the nation, all the favour of God is suspended on this one branch of moral obedience.   To judge of the force of this, contrast it with the same prophet's declaration concerning ceremonial observances : " For I spake not unto your fathers, nor commanded them in the day that I brought them out of the land of Egypt concerning burnt-offerings or sacrifices.   But this one thing commanded I them, saying, Obey my voice,

---

[1] Isaiah lviii. 10, 13.   [2] Jer. xvii. 19—27.

and I will be your God, and ye shall be my people."[1]

Agani, mark how the prophet Amos reproaches the degenerate people with an impatience of the holy services of the Sabbath and other festivals : " Hear this, O ye that swallow up the needy, even to make the poor of the land to fail, saying, When will the new moon be gone that we may sell corn, and the Sabbath that we may set forth wheat ![2]

The prophet Ezekiel follows. He lived later than Jeremiah and Amos. The Babylonish captivity had now begun; and the peculiar aggravation of the people's sins is represented to be their profanation of the Sabbath : " Moreover, I gave them my Sabbaths to be a sign between me and them, that they might know that I am the Lord that sanctify them. But the house of Israel rebelled against me ; my Sabbaths they greatly polluted : then I said, I will pour out my fury upon them in the wilderness to consume them." The charge is repeated again and again in the course of the expostulation, and is connected with the sin of idolatry and of direct contempt of the majesty of the Lord : " They despised my judgments and walked not in my statutes, but polluted my Sabbaths ; for their heart went after their idols."[3] Similar charges are reiterated in subsequent chapters of this and the other prophets, and like threatenings denounced.

And what was THE PARTICULAR REFORMATION which Ezra, and Nehemiah, and the prophets after the captivity, were most anxious to effect upon the first return of the people from Babylon ? We are now come to the last trace of prophetical revelation. The Old Testament canon is closing. What do the last inspired teachers and leaders testify ? What was their chief care ? What their main object ? Was it not to restore the house of God's worship? to rebuild the temple? to recall the people to the sanctity of the

___

[1] Jer. vii. 22, 23.　　　　[2] Amos viii. 11.
[3] Ezek. xx. 12, 13, 16.

Sabbath ?   I omit other points, to exhibit the noble
conduct of Nehemiah when he found the men of Tyre
bringing fish and selling it on the sacred day.   Mark
his warmth of reproach.   Observe his appeal to the
past history of the nation.   Notice that the whole
transaction rests, not on any ceremonial rite omitted
or despised, but on the violation of the grand fundamental duty of the religious rest of God.   " In those
days saw I in Judah, some treading wine-presses on
the Sabbath, and bringing in sheaves, and lading
asses; as also wine, grapes, and figs, and all manner
of burdens, which they brought into Jerusalem on the
Sabbath-day; and I testified against them in the day
wherein they sold victuals.   There dwelt men of
Tyre also therein, which brought fish and all manner
of ware, and sold on the Sabbath unto the children
of Judah and in Jerusalem.   Then I contended with
the nobles of Judah, and said unto them, What evil
thing is this that ye do, and profane the Sabbath-day ?
Did not your fathers thus, and did not our God bring
all this evil upon us, and upon this city? yet ye
bring more wrath upon Israel by profaning the Sabbath.   And it came to pass, than when the gates of
Jerusalem began to be dark before the Sabbath, I
commanded that the gates should be shut, and
charged that they should not be opened till after the
Sabbath; and some of my servants set I at the gates,
that there should no burden be brought in on the
Sabbath-day.   And I commanded the Levites that
they should cleanse themselves, and that they should
come and keep the gates, to sanctify the Sabbath-
day." [1]

Thirty or forty years after this, THE PROPHET MA-
LACHI utters the last predictions, and gives the last
warnings, before the coming of Messiah.   And on
what does he so much insist, as on the contempt into
which the ordinances of God were sunk, and on the
indignation of the Almighty which was about to fol-

---

[1] Nehemiah xiii 15, 21, 22.

low? They " offered polluted bread." No one
would " shut the temple-doors for nought." They
said, " The table of the Lord is contemptible." They
said, " Behold, what a weariness is it !" " And ye have
" snuffed at it, saith the Lord of hosts." " Ye have
said, It is vain to serve God, and what profit is it that
we have kept his ordinances." " Therefore," adds the
prophet, " the day cometh that shall burn as an oven ;
and all the proud, and they that do wickedly shall be
as stubble." [1]

Such is the estimate which we are led to form of
the essential moral character of the law of the Sabbath, from a review of every part of the Old Testament. More than three thousand six hundred years
since the first Sabbath have now elapsed. The sacred
institution stands on the margin of the New Testament dispensation. We naturally inquire, then,
what we might expect to be its dignity, if we find
nothing directly to the contrary, in the kingdom of
Messiah? It derived not its authority from the Levitical law, it could lose, therefore, none of its sanctity
by the abrogation of it. The same respect would be
due to it as before that intervening dispensation.
Whatever the Sabbath was when it entered the Mosaic ritual, that would it be when it came from it.
The cessation of the ceremonial law would no more
release the worshipper of God from the observation
of a weekly rest, than it would cancel the injunction
of filial piety, or the prohibition of theft, murder,
adultery, false witness, or concupiscence. The importance of all we have been considering is in this
view very material. We have shown its divine institution in paradise, the traces of its observance during
the patriarchal ages, its re-enactment in the wilderness
before the Mosaical economy, at the miraculous fall
of manna. We have also noticed its solemn incorporation in the ten commandments—the awful glories

[1] Mal. i. 6, 7, 13; iii. 14; i. 1.

of that promulgation—its dignity above all the ceremonies of the Jewish religion—its essential and perpetual obligation as inculcated by the prophets, and
destined to form a part of the gospel age.   It comes
forth, therefore, from the hand of Moses with all its
pristine authority, which it had, in fact, never lost as
to any portion of the human race, except as the corruption of man had perverted or forgotten the original
institution.

Nay, it enters the gospel dispensation with more
than its patriarchal majesty and obligation.   It has
been accumulating, not diminishing, its claims upon
men, by all the testimonies to its essential importance
which Moses and the prophets gave.   It has acquired
new force, new evidence, new illustration, by its position under an economy which, if it had been merely
a ceremony, would have buried it amid a thousand
surrounding rites.

The gospel will, therefore, we may conclude, secure
to the original institution of the Sabbath more ample
scope, higher obligations, and a more elevated position
of dignity and importance.   The gospel is the last
and most perfect dispensation—the completion of all
the preceding, the time of enlarged privilege, of
superabundant grace !   If, therefore, a weekly day of
repose and religious worship was granted to the
saints of the patriarchal dispensations—and if even
under the law of bondage this blessing was continued
to the Jew, much more will it be vouchsafed to the
Christian,—much more will it accompany " the law of
liberty."   We may be sure that the boon is not revoked;
we may be sure that man is not doomed now to seven
days' labour instead of six; we may be sure that his
time for worshipping God is not abridged, nor the
pledge of the covenant of grace lessened and restrained.

But this is not all.   The Sabbath had been increasing in its moral influence upon man from the first institution.   Every fresh motive to the love of God,
every ray of glory from Mount Sinai, every prophecy

of a future Saviour, had been augmenting proportionably his duty, by affording him more copious aids in fulfilling it.   Christians, then, being favoured with a clearer knowledge of the divine will, having more motives to love and serve God, having a more abundant effusion of the Holy Spirit, than under any preceding period, we may be sure that their character will be superior, their delight in the worship of God more warm, their celebration of God's praises in creation and redemption proportionably more fervent.   Yet, if a sabbatical institution is not binding upon Christians, we must reverse the supposition.   We must forget the devotion of the patriarchs, the spiritual fervour of the psalmist, the zeal for the Sabbath which animated Nehemiah and Ezra, the delight in its duties foretold by Isaiah as marking the gospel age ; and the Christian must take his station below the Jew in spirituality and love.   But this can never be the case.   We may conclude that if one day in seven was the measure under more imperfect dispensations, a less term cannot suffice under the influence of so many motives and inducements to a higher degree of love in the worship of God.[1]

We shall want, therefore, no enactment, no express command in the New Testament.   Things will go on as they did before the Mosaic economy, except as a richer effusion of grace will render the Sabbath a more delightful season of repose than in the preceding ages. The worship of the New Testament will be, we may conclude, a restoration of the patriarchal in its primitive simplicity and purity, dropping the incumbrances imposed during the time of the law, and acquiring all the new influence and obligations which the infinite benefits of the gospel confer.

And thus, as the patriarchal sacrifices passed on into the passover and numerous offerings of the law during the term of that intervening dispensation, and then emerged in the simple evangelical supper of our

---

[1] Archd. Pott.

Lord—as the patriarchal circumcision reserved its rites during the same economy, and then yielded to the sacrament of baptism—as the patriarchal institution of marriage, suspended on account of the hardness of the people's hearts during the Jewish age, was re-established and came to its full effect in the Christian law of marriage,—so the patriarchal day of rest, with its worship of God, its celebration of the wonders of creation, and its provision for the religious repose of man, after having been annexed for a period to the national covenant of the Jews, was restored to its first design in the Christian Sabbath.

A re-enactment in the New Testament would be a denial, by implication, of its previous institution and authority. Nothing is re-enacted in the gospel. The moral law, the essential duties of religion, the relations of man to his Maker and Benefactor, the necessity of a season for divine worship, the proportion of time destined for it from the creation, all the precepts of the decalogue—remain unchanged. They are not again formally promulgated. Creation and Mount Sinai suffice. They go on of course, and the Sabbath with them, if no express and formal abrogation of it be found in the gospel.

But we are anticipating our next discourse. Our object is merely to bring up the sabbatical rest to the threshhold of the New Testament, and to leave it there, ready to enter.

Let us then turn from these discussions to some practical points which may affect our hearts.

1. Let us learn to give to the holy day of rest that PROMINENCY IN OUR ESTEEM which Moses was instructed to give it in his dispensation. Christian brethren, let the gospel be as influential upon us to observe the day of rest and holy worship, as the law was of old. Let not the Sabbath be sunk amidst external observances, ordinary rites, an outward adherence to a national creed, the common decencies of religion. Let it be exalted and placed aloft as the Queen of days. Let the admiration of the Jew, blind as it often was, be

a stimulus to the more enlightened devotion of the
Christian.   Let the mercies of God in the redemption
from the Egyptian captivity, which bound with additional motives the Sabbath upon the ancient people,
teach us how the mercies of a spiritual redemption
from sin and death should bind on us the sanctification
of that day when they are especially celebrated.   Let
the perpetual inculcation of this duty by Moses, on all
occasions, in every connexion, by every species of motive, lead us to urge it upon our children and households
on every fit opportunity.   Let the solemn promulgation of it in " The Ten Cemmandments" be the rally-
ing point of all our arguments, and the brief and
conclusive evidence of the perpetuity of the institution.

II. And to this end, let us IMBIBE THE SPIRIT OF
LOVE AND DELIGHT in the worship of God, which the
Psalms and Prophets display.   We never can imitate
the earnestness of Moses, nor place the Sabbath on
the prominency where he exhibits it, unless we join to
it the holy David's love to God, and the sublime
Isaiah's spiritual joy in his service.   O, how much are
our Sabbaths, practically speaking, below those of the
saints of old.   How much is our repose of soul in
God, our fainting of heart after his courts, our view of
the happiness which religion communicates, inferior to
the feelings which these holy men experienced !   Let
us pray, let us seek for such a spiritual state of heart,
for such a real choice and preference of God in Christ
Jesus, and such a delight in the contemplation of his
glory in creation, providence, and redemption, as may
enlarge our hearts and "lift them up in the ways of
the Lord ;" as may render the Sabbath a delight, as
may surround it with the honour and esteem which are
its due, and make "one day in God's courts better
than a thousand."   Then, then should we indeed sanctify our Sabbaths.   Then would disputes soon cease.
Then should we abstain naturally and with choice,
from "doing our own ways, finding our own pleasure,
or speaking our own words."   And what, indeed, does

D

the love of our Saviour Christ, and the grace of the
Holy Spirit do for us, if they do not raise us out of the
world, and unite us with the spiritual church in religious adoration ?   This is the secret of true religion.
It reigns by love, it subdues by the sense of benefits, it
calms and purifies the soul, it turns the current of the
affections towards God, it pays cheerfully and with delight the tribute of one day in seven, as the Lord's portion and share out of man's time and efforts, and
for the training and discipline of the soul for an eternity
of worship in heaven.

III. But add to these motives THE AWFUL INDIG-
NATION of Almighty God against the contempt of
his name and his day.   Judge from the terrors of
Mount Sinai and the denunciations of the prophets
against the sin of polluting the Sabbath, what is the
esteem in which the Lord holds it.   I would urge
upon my own conscience, and that of others, the guilt
of that weariness in the service of God, that contempt
and neglect of its spiritual benefits, that inward disgust and pride which harden the heart against penitence and a return to God, that conceit and self-reliance
and self-satisfaction which engender dislike for divine
worship and religious repose.   I would urge the criminality, the peculiar criminality, under the spiritual
dispensation of the New Testament, of those sins
which Moses and the prophets condemned with so
much vehemence under the less perfect economy of
the law.   The greater ease and liberty of the gospel
and our freedom from the bond of ceremonies, only aug-
ment the guilt of that enmity against the holy nature
and blessed will of God, from which contempt of his
worship springs.   We have now no multiplied festivals
to observe, no difficult and expensive offerings to present, no perpetual oblations to go through with, no
sabbatical years to observe.   The simple and noble
worship and repose of one day in seven is what God
commands—or rather grants us as a boon—and only
enjoins when we refuse thus to receive it.

Awaken, then, Christian brethren, from the torpo

and lukewarmness which too much mark the age in which we live. A philosophic conceit, the pride of intellect, indifference to truth, a selfish calculating love of ease and indulgence, a blindness to the magnitude and dignity of the claims of our invisible Benefactor—these are our sins—and these were the sins of the days of Ezekiel and Malachi under the old dispensation. And from these sins, a readiness to listen to objections against the Sabbath springs. Who would ever have endured the fiction of an anticipation in the narrative of the glorious work of creation,[1] or of the Sabbath being a merely ceremonial rite, if an indifference and weariness for spiritual things had not predisposed the mind to seek any excuse for its worldliness and unconcern. But let us be aroused to real penitence. Let us view the guilt of contemning God in its true light. Let our hardness of heart, and pride of intellectual distinction, yield to the sweet influences of grace, and we shall honour God in the day which from the creation has been dedicated to him. The anomaly of a Christian loving God and undervaluing the day of God, has never yet been known. But further,

IV. Let us IMITATE THE HEROIC ZEAL of Ezra and Nehemiah in vindicating the sanctity of the Sabbath. Surely the Christian cannot hesitate as to his duty, after considering the conduct of these inspired men. Each should do what his talent and influence in society enjoin and permit. It is the principle upon which I insist. If we cannot absolutely shut the gates of our great cities to the entrance of merchandize, we may do something to lessen the evil. We may shut the door of our houses—we may prohibit the purchase or reception of articles of consumption by our servants and dependants—we may encourage those upon whom we have any influence, to observe the sacred day. Let only the zeal, the courage, the firmness, the disinterestedness of Ezra

---

[1] No man ever thought of anticipation in this place, who was not first anticipated with manifest prejudice, says an old writer.

D 2

and Nehemiah be connected with their piety and love to the house of their God, and much would be done. How have national revivals of religion been brought about in other times? In the days of Samuel, in those of Hezekiah or Jehoshaphat or Josiah? The magistrates and ministers of religion took the lead. Men like Ezra and Nehemiah rose up with holy determination and simplicity. Public conscience and sentiment were addressed. Gross infractions of the day of rest were discouraged. Prayer was offered up at the throne of mercy. God answered the petition, and truth and holiness were again established.

V. I add only one more thought; that as the guilt of Sabbath-breaking and of idolatry were united of old in the practice of the people, and in the threatnings of the holy prophets, we should especially dread that FALSE VIEW OF THE CHARACTER OF GOD AND OF THE NATURE OF CHRISTIANITY which are generally associated with the violation of the Lord's day. To worship God aright, is to adore him in his perfections, in his manifestations of himself in his word, in his infinite right over man, in his holy law, in his eternal judgment, in the revelation of a way of salvation through the atonement of Christ and in the operations of the divine Spirit, in the communion with himself to which he admits the devout worshipper. All other worship is idolatry in its proper sense. It is the setting up idols in our heart. It is worshipping a God of our own imagination. Now mark the alliance of all this with the sin of neglecting and violating the holy Sabbath. We throw off the day of religion, because we throw off the God whom that religion regards. We set up the god of the infidel, or of the Socinian, or the careless worldly professor, which is such an one as himself; and then we worship that idol, by vanity, by carnal indulgence, by the neglect of all the spiritual duties of the Christian Sabbath. Let the God of the Bible be enthroned in the heart, and the Sabbath which that God blessed and sanctified, will be duly honoured. To love him, to glorify him, to worship him, to meditate on his works, to prepare for the enjoyment of him for ever, will fully occupy that sacred portion of time which he has appointed for those ends. Faith in the object of worship will produce the sanctification of the day of worship. And thus shall we join the instructions of the Old Testament on the subject of the Sabbath, with the grace and strength furnished in the New, and have the patriarchal and Christian day of rest united and fulfilled in all their blessings.

SERMON III.

MARK II. 27, 28.

*And he said unto them, The Sabbath was made for
man, and not man for the Sabbath :*
Therefore the Son of man is Lord also of the Sabbath.

WE now come to a most important part of the argument for the divine authority and perpetual obligation
of a day of weekly rest. There has hitherto appeared
but little of real weight, or even of plausibility, in the
objections raised by our opponents. The fiction of an
anticipated history is so groundless, and the attempt to
evade the authority of the fourth commandment so
violent, that we may almost wonder that any professed
believer in Christianity should have advanced them.
But the case is different, as it respects the gospel dispensation : our Lord undoubtedly introduced material
changes in the observation of the Sabbath as prevalent at the time of his ministry. Undoubtedly he relieved it from many restrictions. On what authority,
indeed, these restrictions had been introduced, is another question—but undoubtedly he relieved it. The
apostles followed, and transferred the time of its celebration, from the last to the first day of the week ; and
abrogated finally the ceremonies and rites of the

Jewish law. All this is considered by many as a repeal of the institution altogether—they view the
Christian Sabbath as a new command resting on its
own basis—and that basis the mere example of the
apostles.

Let us then calmly consider this part of the subject.
The authority of our Redeemer, as " Lord of the Sabbath," to abrogate or dissolve any divine ordinance, is
cknowledged on all hands.

Here it will be convenient to divide the question
into two parts—The divine authority of the Sabbath
itself under the Christian dispensation—and The ground
on which the day of its observation was changed. In
other words, we must answer two questions : Have we
a Sabbath under the gospel? and, Is that Sabbath
the Lord's day? The first will occupy the present discourse.

Now if the statements we have made in our preceding arguments be at all valid, this question will almost
answer itself. For we left the Sabbath on the margin
of the Old Testament, ready to step over into the
Evangelical dispensation. We had brought up the
proof of its continued obligation from its first enactment in paradise, to the very line of separation. The
glories of the six days' work, succeeded by a seventh
day's repose, as inscribed on the order of creation—the
insertion of the law of the Sabbath into the ten commandments—its distinct and lofty position above the
ceremonies of Moses in the very midst of that economy—its inculcation by the prophets as of essential
moral force, and as about to form a part of the Messiah's kingdom ;—all this implies that Christ's religion
would not be deprived of its day of rest—that the
most perfect dispensation would not be inferior in privilege to the less perfect—that where all is grace, and
light, and universality, we should not be allowed a
smaller portion of time for the immediate honour of
our God, and communion with him, than where bondage and fear prevailed.

And this we shall accordingly find to be the case.

We shall see the ten commandments, and the Sabbath amongst the number, recognized by our Lord and his apostles—we shall observe our Saviour honouring it on all occasions by his practice, and vindicating it from unauthorized traditions injurious to its real design. We shall find that nothing with respect to it is abrogated under the gospel, but those temporary ceremonies and statutes which constituted the peculiarities of the Jewish age. We shall perceive that the especial promise of the New Testament has for its object to render its duties more practicable and delightful, and thus increase tenfold their obligation.

That is, we shall discover that the solemn axiom delivered by our Lord in the text, together with the caution and inference connected with it, lays down the true principle on which the Christian day of rest is to be enforced.

The sabbath was made for man; was originally granted him as a boon—was appointed for his necessary repose from worldly toil and care—was made, not for the Jew merely, but for man as man; for man as consisting of body and soul; as requiring rest and refreshment for the one, religious instruction for the other; as created for his Maker's glory, and destined for eternal happiness or misery.

What a noble declaration of the perpetual design and authority of the institution! Of all our Saviour's axioms, few are more clear, definite, important, universal. It takes for granted that there would be a Sabbath under his dispensation; and it defines its purposes, that it was made for the advantage and benefit of man—for his highest welfare both as to his body and soul.

Nor is the caution which our Lord adds less appropriate, considering the austerities which the Jewish masters had imposed; NOT MAN FOR THE SABBATH. Their error lay in overlooking the grand moral end of the institution. They taught that " man was made for the Sabbath." Our Lord recalls the institution to its first and true design; he teaches that it was not a rite ending in itself, and to which all the moral purposes of it should yield ; but that God would "have mercy and not sacrifice," and that when the real spiritual and exalted interests of man, for which it was appointed, required a suspension of any of its outward observances, that suspension was lawful.

The axiom and caution explain all our Lord's conduct. The fundamental law of the Sabbath remains unchanged : as it began, so it will end only with the world itself. But the embarrassments and trammels of human fancy are dissolved, and its simplicity is restored.

The inference follows of course ; THEREFORE THE SON OF MAN IS LORD ALSO OF THE SABBATH. For the institution having originally been made for the good of man ; and "the Lord of the Sabbath" having become, by his incarnation "the Son of man," for redeeming him from death, for introducing the last dispensation, and ordering all things in that dispensation for his best welfare—" THEREFORE the Son of man is Lord also of the Sabbath," to expound as legislator its injunctions, to annul with authority the impositions introduced contrary to its genuine spirit, to leave it as one of the distinctions and privileges of his universal and spiritual kingdom.

Proceed we, then, to consider the divine obligation of the weekly day of rest under the gospel, as apparent from

I. THE RECOGNITION OF THE TEN COMMANDMENTS, AND OF THE FOURTH AMONGST THE NUMBER, which our Lord and his apostles make.

It will be recollected, that the moral law had for fifteen centuries been known as a distinct code, under the titles of " The Tables of the Law," " The Commandments," " The Law," and similar appropriate names, which, as we have already remarked, meant the same, with reference to other commands; as " The Bible" with regard to other books. It need scarcely be noticed, also, that " The Commandments" were divided

into two parts, the first containing four precepts and
no more, the second six; the whole being ten ; and
that the first series was summed up in the well-known
command of the love of God, and the second of the
love of our neighbour.

Now if our Lord and his apostles recognize the
perpetual authority of the whole moral law as a matter of course; if they refer to it as known by the collective name or names which we have noticed ; if they
divide it into the two great commanding precepts of
the love of God and man; if they refer to some of
them in a manner which proves that the order of the
ten commands was the same as when promulgated from
Mount Sinai; if they declare that the gospel abrogated
none of the precepts, but enlarged their scope and enforced their authority ; and if, finally, they denounced
their displeasure against those who should teach any
relaxation of the least of these enactments;—then the
whole ten commandments, the fourth included, are of
plenary force under the gospel.

And need I remind you that when one came to Christ
and said, " Good Master, what shall I do that I may
inherit eternal life?" our Lord at once replied, as a
matter perfectly familiar, "Thou knowest THE COM-
MANDMENTS"—" if thou wilt enter into life, keep
THE COMMANDMENTS,"—and when the inquirer demanded which, Jesus recapitulated five; thus expressly recognizing the whole code?[1]   Need I tell
you, that on another occasion, he summed up the
two tables, as Moses so frequently had done in the
Pentateuch, into the love of God and the love
of our neighbour, adding, as if to strengthen his recognition of them—" On these two commandments hang
all the law and the prophets?"[2]

Need I tell you that at another time he reproached
the Pharisees with having " made void" one commandment, the fifth, " through their tradition?" Need I
remind you, above all, that he declared in one of his

[1] Matt. xix. 16;   Mark x. 17;   Luke xviii. 18.
[2] Deut. vi. 5; Lev. xix. 19; Matt. xxii. 36—40.

most solemn discourses—that on the Mount—that he
"came not to destroy the law and the prophets, but to
fulfil"—that "till heaven and earth should pass, one
jot or one tittle should in no wise pass from the law
till all be fulfilled"—that "whosoever should break one
of the least of these commandments and should teach
men so, should be called least in the kingdom of heaven"—and that "unless the righteousness of his disciples should exceed the righteousness of the Scribes
and Pharisees, they should in no case enter into the
kingdom of heaven?" Can any thing be more express
upon our argument than such declarations; especially
as our Saviour leaves us in no doubt of what he meant
by the law, but proceeds to explain several of the ten
commandments?[1]

And why should I detain you with going over the
same ground as to the apostles? Do they not every
where acknowledge, without addition or diminution,
the same decalogue? Does not St. Paul say, "He
that loveth another, hath fulfilled the law?" and
then, after enumerating five commands, does he not
add, "And if there be any other commandment,
it is briefly comprehended in this saying, "Thou
shalt love thy neighbour as thyself?"[2] And though
he quote not separately, any more than our
Lord, the particular precepts of the first table, yet
can any one suppose, that when he sums up the
second table, as we have seen, in the love of our
neighbour, he meant to exclude the first table or any
precept of it, any more than our Lord meant to exclude it, who actually quotes the Mosaic summary of that
first table? But I need not dwell on so clear a point.
I need not enumerate the passages where St. Paul and
his brother apostles cite or refer to the moral law, as of
divine and perpetual authority under the gospel. What
indeed is sin "but the transgression of the law?"[3]
What is the Christian's whole state of duty, but "the
being under the law to Christ?"[4] And how would the

[1] Matt. v. vi. vii.   [2] Rom. xiii. 8.
[3] 1 John iii. 4.   [4] 1 Cor. ix. 21.

apostle have "known sin, except the law had said, thou shalt not covet?"[1] I add, therefore only, that St. Paul, when writing to the Ephesians, a Gentile church, assumes their acquaintance with the very order of the precepts of the decalogue, as well as their authority, when he states concerning filial obedience, that it is "the first commandment with promise;"— thus recognizing the usual arrangement of the decalogue, and proving that no commandment had been changed or dispossessed of its place.

Now this carries the whole question. If Christ and his apostles came not to relax, or abrogate, or destroy the moral law, but to vindicate, explain, and enforce it, then the ten commandments in every one of their number—and the fourth equally with the rest—is established and recognized—the law of the Sabbath is as authoritative as the law against theft, murder, or adultery. The code is one entire, inseparable body of moral precepts. "Whosoever," says St. James, in language which implies all we are contending for, "shall keep THE WHOLE LAW, and yet offend in one point, he is guilty of all: for he that said, Do not commit adultery, said also, Do not kill. Now if thou commit no adultery, yet if thou kill, thou art become a transgressor of THE LAW."[2]

After the argument of the preceding discourses, it seems only trifling to object that our Lord has not expressly quoted the fourth commandment. The mere silence of Scripture will not surely be again alleged. And we are to remember that several other of the precepts of the decalogue are equally omitted— and that as the fault of the Jews with regard to the Sabbath, was not in defect, but excess—as they considered the fourth commandment as surpassing every other in dignity—as they boasted of a most minute and punctilious observance of it—and loaded it with innumerable traditions; our Lord had only to restore it to its original simplicity, and set it forth by his doc-

[1] Rom. vii. 7.   [2] James ii. 10, 11.

trine and example in its native loveliness. And this is precisely what he did. The neglect into which the original law had fallen before the Mosaical dispensation, was supplied by exactly what was then required, an express promulgation—a strong, direct, detailed command inserted amongst the other moral precepts. The excess which had been generated by the superstition and formality of the Jews before the gospel economy, was corrected by exactly what was required, the gracious conduct of our Lord. For,

II. HE HONOURED THE SABBATH ON ALL OCCASIONS, AND NEVER VIOLATED ITS SANCTITY, according to the true import of the moral and ceremonial enactments of Moses; but merely brought it back to its genuine spirit and design, from the uncommanded austerities of the Jewish doctors—a conduct which the apostles also perfectly understood and imitated in their own practice.

On eleven occasions is our Lord's doctrine and spirit with regard to the Sabbath recorded. These are distributed over his ministry. Between the first and second passover we have three: the sermon at Nazareth;[1] his teaching at Capernaum,[2] and his healing Peter's wife's mother.[3] We have four between the second and third passover: the miracle at the pool of Bethesda;[4] the plucking the ears of corn;[5] his restoring the withered hand;[6] and his second teaching at Nazareth.[7] The remaining occasions occur between the third and fourth passover—the last of his ministry: his defence of the miracle at the pool of Bethesda;[8] his healing of the man blind from his birth;[9] of the woman eighteen years infirm[10]—and the man afflicted with the dropsy.[11]

Now, if on calmly examining all these narratives, we

[1] Luke iv. 16—22.   [2] Luke iv. 31—37.   [3] Luke iv. 38—41.
[4] John v. 5. ad fin.   [5] Luke vi. 1—5.   [6] Matt. xii. 9—21.
[7] Mark vi. 1—6.   [8] John vii. 21, ad fin.   [9] John ix. 1. ad fin.
[10] Luke xiii. 10—17.   [11] Luke xiv. 1—6.

should find that our Lord always honoured and kept
the Sabbath; that he performed miracles of healing
upon it, only as occasions arose, and in order to confirm his doctrine, and ensure faith in his messiahship;
that these acts were never in violation, but entirely in
accordance with the Mosaic law; that they were especially designed to relieve the institution from the oppressive traditions of the Scribes and Pharisees; that
no objections were taken against them at first, and
afterwards only as pretences to cover their malignity
and hatred to his divine mission; that our Lord's de-
fences of himself and his disciples proceeded on what
was the real import of the fourth commandment, though
misunderstood; and assumed that the Sabbath itself
was of perpetual obligation; and if all this be confirmed by our Lord's caution concerning the flight of
his disciples at the destruction of Jerusalem, and by
the conduct and doctrines of his inspired apostles at
the first promulgation of the gospel—then it will be
admitted that our Saviour, so far from relaxing the
fourth commandment, or abrogating the essential law
of the Sabbath, vindic·ted it, established it, and left it
in more than its origina authority.

We begin with the three incidents occurring before
the second passover.   On the very first of these
we are told that our Lord "went, AS HIS CUSTOM WAS,
into the synagogue on the Sabbath-day, and stood up
for to read."   This marks a habit—a habit acted upon
in his own city, "where he had been brought up."
The divine discourse cited from the prophet Isaiah
followed; and thus the highest honour is put upon
his Father's institution.   Capernaum is the next
scene presented to us.   "He taught the people on the
Sabbath-days," is the record; betokening again a custom, a course of instruction.   But a dæmoniac is
present, and cries out to the disturbance of the worshippers; the devil is rebuked with a word, quits the
possessed sufferer, bears unwilling testimony to our
Saviour's messiahship, and diffuses his fame; so that

the evangelist notes the fulfilment of the prophecy :
" The people which sat in darkness saw a great light."[1]
No idea of a breach of the fourth commandment enters
a single mind, no clamour is raised, no accusation is
brought against him.   The Sabbath is exalted by our
Lord's conduct on it.   On the same evening, retiring
from the synagogue and entering Simon's house, he
heals his wife's mother of a fever; and afterwards,
when the sun was set and the Sabbath past,[2] multitudes
of sick were brought to him, and were healed—for on
no occasion were crowds collected even for this beneficent exertion of power, on the Sabbath : the miracles
are separate acts, occurring incidentally, and forming
a part of our Lord's doctrine and instructions as
Messiah.

Between the second and third passover, similar deeds
of mercy occur, and are now seized on by the Pharisees
and Scribes as pretences for displaying that hatred to
his person and mission which his miracles and doctrines
had by this time inflamed.

At the pool of Bethesda, the impotent man, after
lying " thirty and eight years in that case," is healed ;
and is commanded, in testimony to the truth of the
cure, or rather as a part of the miraculous act, to
carry away with him the miserable rug or covering on
which he lay,—which it was customary for the poor
to take with them from place to place, and which, if
left behind at the pool, would have been lost, though
probably his only possession.[3]

---

[1] Matt. iv. 14—16, for it was on that occasion.
[2] The Jewish Sabbath ended at sunset.
[3] The beds of the poor in the Holy Land were often mattresses,
rugs, and coverings, used during the day for raiment—" If thou
take at all thy neighbour's raiment to pledge, thou shalt deliver
it to him by that the sun goeth down : for that is his covering
only, it is his raiment for his skin: wherein shall he sleep."—
Exod. xxii. 26, 27.   Similar customs prevail in hot countries now.
" Mattresses, or something of that kind, are used (in Palestine)
for sleeping upon."   They are rolled up, carried away, and
placed in cupboards till they are wanted at night."   " In many

His disciples passing through the corn-fields, (most likely to or from the synagogue,) and having nothing with them to eat, and no opportunity of procuring victuals, pluck the ears of corn to satisfy the pressure of instant hunger.   The man with the withered hand is restored, our Lord knowing the secret thoughts of the Pharisees who were watching him, and asking them, before he performed the cure, whether it was "lawful on the Sabbath to do good or to do evil—to save life or to destroy it." Their silence is the plainest admission that it was permitted to heal on the Sabbath-day.   Lastly, his second instructions at Nazareth are recorded, no instance of healing occurring; and the offence arising from his mission and character, breaking out notwithstanding.

Now in this second series of cases, can any one really maintain that there was any violation of the Sabbath, moral or ceremonial, by such conduct and doctrine in such a person as our Lord—a messenger from heaven, one who was executing the office of Messiah, one who sustained his divine message by these divine acts? Were they not, on the contrary, in the highest degree calculated to honour and distinguish the day of religious worship, did they not tend to the immediate glory of his heavenly Father, and promote all the highest ends of the Sabbath? Were not the attendant multitudes thus enabled to witness his mighty deeds; and did not even the false accusations of the Pharisees lead to a more close examination of the truth of the miracles performed?

But to reap and gather in corn is a breach of the rest of the Sabbath!—but to bear and carry burdens is a breach of the ceremonial law! Yes; and of the moral also. But the plucking a few ears of corn,

parts of Spain the country people sleep upon mats of rushes or straw, which they roll up in the morning and take with them."—*Harmer and Rocca in Burder.*

Accordingly our Lord said to the paralytic, almost as a matter of course, if his cure were wrought, and as a part of that cure, "Arise, take up thy bed and walk."—Matt. ix. 6.

when passing through a field and pressed with hunger, is not reaping—and to carry to one's house a mat-bed as a part of a miraculous cure, from a pool, where if left it would instantly have been lost to its possessor, is not bearing burdens.   Between the reaper gathering in his field, and the disciples' conduct, there was as great a difference as between "the men of Tyre bringing fish and all manner of ware to Jerusalem,"[1] and the impotent man bearing off his bed to his house, in proof of a miraculous restoration to health.

We pass to the third series of our Lord's conduct and works on the Sabbath—those immediately preceding his passion.   On the first of these occasions he vindicates the cure of the impotent man which had been wrought a year, or a year and a half, previously, at the pool.   The restoration of the man blind from his birth, whom he met as he was passing by, forms the second.   The next is the loosing from her infirmity the woman who had been bowed together for eighteen years by Satan, and who, though she in no wise could lift up herself, had yet come to the worship of the synagogue.   The last was the cure of the man that had the dropsy, who was present in the house where our Saviour was eating bread—the Pharisees watching him—and Jesus pausing to ask them, before he relieved the sufferer, "If it was lawful to heal on the Sabbath-day?"   Upon which, "holding their peace," as they must needs do, as they knew that it was no violation of their law, he "took him, and healed him, and let him go."[2]

Such are the separate narratives, which sufficiently vindicate themselves, considering the mission which our Lord was fulfilling, and the habitual observation of the worship and law of the Sabbath which he maintained.

But, mark the GENERAL GROUNDS ON WHICH HE DEFENDS his conduct, and that of his disciples, in the

---

[1] Neh. xiii. 16.   [2] Luke xiv. 1---6.

second series of his works,[1] for the first excited nothing
but admiration. Mark how he appeals to their own
law, their own usages, as recorded in the sacred books
—the example of David, the example of the priests
preparing the sacrifices—the divine decision, " I will
have mercy and not sacrifice ;" concluding the defence
with the words which form the text of this discourse—
"The Sabbath was made for " the highest good of
" man ;" " not man for " the good of "the Sabbath—
therefore the Son of Man is Lord also of the Sabbath,"
to explain its true ritual, and bring it back to its true
design.

Notice also another ground of our Lord's vindication,
the common necessities of our nature, which no law of
God can be supposed to prohibit : " Thou hypocrite,
doth not each one of you on the Sabbath loose his ox
or his ass from the stall, and lead him away to water-
ing ?"[2] —" What man shall there be among you, that
shall have one sheep, and if it fall into a pit on the
Sabbath-day, will he not lay hold on it and lift it out ?
How much then is a man better than a sheep ?"[3] Such
language proves that it was the false and hypocritical
interpretations of the Pharisees which our Lord meant
to oppose.   And, indeed, the effect of his remonstrances was so pointed, that on one occasion we are
told, "his adversaries were ashamed, and could not
answer him again to these things; whilst all the people
rejoiced and glorified God."[4]

That these actions and cures on the Sabbath were
contrary to THE NOTIONS AND FALSE GLOSSES OF

---

[1] "Have ye not READ what David did when he was an hungred,
and they that were with him, how he entered into the house of
God, and did eat the shew-bread, which it was not lawful to eat,
neither to them that were with him, but only for the priests?   Or
have ye not read IN THE LAW how that on the Sabbath-days the
priests in the temple profane the Sabbath and are blameless? But,
I say unto you in this place is one greater than the temple.   But
if ye had known what this meaneth, I will have mercy and not
sacrifice, ye would NOT HAVE CONDEMNED THE GUILTLESS."
[2] Luke xiii. 15.   [3] Matt. xii. 11, 12.
[4] Luke xiii. 17 ; xiv. 6.

THE JEWISH DOCTORS, I admit. The hatred of the people, and especially their rulers, to our Saviour's character and mission, was the real cause : but the uncommanded traditions of the Pharisees afforded them a pretext. And when we consider the extent to which this vexatious and hypocritical system had been carried, and the immense importance to an universal and benignant religion like Christianity, to have one of its chief glories, the day of rest, placed on its true footing, we cannot wonder at the course which our Saviour pursued. The law of the Sabbath had been loaded by the masters with unreasonable and minute observances. " You will see in their oral law," says Dr. Wotton, " an incredible minuteness in things seemingly the most trivial; but all subservient to one main end, which was to teach men how to evade the law, when they seemed most solicitous to observe it."[1] Take as an example the absurd reason assigned for the institution itself by Philo the Jew: " Now, why God chose the seventh day, and established it by law for the day of rest, you need not ask at all of me, since both physicians and philosophers have so often declared, of what great power and virtue that number is, as in all other things, so specially on the nature and state of man. And thus you have the reason of the seventh-day-Sabbath."[2]

Now the exact points which our Lord determined to fall within the Mosaical law, are those which the Jewish lawyers had prohibited. They excused themselves, for instance, from offices of piety and charity to their neighbour, though they allowed the law its fair import when their own ox or ass was to be fed or rescued from danger—that is, they took advantage of the Sabbath to veil their own selfishness. They held, again, that no ointment should be applied to a wound, and that in chronical diseases the persons afflicted should endure them a day longer, rather than attempt a cure on the Sabbath : but they allowed circumcision to be performed

[1] Wotton's Mishna.   [2] Heylin in Ecl. Rev. 1830.

on the same day.   Do we wonder, then, that our
blessed Lord healed on the Sabbath-day—do we wonder that he selected chronical complaints as the object
of his compassion—do we wonder that he bid the impotent man to take home his humble bed—do we wonder that he made clay and anointed the eyes of the
blind?   These actions were designed to sweep away
the rubbish of human tradition, which perverted the
true design, and encumbered the real duties of the
Sabbath.

In all this our Lord made NO ALTERATION IN THE
MOSAIC LAW, he relaxed no part of the divine commandment, he repealed no particle of the ceremonial
usages, (this belonged to the apostolic day,) it was not
the Christian but the Jewish Sabbath which he vindicated, and brought back to its original design by
showing that works of necessity and charity were
entirely consistent with the letter as well as spirit of
the fourth commandment, as well as with the ceremonial
and judicial statutes of Moses.

Indeed all our Lord's REASONINGS SUPPOSE THE CON-
TINUANCE OF THE DAY OF REST IN ITS ESSENTIAL
MORAL OBLIGATION UPON MAN.   The idea of a
worshipper of God without a Sabbath never entered
the mind of Jew or Christian in any age—much less
in that of our Saviour.   Why regulate, why amend,
why modify the false usages, if all was about to be
abrogated?   Why contend so warmly against the inventions of the traditionary masters?   Why lay down
distinctions between what is lawful and what is unlawful to be done? [1]   Why determine that works of mercy
and charity are allowable, thus implicitly prohibiting
all other works?   Why not silence the Pharisees by
declaring that the Sabbath was a merely temporary
observance, about to vanish before the permanent law
of the gospel?   When our Lord, therefore, instead of
all this, defends himself and his disciples by a mode

[1] Mark the expression, " Wherefore it is LAWFUL to do well
(to heal the sick and similar acts) on the Sabbath-day."—Matt.
xii. 12.

of argument in which the permanence of the Sabbath is assumed, we conclude that he meant to teach that the moral obligation of it remained, and would remain under the gospel age.

It is thus he EXPLAINED AND VINDICATED OTHER COMMANDS, taking for granted the validity of the commands themselves, and adding his authoritative expositions. Who ever thought that his extension and new application of several precepts of the moral law, in the sermon on the Mount, was intended to weaken the force of the original commands? Who ever imagined that when the traditions concerning the fifth precept were exposed, and the pretence of Corban swept away, that one iota of the law itself was removed?

And all this receives confirmation from our Lord's SUPPOSING THE CONTINUANCE OF THE SABBATH at a period when all real obligation to a Jewish institution would long have ceased. In foretelling the destruction of Jerusalem, and directing the flight of his disciples (not the Jews generally—but his disciples —Christians—and this in a private and confidential conference, and applying to a calamity nearly forty years distant, when the ceremonial and civil law of the Jews would long have been publicly abrogated by the mission of his apostles) he bids them to pray, " That their flight be not in the winter, NOR ON THE SABBATH-DAY;" as these two impediments, the one from the nature of the season, the other from the obligation of the fourth commandment, would obstruct their escape. The observation cannot be expounded of any superstitious fears of violating a ceremonial or Mosaical precept, or even the tradition of the elders; because flight under imminent peril was allowed. The argument, therefore, seems of mighty force.

But how did THE INSPIRED APOSTLES UNDERSTAND their Master's doctrine? What was their conduct immediately upon the descent of the Spirit, and in the interval between the abrogation of the ceremo-

nial law and the change of the day of rest, from the
seventh to the first of the week? Did they, or did
they not, honour the Sabbath? A very few words
will suffice on this point: because no one ventures to
deny that their devout observation of the Jewish rest
extended even beyond the time when the Christian (as
we shall prove in our next discourse) superseded it.
They were so far from neglecting the Sabbath, that
they kept for a period, in order to conciliate the Jews,
both the Mosaical and Christian. I speak not of the
holy women who, embued with their Lord's doctrine,
and guided by his conduct, hesitated not a moment to
" rest the Sabbath-day ACCORDING TO THE COM-
MANDMENT;"[1] eager as they were to provide spices
and ointments for his body. I dwell not upon the
notice of the sacred day, which occurs naturally
and without effort, in the Acts of the Apostles, even
where the Jews are not concerned: " And the Gentiles
besought that these words might be preached unto
them the next Sabbath. And the next Sabbath almost
the whole city came together to hear the word of
God."[2] Nor will I do more than refer to the apostle's habit, copied from that of his divine Lord, of
sanctifying this most ancient of institutions: "and Paul,
AS HIS MANNER WAS, went in unto them, and three
Sabbath-days reasoned with them out of the Scriptures. And he reasoned in the synagogue EVERY
SABBATH."

So contrary to the truth of the case is it, to suppose that our Lord and his apostles abrogated the law
of the Sabbath—THEY DID NOT EVEN RELAX IT.
It wanted no relaxation. Like every other, the fourth
commandment was " holy, just, and good." It contained in itself all that principle of suspension in
cases of real necessity, which the mercy of the Almighty from the first intended, and which the tenor of
the precept was meant to include. Not even the ceremonial and temporary appendages of the Mosaical

<hr>

[1] Luke xxiii. 56.   [2] Acts xiii. 42—45.

economy were violated by our Lord.   All his conduct
exalted and honoured the day of his heavenly Father,
and vindicated it from the false glosses of the masters,
which, injurious as they were to the Jewish religion,
would have " eaten as doth a cancer" into the Christian—and, in fact, would have been a fatal obstruction
to its universality.

To relax, indeed, any one of the moral and essential rules of human duty, would have been the very
thing which OUR LORD MOST POINTEDLY CONDEMNED
in his sermon on the Mount—it would have been a
curse, not a blessing, to man.   The moral law is in all
its parts a transcript of the divine goodness, and the
materials of human happiness.   What man wants is,
not an alteration of the moral law of his Maker, but
pardon, grace, salvation—motive and strength to love
God and to keep his commandments, and more particularly that which is rather a boon and gift than a precept—which was MADE FOR MAN; and which, when
cleared by the Lord of the Sabbath from the austerities which perverted all its designs and evaporated all
its spirit, is set forth in his kingdom in more than its
original dignity and glory.

III. We proceed, then, to our next point, which is
indeed implied in what we have already proved—That
nothing is abrogated under the Christian dispensation
with respect to the Sabbath, but THOSE TEMPORARY
AND FIGURATIVE ENACTMENTS WHICH CONSTITUTED
THE PECULIARITIES OF THE JEWISH AGE.

For that these are abrogated it is important for us to
remember.   We maintain not now the Jewish Sabbath, nor the Mosaic Sabbath, nor the ceremonial
Sabbath.   Here we request a particular attention.   It
is a misconception almost constantly made.   The moment we defend the original institution of the Sabbath
in paradise, and its perpetuity and authority as a part
of the moral law, we are suspected of leaning towards
the Jewish Sabbath.   And when we go on to show
that our Lord never violated the Mosaic enactments

but honoured them in his whole ministry, and left the Sabbath in its full force, we are condemned at once as bringing in again the abrogated ceremonies. We.assert, then, just as strongly, that the Jewish Sabbath is abolished, as we maintain that the primitive and patriarchal is restored and reanimated with the peculiar grace and motives of the Christian dispensation. The moral, essential law of the day of rest remains, nay is increased in obligation, like every other precept of the decalogue; the ceremonial and judicial super-additions have passed away with the dispensation which gave them birth.

Our argument from the example and doctrine of our Lord went, indeed, to prove, not only that he recognized the moral law of the fourth commandment, but that he also honoured its Mosaical ceremonies, because he was " a minister of the circumcision for the truth of God." What we now assert is, that after the resurrection of Christ, and the descent of the Holy Spirit, the gospel-day burst upon the world, and dissipated " the shadows" of the Jewish law—the Mosaic covenant " decayed and waxed old and was ready to vanish away," and the evangelical covenant took its place—all that part of the sabbatical observances which was temporary and figurative, and dependant on the Jewish theocracy, was carried away; and nothing left but the primary essential law of one day's religious rest, after six days' labour, as first promulgated in paradise, as re-established and reduced to a written precept in the moral law, and as explained and vindicated from Pharisaical impositions by our gracious Redeemer. We have now a better covenant, a nobler mediator, a more glorious high priest, a more free and unembarrassed way of access, a richer sacrifice; other altar, temple, worship, and sacraments; a new and simpler sanctification of the season allotted for all these duties. The introductory dispensation is taken out of the way, the scaffolding removed, the emblems abrogated; and the last dispensation, the spiritual building and perfect atonement, are come.

The Jewish Sabbath is no more in force SINCE, than it was BEFORE, the Mosaical economy. The double sacrifices, and indeed all sacrifices of animals; the shew-bread; the holy vestments; the Levitical priest-hood itself; the civil and judicial statutes; the signs and badges of a national covenant; the ceremonial ablutions; the limitation to the particular day of the seven for its observance; the spirit of bondage; the whole manner and tone of worship as suited to that servile and imperfect state of things, are gone. These, if now insisted on (and possibly they have been in some periods of the Christian Church) may be justly denominated, carnal ordinances; " weak and beggarly elements; a yoke which neither we nor our fathers were able to bear."[1] We are, in all these and similar respects, to stand fast in "the liberty where-with Christ hath made us free, and not be entangled again in the yoke of bondage."[2]

The converts, indeed, from the Jewish people were permitted to observe for a season the injunctions of the Mosaic institutes—and those connected with the Sabbath amongst the number—supposing they relied not upon them for justification. Thus St. Paul circum-cised Timothy, fulfilled his vow as a Nazarite, kept the Jewish Sabbath after the Christian had commenced, walked unblameably in the ordinances; that is, "to the Jew he became a Jew, that he might gain the Jews; to them that were under the law, as under the law, that he might gain them that were under the law."[3]

But the authority of all that was ceremonial, was void, and the practice gradually ceased. The Gentile converts were strongly urged to resist all imposition of the antiquated yoke, and were taught the true spi-rituality of the Christian. " Blotting out the hand-writing of ordinances that was against us, which was contrary to us, and took it out of the way, nailing it to his cross." Such is the apostolic declaration; to which succeeds the inference—" Let no man, therefore, judge

---

[1] Gal. iv. 9; Acts xv. 10.   [2] Gal. v. 1.   [3] 1 Cor. ix. 20.

you in meat, or in drink, or in respect of an holy-
day, or the new-moon, or of the Sabbath-days; which
are A SHADOW OF THINGS TO COME; but the body is
of Christ." [1]

And yet more pungently to the self-justifying Gala-
tions: " How turn ye again to THE WEAK AND BEG-
GARLY ELEMENTS, whereunto ye desire to be in bondage! Ye observe days, and months, and times, and
years. I am afraid of you, lest I have bestowed on
you labour in vain." [2]

So, with his wonted tenderness where sincerity of
faith appeared, to the unestablished Roman converts,
" Him that is weak in the faith, receive ye, but not to
doubtful disputations. For one man believeth that he
may eat all things; another who is weak, eateth herbs.
One man esteemeth one day above another; another
esteemeth every day alike : let every man be fully persuaded in his own mind." [3]

How these passages could ever be supposed to be
meant to abolish the moral and essential law of the
Sabbath, (or THE LORD'S DAY, which was the name it
assumed immediately upon the Resurrection's drawing
it to the first day of the week,) it is difficult to conceive.
No doubt, if the anticipated history be received, and
if the assertion of the merely-ceremonial nature of the
Sabbath be admitted,-this or any other consequence may
be shown to follow. But having now a right to take
for granted the actual institution of the day of rest in
Paradise—its actual moral character and obligation,
from its incorporation into the decalogue—its essential
dignity and importance even when surrounded with the
appendages of the intervening economy of Moses—its
inherent authority as urged in the most evangelical
of the prophecies—and its entire simplicity and
force when purified from the corruptions of the Pharisees by our Saviour;—having a right to take all this
for granted, the passages just cited strongly confirm
our general argument, by showing that nothing but

1 Col. ii. 14—17.   2 Gal. iv. 7—11.   3 Rom. xiv. 1, 5.

the ceremonies and shadows connected with it are dispersed; the substance of course still remaining.

In fact, what took place with regard to the fourth commandment, happened, as we have already observed, to all the others. The moral law assumed, as it entered the Mosaic dispensation, her robes of emblematic and civil ceremony. Each commandment was adorned with appendages. When that dispensation ceased, she put off her robes, and reassumed her original simplicity of attire. And now the Queen of days approaches us with that native majesty and authority which was veiled, but not lost, during the figurative age;—a majesty and authority, which was derived from her first coronation in Paradise, which was augmented by the public proclamation of her rights on Mount Sinai, and which she retains with increased privileges and prerogatives under the New Testament.

IV. For this is the last point which establishes the dignity and glory of the weekly day of religious rest under the Christian dispensation, THAT THE DISTIN-GUISHING PROMISE OF THE NEW TESTAMENT HAS FOR ITS OBJECT TO RENDER THE DUTIES OF THE SABBATH MORE DELIGHTFUL, AND THUS INCREASES TENFOLD THEIR OBLIGATION.

For what is the distinguishing promise of the New Testament? What is the characteristic of the gospel? Is it not the larger grace of the Holy Spirit? Is it not that it is " the ministration of the Spirit?" And what is the most important office of the divine Spirit? Is it not to write this very law, these very ten commandments and none other, this very decalogue which was effaced from the heart of man by the fall, and which was republished with so much solemnity on Mount Sinai, and written on tables of stone with the finger of God, and deposited in the ark— is it not TO WRITE THIS LAW UPON THE HEART OF MAN? And would our Lord have promised the Holy Spirit for this purpose, if he had himself relaxed any part of this law? And does

not this promised aid increase the obligations of this
law upon man, and exhibit its importance with a tenfold force ?

Read the apostle's comment in the 8th chapter of
his epistle to the Hebrews, where he describes the new
covenant, and contrasts it with the old ; " Behold, the
days come, saith the Lord, when I will make a new
covenant with the house of Israel and with the house
of Judah; not according to the covenant, which I
made with their fathers, in the day when I took them
by the hand to lead them out of the land of Egypt;
because they continued not in my covenant and I regarded them not, saith the Lord. For this is the covenant that I will make with the house of Israel after
those days, saith the Lord. I will put my laws (the
very decalogue of which we speak) into their mind,
and write them in their hearts." [1]

And accordingly is not the first commandment, to
worship one God, thus written upon the heart? Is not
the second, to worship him not with graven images?
Is not the third, not to take his awful name in vain?
And so of all the others? And is the fourth then
omitted? Is there a gap, a failure in the divine code?
Was the fourth precept inserted in the decalogue by a
mistake? Are there ten commandments in the law,
and only nine written on the heart? Is the institution
of the Sabbath engraven and exhibited in the very
order of the first creation, and not engraven in the
order of the new creation? [2] Is the soul of man
formed to this heavenly temper in all other respects,
and has he no taste for devoting the seventh portion of
his time for the immediate service of his God? No,
my brethren, we have no abrogation of the immutable
law of God under the New Testament. On the contrary, the office of the Holy Spirit is to infix it deeply
in all its parts on the inmost soul of man. This confirms and clenches all our preceding arguments; and

[1] Heb. viii. 8—10.
[2] "If any man be in Christ he is a new creature;" or, NEW
CREATION.----2 Cor. v. 17.

especially that from the conduct and doctrine of our Lord, by whom the Spirit was sent for the comfort and guidance of the church.

The apostle yet more distinctly teaches us this, when he says, that the Christian is an epistle of Christ, and refers to the two tables of the law as transcribed on the human heart, and to the Holy Spirit as the divine Author of the transcription. Mark, I entreat you, his language: " Forasmuch as ye are manifestly declared to be the epistle of Christ, ministered by us, written not with ink, but with the Spirit of the living God; not IN TABLES OF STONE, but IN FLESHLY TABLES OF THE HEART."[1]   Here then are the two tables of the law—the first and second—the one containing the precepts of the love of God; the other, those of the love of man.   Here is a precise transfer of this law, a removal from mere tablets of stone, to the fleshly tablets of the heart.   In this transfer, do any of the commandments fall away?   In the Christian's heart, the two tablets are re-impressed, the two tablets as they came from the hand of God.   And has the fourth commandment disappeared in the passage through which all the rest have found their way from the tablets of a literal inscription, to those of the Christian's heart?   No, my brethren, if " there were a window in the Christian's bosom, you would see the fourth commandment filling as large a space of that epistle which is written not with ink, but with the Spirit of the living God, as it does in the decalogue of Moses."[2] You will find the Christian saying, " I delight" in this, as well as every other part of " the law of God, after the inner man;"[3] you will find him acknowledging with St. John, " His commandments are not grievous;"[4] you will find him saying with the Psalmist, " Therefore hold I straight ALL thy commandments, and all false ways I utterly abhor."[5]

Now just in proportion as the Holy Spirit is the

[1] 2 Cor. iii. 3. ·   [2] Chalmers.
[3] Rom. vii. 22.   [4] 1 John v. 3.   [5] Psalms cxix. 128.

grand peculiarity of the Christian dispensation, is the obligation of all the commandments, and therefore of the fourth, increased.   We stated in a former place, that the new motives which the advancing privileges and light of the church continually afforded, were so many additional claims of the day of rest upon man. But how much more are these claims strengthened by the aid now vouchsafed by the Holy Spirit—this aid being the distinguishing object of all his operations—producing a transfer of the law of the Sabbath from stony to fleshly tables ; and thus ending in a far lighter burden as to external service, and a far weightier obligation in respect of love and gratitude ?

But it is time to close the discussion, which has been necessarily long.   A case has been made out which commends itself, I trust, to every attentive hearer, and which strengthens the proofs of our preceding discourses, and carries on the argument to a moral demonstration.   I have dwelt at length on the conduct and doctrine of our Lord, because it is the only point where any reasonable doubt can be entertained.   The first blush of the other objections condemns them. But the objection raised from this has its plausibility ; it demanded and has rewarded our examination.   I feel confident that in the main the view now presented is the true one.   If any doubt is suffered to rest on the question, whether our Saviour violated the ceremonial law of the Sabbath, it is a subordinate point. Supposing he did violate the letter of this law, it was as " the Lord of the Sabbath," in the discharge of the highest of all commissions—that of the Saviour of mankind.   The topics which would remain would still be conclusive—that our Lord honoured and reverenced the institution itself—based his defence of what he did and said with regard to it on the Old Testament, and the admitted usages of the Mosaic dispensation—only opposed the false commandments of the traditionary doctors—and left the moral and substantial duty untouched.   These points would be admitted.   Add then, to these, the express recognition of the ten commandments by Christ and his apostles—the conduct of the apostles in honouring the Sabbath after his example—and the special office of the Holy Ghost under the gospel, augmenting the obligation, whilst it facilitates the discharge of its duties—and we have an accumulation of evidence which requires no aid from the question of our Lord's exact conformity to the ceremonial law.

Let any one apply the argument as thus deduced from the reasonings and conduct of Christ concerning the moral law of the Sabbath, to any statute of human legislation which had been loaded with unauthorized usages, and let him ask himself, what would be the necessary effect of such reasoning and such conduct upon the authority of the original provisions of the statute; and he would instantly say, the establishment of that authority in its real and paramount force.

I conceive that the duty of dedicating one day in seven to the worship of Almighty God, was so wrought into the consciences of all his true servants in every age, after its re-promulgation in the moral law had revived the memory of its glory as infixed in the order of creation—and that the observance of it was so reasonable in itself, so necessary to man, as man, and so delightful also to the devout mind—that the thought would never have occurred to any creature, that our Lord abrogated the fourth commandment. The Jews accused him of breaking it, but never of denying its obligation or sapping its claims. The Jews at the time of Christ were indignant even at the violation of their oral precepts concerning the Sabbath, and they carried their prejudices with them into the Christian church. The Gentile converts had all been accustomed to religious festivals and days of repose—the corruptions and faint vestiges of the original Sabbath. All therefore were prepared for keeping the fourth, as well as every other of THE COMMANDMENTS. There was no one to deny its divine authority; and when the gra-

cious interpretation of its true import by our Lord,
and the change of the day to the commemoration of
his Resurrection (as we shall see in the next discourse) were acquiesced in, the ends of the institution were fulfilled in the celebration of the divine
praises in creation, in redemption, in grace, and in the
anticipations of the heavenly repose.

I. Yield, then, Christian brethren, to these accumulated proofs.   Open your hearts to the Lord Jesus,
that he may re-establish there the authority of the
day of his heavenly Father.   Consider the many additional motives to its observance which flow from the
grace and compassion of your Redeemer; mark his tenderness in asserting the day of rest for its proper spiritual purposes; observe his permission of those works
of real necessity and mercy which render an attendance
on them more practicable.   You have not a Saviour
who allows the Sabbath to be buried under the rubbish
of human commandments.   You have not a Saviour
who, from indifference or cowardice, fears to put down
the pharisaical imposers of austerities.   No.   Behold!
he enters the synagogue on the holy Sabbath—he
teaches; he applies to himself the divine prophecies
concerning the Messiah; he heals the sick in confirmation of his doctrine; he rebukes devils, and they leave
the possessed and proclaim his name and glory.   It is
the Sabbath: and it is in this way that the Messiah
distinguishes and honours it.   He vindicates his disciples plucking the ears of corn—he anoints the eyes
of a blind man with clay—he bids the dropsy quit the
frame of one patient, and bids another extend his
withered arm—he commands the devout worshipper,
bowed for eighteen years, and she raises herself to
glorify God—he strengthens the impotent man, after
thirty-eight years of hopeless dejection, to carry mira-
culously his couch, and in that act to prove his cure.
Blessed Jesus! in all this we see thee to be a "merciful
and faithful high priest."   In all this we see thy pity
in vindicating the day of rest to its proper purposes.

In all this we see, not the lawgiver, not the prophet, not Moses, not Elias—but JESUS, the wise and merciful Saviour of mankind. Hadst thou not, O Saviour, thus cleared up the law of the Sabbath by this thine holy example and doctrine, how long might thy church have been perplexed with doubts—how much might superstition and tyranny over the conscience have prevailed! How little might have been left to man of the real design and consolation of the day of rest! But now thou hast vindicated the truth. Now thou hast taught, not only that "THE SABBATH WAS MADE FOR MAN," but that "MAN WAS NOT MADE FOR THE SABBATH." Now we have nothing to do under thy new dispensation, but drop the temporary ceremonies of the Mosaic law, and return to the simplicity of the patriarchal worship, inspired and elevated with the grace of thy all-bountiful Spirit.

II. And here let us learn, Christian brethren, to shun the INGRATITUDE OF MAKING USE OF THE COMPASSION OF OUR SAVIOUR, TO THE TACIT DISPARAGEMENT OF THE SABBATH ITSELF, which our Lord, as we have seen, has honoured by the very acts which were alleged as infringing its sanctity. If the intention of our Saviour was, as I am fully convinced every fair and unprejudiced hearer will admit, to magnify his heavenly Father's institution—if every denunciation against the hypocrisy and severity of the Pharisees was so much of real dignity and authority added to the Sabbath; then let us beware of the guilt of abusing all this to unrighteousness and irreligion. What avails that God allows works of necessity and mercy to be done on the Sabbath, if your practice desecrates the whole day by works of folly and sin? What avails it that God will "have mercy and not sacrifice," when you give him neither?[1] Surely no abuse of the divine goodness can be more criminal than to take occasion from a sympathy so exuberant, to rob God of his due, our souls of their best blessings, the poor of

---

[1] Ogden.

their season of repose, the church of the edification of our example.   Surely this is a branch of that practical antinomianism which "turns the grace of our Lord Jesus Christ into lasciviousness."   And be it well remembered, that if we once violate conscience in our search after truth, there is no telling whither we may wander.   The calm examination of the question of the Sabbath is our bounden duty.   I am endeavouring to assist you in the inquiry.   At the points where mistakes may arise, I have put you on your guard.   Time for settling the judgment I readily allow : differences on minor branches of the argument I cheerfully concede.   But this I must remind you of ; fear, reverence, faith, simple subjection of soul to the truth, are essential to all religious inquiries.   Yield, then, to the call of grace.   Abuse not the mercy of your Saviour. Rather implore that spiritual influence of the grand Comforter, which may render the duties of the Christian Sabbath a delight and joy.

III. And this is our last point of application.   The Jewish Sabbath is no more.   It is for the Christian we plead—THAT CHRISTIAN SABBATH FOR WHICH THE HOLY SPIRIT IS ESPECIALLY GIVEN.   The yoke, not only of pharisaical impositions, but of ceremonial observances, is broken off your neck.   The law of the Sabbath is now a law of love, a law of gratitude, a " LAW OF LIBERTY," as the apostle James terms it, in common with the whole moral law.   You must imbibe this filial and gracious spirit, in order to have the true conception of the importance of the institution, and the right feelings for rejoicing in it.   The despite done to the Holy Spirit is one cause of the neglect of the sacred day.   You seek not his influences to enlarge and purify the heart.   You seek not his consolations to animate your devotion.   You complain that the Sabbath is a heavy day, to be got over as well as you can.   You have no taste for its spiritual duties, no joy at its return, no repose in its divine anticipations.   What does this go to prove ?   That you are yet in the state of fallen nature—and that, as such, you " receive not the things of the Spirit of God, for they are foolishness unto you, neither can you know them, because they are spiritually discerned?"[1] What does this prove, but that you want the love of God, the spiritual life, the vital perceptions of a soul quickened by the Holy Spirit? Proceed then no further. Persist not in a course which only condemns your state of heart. Seek the illuminating and sanctifying influence of the Spirit. Almost the first truth you will discover, will be the glory and majesty of the Sabbath; and the next, that the exercises of that day are the festival and nourishment and element of the renewed and holy heart. Yes, all the transport of the Psalmist, all his repose and joy in God, all his mourning when banished from his courts, all his longing, yea, fainting after his house, all his perception of satisfaction, and relief, and holy pleasure in his service, will be experienced, in proportion as the vivifying Spirit quickens your soul. Men who are formal in religion naturally betray an indifference to the means of grace. As these means have little practical influence upon them, a small matter induces them to dispense with the incumbrance; but the sincere Christian has his delight in the Sabbath, and in the public and private ordinances of religion; he is "planted in the house of the Lord;" HE IS AT HOME THERE; his best pleasures, his warmest hopes, his most tranquil repose, his plenary satisfaction of soul, his liveliest pledges and anticipations of a heavenly rest, are drawn from the sacred and most gracious institution, in the services of which he waits to be prepared and ripened for that upper temple, those heavenly mansions, where he "shall dwell in the house of the Lord for ever."

----

[1] 1 Cor. ii. 14.

SERMON IV.

THE SABBATH TRANSFERRED BY DIVINE AUTHORITY FROM THE SEVENTH TO THE FIRST DAY OF THE WEEK, OR LORD'S DAY.

REVELATION i. 10.

I was in the spirit on the Lord's Day.

WE have now completed all that is essential in the first division of our general subject. We have proved the divine authority and perpetual obligation of a weekly religious rest. We have traced it from its institution in Paradise to the time of the Mosaical dispensation. We have considered its insertion in the ten commandments, and the dignity assigned to it by Moses and the prophets, as of essential moral obligation. We have also shown that it was vindicated by our Lord from the corruptions of the Scribes and Pharisees, and left in more than its primeval importance and authority. We might now pass on to the second or practical division of our subject, if we were not called on first to consider the transfer of the day on which the Sabbath under the gospel is kept, from the last to the first of the week. As the stress of the law has from the beginning been shown to lie on the proportion of time between the working days and the day of rest, the mere change

of the particular period in the week when we celebrate our Sabbath, cannot in itself be considered important.   So long as one day is sanctified out of every
seven, the purport of the institution is accomplished.
Still it is necessary to explain the manner in which the
alteration took place.   For as the seventh day in order
was fixed by the Almighty himself after the work of
the creation, and as the Jew observed the same, or at
least considered his six days' work to precede, and not
follow his Sabbath, it is important to show the authority
which retarded its celebration under the gospel, and
fixed it one day later than the Jewish usage.   Any
change in a divine command, though in a point of
itself subordinate, requires a sufficient reason, or we are
guilty of altering, of our own minds, an authoritative
rule of Almighty God.

We shall show, then, in the present discourse, that
our day of religious rest, under the gospel, is not the
Jewish Sabbath, but the Lord's day.   We shall
show that the change from the seventh to the first
day of the week, was made on the authority of
Christ and his apostles.   We shall show that the transfer took place naturally, and almost necessarily, from
the events attending the accomplishment of redemption.
These points will of necessity occupy time—perhaps
more than any preceding topic.   But they will deserve
all our care ; as the alteration in question, non-essential
as it is in itself, has perhaps more disturbed the minds
of uninformed Christians, and more aided the cause of
those who oppose the divine authority of the Christian Sabbath, than all the other objections together.

To proceed, then, in order, we shall first direct your
attention to several PREPARATORY CIRCUMSTANCES
in the history of the law of the Sabbath, which lay a
probable ground for the change of the day : and then,
secondly, the manner in which THE CHANGE ITSELF
WAS GRADUALLY INTRODUCED.

I. The preparatory circumstances are numerous.

For, first, the PROPORTION OF TIME, which we have more than once alluded to, is not only an obvious part of the first institution in Paradise, but is so prominent in the wording of the fourth commandment, and in its different republications, as to lay a probable ground for the change of the day of celebration, if any paramount reasons should occur. If out of seven days, one be sanctified to holy rest, the spirit as well as the terms of the law are satisfied. In the general course of nature, indeed, labour precedes repose; and in the primitive institution, the day of the Sabbath fell, from the order of creation and the example of the Almighty, upon the seventh, or last of the week. But even here the proportion of time between the working days and the day of rest, is laid as a foundation for the whole. The distribution of the work of creation over six days, marks the reason why the seventh was given to repose; and shows that the essence of the institution would be preserved, if after six days of labour, one of rest should succeed. Accordingly, in the revival of the Sabbath at the period of the fall of manna, not one word is said of the last day or the first day. All you can collect is, that they were to gather manna six days, and make a Sabbath of the seventh. Again, the fourth commandment, as we have said, is so worded as to admit of the change of the day of rest, without at all violating the institution. And this the divine lawgiver doubtless so arranged, with a view to the alteration which the gospel would introduce. The Jew could never have determined from this command on what day his first Sabbath was to be kept. It enjoins no more than that the interval of time between rest and rest should be six days. The proportion of the days is the essential point. The Christian Sabbath, in the sense of the fourth commandment, is as much the seventh day, as the Jewish Sabbath was the seventh day. It is kept after six days labour, as that was. It is the seventh day, reckoning from the beginning of our first working day, as well as their Sabbath was the seventh day, reckoning from the beginning of their first working day.[1] So, in all the recapitulations of the fourth commandment, the substance is the proportion of time which we dedicate to God—a seventh portion with respect to six days' labour—and therefore the six days' labour are always noted when the seventh is spoken of.   The day when we begin to compute is, abstractedly speaking, of very little consequence.   Our Lord's day may be called the seventh in relation to the six days' work, as well as the first in reference to the Jewish Sabbath, which preceded it.   This single circumstance clears the whole question.

2. But there is, in the next place, the highest probability that the exact computation of time from the creation was LOST DURING THE BONDAGE OF EGYPT, and that the Jewish Sabbath was reckoned from some other day—the day of the redemption, for example—and not from the day when the Almighty rested after the creation.   If this be the case, we are thrown yet more completely upon the proportion of time.   Two thousand five hundred years of an unwritten law, closed with centuries of oppression in the Egyptian captivity, had in all probability disturbed the exact reckoning of weeks.   An irregular observation of the sacred day had crept in previously—the impossibility of generally celebrating it at all, was doubtless one consequence of their task-masters' exactions ; [2] and thus, though the institution was by no means effaced

---

[1] " The fourth commandment does not determine which day of the week we should keep as a Sabbath ; but only that we should keep every seventh day, or one day after six.   It says, ' Six days shalt thou labour, and the seventh thou shalt rest ;' which implies no more than that after six days of labour, we should upon the next to the sixth rest.   The words no way determine where these six days should begin, nor where the rest of the Sabbath should fall : that is supposed to be determined elsewhere.   The precept in the fourth commandment is to be taken generally of such a seventh day as God should appoint, or had appointed."—*J. Edwards*,—and so Dean Milner.

[2] Cogitavi Egypto ubi serviabas, etiam ipso sabbato per vim te esse coactum ad labores.----*Manasseh Ben Israel, on Deut.* v. 15.

from their memory, the order of weeks was most likely interrupted. Nothing is more difficult than to preserve, in an early state of science and civilization, the accurate calculation of festivals, especially when recurring frequently, and admitting of an insensible removal from their relative position, by changes in the revolutions of the heavenly bodies. The alteration is in such a case slight, and the order of things is tolerably well kept up. Many learned men, therefore, agree in thinking that it is highly improbable, that the day observed as the first Sabbath after the deliverance from Egypt, was precisely the same as the day on which the Almighty rested after the creation of man. They think it more likely that the redemption from bondage was the period whence the new reckoning dated.[1]   Certain it is that the ten commandments are prefaced with a reason drawn from this great benefit— "I am the Lord thy God which brought thee out of the land of Egypt, out of the house of bondage."[2]   And, what is more important, at the recapitulation of the law forty years afterwards, the same preface to the decalogue is retained, but the motive enforcing the fourth commandment is no longer drawn from the work of creation, but from that of redemption, as if that were the reason and date of the particular day on which the celebration was renewed. "And remember that thou wast a servant in the land of Egypt, and that the Lord thy God brought thee out thence through a mighty hand, and by a stretched-out arm; THEREFORE the Lord thy God commanded thee to keep the Sabbath-day."[3]   Not a word is here said about the creation, as when the institution in paradise was cited in the first promulgation on Mount Sinai; but the Sabbath is ex-

---

[1] J. Mede, Grotius, Abp. Bramhall, J. Edwards, Dean Milner, Scott, all think the reckoning was lost, and was re-commenced at the fall of manna, Exodus xvi. And most of them conceive the new computation began from the day of Egyptian redemption.

[2] Exod. xx. 11.   [3] Deut. v. 15.

pressly appointed to commemorate the mighty deliverance from Egypt. It is probable, therefore, that this
was the day whence the new computation started.
When the divine Saviour, then, appeared and wrought
out an eternal redemption, it was natural, it was almost necessary, that the day should be changed from
the commemoration of the type to the commemoration
of the antitype. The Sabbath then follows the
mightiest benefit in each dispensation. In the patriarchal, creation ; in the Mosaical, the redemption from
Egypt; in the Christian, the spiritual redemption in
the death and resurrection of Messiah. The essential
point, the proportion of time, is untouched throughout.
But let us proceed to observe,

   3. That these things being so, the VERY FREEDOM
AND UNIVERSALITY OF THE GOSPEL DISPENSATION
would lead us to think that the same principle would
be carried on, that the precise day of the week on
which the Sabbath should be kept, would be less insisted on, and that a rule would be laid down applicable to all nations, in all ages, and in all parts of the
world. While men were few, and lived nearly in the
same quarter, as before the dispersion of Babel, and
during the Mosaical economy, it would be easy to keep
a pretty exact computation of the succession of time,
as soon as the date from which the reckoning was to
begin was given—or if the date was lost, as it probably
was during the bondage of Egypt, as soon as the new
æra was once determined on. But consider how different is the nature of the case under the gospel.
Here you have not a distinct line of patriarchs, or a
favoured nation under a theocracy, but a dispensation
designed for the whole race of mankind, whose disciples are multiplied in every quarter of the globe, and
live under all meridians, and with every variety of
civil government and scientific improvement. An appointed season dependent on a succession of days, and
losing its validity if the day be miscalculated, seems,
therefore, not very likely to be established under such
a dispensation. Of two navigators sailing round the

world in opposite directions, one would lose and the
other gain a day in his computation—there would be
a variation of two days.   Now, which would be the
seventh day of the week to each of the navigators?
When Pitcairn's Island in the South Seas was visited
a few years since by an English ship, our voyagers, on
the day when they arrived, which was Saturday, found
the 'islanders observing Sunday; the English ship and
the islanders having arrived at the island by sailing
from England in opposite directions.   Under the gospel, then, we might expect that our duty would be
fixed upon a plain and easy computation;   that after
six days of labour there should succeed one day of
rest, without troubling men in all the regions of the
earth, and under all circumstances, with reckoning up
the course of weeks or the order of days from the beginning, which it would be utterly impossible for them
to settle, if it were material.

How admirably the wisdom of God has provided for
this in the arrangement and wording of the law of the
Sabbath from the first, I need not observe.   Nor is it
necessary to remark how naturally the change of the
Jewish day of observance, to the Christian, would fall
in with this design, and expedite the practical execution
of it.

I think one would allow these remarks to be almost
enough for the point in hand.   Suppose any should
say, the day of celebrating the sacred rest of religion
has been changed under the gospel to honour our
Lord's accomplishment of redemption, and has been
so kept, as nearly as possible, by the whole church of
Christ from the very age of the apostles; the essential
law of the Sabbath, the proportion of time, being always preserved inviolate; I should conceive such a statement would be satisfactory.   Nor do I think any thing
would have been objected to such a statement if the
Jewish seventh-day-Sabbath had not been assumed to
be the same with the seventh-day-Sabbath in paradise.
This confuses the subject.   It seems to make the
seventh day a fundamental matter; whilst the real sub-

stance of the institution, the measure of working and resting days, is forgotten. Doubtless, also, those who had first feigned an anticipated history, and then banished the Sabbath from the moral law, and lastly, accused our Saviour of repealing that command, have been ready enough to seize on the merely non-essential circumstance of the change of the day of celebration, to prop up their falling cause. And thus it has happened that this subordinate, has in truth become a primary, question, from the accidental importance attached to it. But we proceed.

4. THE WORD OF PROPHECY does not, indeed, expressly announce a change of the day of the Sabbath, but it affords such intimations as are quite consistent with such a transfer. The "old creation"—the state of things under the law—shall not be remembered, but the "new creation"—the state of things under the gospel—shall.[1] The Christian church shall have her ministers, solemnities, sabbaths, and holy ordinances, all referring directly to the Messiah. A new dispensation shall be introduced, in which the alteration shall be so great and extensive as to be fitly compared to "new heavens and a new earth," which shall efface the memory of the old. Read the glowing language itself: "Behold, I create new heavens and a new earth; and the former shall not be remembered nor come to mind." "As the new heavens and the new earth which I will make shall remain before me, saith the Lord, so shall your seed and your name remain. And it shall come to pass, that from one new moon to another, and from one Sabbath to another, shall ALL FLESH come to worship before me, saith the Lord."[2]

But a more explicit prediction, embracing the change of the day of celebrating the Sabbath, or, at the least, giving an intimation of it, is found in the 118th Psalm. "The stone which the builders refused

[1] Called in the Epistle to the Hebrews, "The world to come," ii. 5.
[2] Isa. lxv. 17; lxvi. 22, 23; and J. Edwards on them.

is become the head-stone of the corner. This is the
Lord's doing, and it is marvellous in our eyes."[1]   Here
the stone spoken of is Christ; the passage being six
times applied to him in the New Testament.   He was
rejected of the builders when he was put to death; he
was made the head of the corner when he rose triumphant from the tomb.   While Christ lay in the
grave, he lay as a stone cast away by the builders; but
when raised from the dead, he became the head of the
corner.[2]   This was a great and marvellous act.   Now
the day when this was done, as we are next taught, is
appointed to be the day of the rejoicing of the church.
"This is the day which the Lord hath made; we will
rejoice and be glad in it."[3]   To what day does the
prophet here refer?   On what day did Christ rise from
the dead?   Was it not on the first day of the week?
Was not this the very day of triumph, the glorious day
of Messiah's being made the head of the corner?   Does
the psalmist refer, then, to any other day?   Or does
he not rather refer to this most distinguished and peculiar one?   To this, no doubt.   And what does he
say shall be the employment of it under the New
Testament?   "THIS is the day which the Lord hath
made; we will REJOICE AND BE GLAD in it."   The
prediction is more decisive, because the celebration of
public worship is the topic which introduces it, "Open
to us the gates of righteousness; I will go into them,
and will praise the Lord: this gate of the Lord, into
which the righteous shall enter."[4]   Here then is an intimation, to say the least, that the Christian day of joy
shall fall on the day of the resurrection of Messiah—
which the Lord's day hath done ever since the promulgation of the gospel.   We dwell not, however, on this
topic.   A further one has greater weight.

    5. In the next and most perfect dispensation of the
divine grace—the gospel—such A COMPLETE REVOLU-
TION ACTUALLY TOOK PLACE IN THE WHOLE STATE

[1] v. 22, 23.   [2] Dr. Lightfoot and J. Edwards.   [3] v. 24.
[4] v. 19. 20.

OF THE CHURCH, that it seems natural that so important a branch of religious observances as the Sabbath, should follow the new order of things. This remark strengthens the intimations of the prophetic word which we have just noted, and falls in entirely with our previous topics—the preparatory circumstances in the terms and arrangements of the law, the probable change of reckoning in the wilderness, and the demands of an universal religion. The Sabbath, in the progress of ages, was continually acquiring new ends by new manifestations of the covenant of redemption ; and those new ends coming to their height in the gospel, justify a correspondent alteration in a subordinate point of the sabbatical institution. " The priesthood being changed," says the apostle, " there is made of necessity a change also in the law."[1] We have a new Mediator, a new covenant, new promises, a new way of access, a new spirit of holy confidence, a new High Priest ; and therefore a new object in the computation of the weekly Sabbath—the glory and triumph of the Mediator in his resurrection. These are termed in the Epistle to the Hebrews, " The world to come."[2] This constitutes what the prophets call, as we have just seen, " The new heavens and the new earth ;" and which St. Peter denominates by the same strong and figurative expression. These form that " dispensation of the fulness of times when God gathers together all things in Christ, both things in heaven and things in earth."[4] Not one thing only is changed, but all. Accordingly, " the former shall not be remembered nor come to mind."[5] The Sabbath, then, probably follows the new course. And this appears the more likely, from the circumstance of the new creation being described as leading to the rest of the Mediator after he had completed it, even as the old creation led to the rest of the Almighty after he had finished his work— a rest granted in each case as a boon to man, and pledging that eternal rest with God in heaven, in

[1] Heb. vii. 12. [2] Heb. ii. 5. [3] 2 Peter iii. 13.
[4] Eph. i. 10. [5] Isa. lxv. 17.

which it terminates, and which is the ultimate felicity
proposed in all the dispensations of grace.   We cannot
enter into the details of the apostle's noble argument
on this subject. [1]   We observe only, that as at the first
creation, the Almighty was pleased to work six days,
and then rest on the seventh, in order to exhibit an in-
structive lesson for man's imitation ; and as his resting
on the seventh day was a sufficient intimation of the
precise day of Sabbath appointed for man ; so in the
second creation Christ wrought his work of restoration
and redemption during his ministry, and then rested,
and was refreshed from that kind of work by which he
laid the foundations of " the new heavens and the new
earth ;" and thus he marked out precisely the new day
of sabbatising under the gospel, the first of the week.
Then " he ceased from his own works, as God did from
his ;" then he entered by his resurrection into his rest :
then he rested and was refreshed, and saw of " the
travail of his soul and was satisfied ;" then he left, in
the new day of Sabbath, a new pledge of heavenly felicity to his church.

[1] " So I sware in my wrath, They shall not enter my rest.   So
we see they could not enter in, because of unbelief.   Let us therefore fear lest a promise being left us," (by the gospel,) " of entering into his rest," (that of the Lord Christ,) " any of you
should seem to come short of it.   For we which have believed,
do enter into rest," (the Christian Sabbath and rest, as a pledge
and preparation of the heavenly.)   " For he spake in a certain
place" (Gen. ii. 2,) " of the seventh day in this wise, And God
did rest the seventh day from all his works.   And in this place
again," (Psal. xcv. 11.) " If they shall enter into my rest.   There
remaineth therefore a rest," (a day of sabbatical rest in earth and
heaven, and the one the pledge of the other,) " for the people
of God.   For he that is entered into his rest," (even Jesus our
Lord, the author of all this new creation,) " he also hath ceased
from his own works" (of redemption and new creation) " as God
did from his," (of the old creation.)   " Let us labour, therefore,
to enter into that rest," (of heaven, of which our Christian weekly
Sabbath is a pledge and foretaste,) " lest any man fall after the
same example of unbelief."   I have inserted a few words of pa-
renthesis from Dr. J. Owen, J. Edwards, Dwight, Scott, Arch.
Pott. &c. who concur in the interpretation ; which is, in fact, the
only one that can stand.

Thus to each dispensation of the divine covenant a peculiar rest was attached—to the patriarchal, to the Mosaical, to the evangelical. The patriarchal was founded in the first creation, after which God ceased from his works, proposed to man a rest with himself in heaven, and appointed a Sabbath as a remembrance of the one and the pledge of the other. The Mosaical dispensation was founded in the redemption from Egypt, when God again ceased from his mighty works of forming and creating a people;[1] proposed a rest with himself to man, and gave him the pledge of it in the Jewish Sabbath. The gospel dispensation is founded in the new creation wrought by the Lord Christ, who redeems, renews, and writes his law upon the heart of man by his Spirit, and introduces a new and more spiritual state of religion. From this creating work Christ ceased, at his resurrection; he was then refreshed in the view of his works, and proposed his own rest to be called after his name, as the sign of the new covenant and the pledge of the heavenly rest (the keeping of a Sabbath, the sabbatising) which remains to his people. And as the day of repose followed certainly the precise order of working and of rest in the first dispensation, and was altered, as we probably conclude, in the Mosaical, to follow the day of redemption; so in the last and most perfect dispensation, it is again changed as to the precise time of its celebration, to dignify the day of spiritual redemption; and thus the patriarchal and Jewish Sabbath become the Lord's day.

We can suppose nothing more fitting, more necessary, so to speak, than so slight and yet significant a change! What! have we a new church, the gospel;

---

[1] "This people I have formed for myself."---Isaiah xliii. 2. And so in many other passages, the Mosaical covenant is termed a creation, the work of God's hands, &c. It is striking also to observe that the last glorious state of the church terminating in the rest of heaven, or perhaps the heavenly state itself, is described in the apocalypse under the same image; "And I saw a new heaven and a new earth."---Rev. xxi. 1.—*Owen, Edwards.*

new ordinances in that church, ceremonial worship taken down and spiritual set up; new sacraments, baptism and the Lord's supper, for circumcision and the passover; a new Mediator, Christ instead of Moses; a new covenant, founded on the better promises of the gospel; a new command of that covenant, to love one another; a new object of divine worship and confidence, the Lord Jesus;—in a word, have we all things new; and have we not a new Sabbath fitted for all this new creation?[1]   Yes, the Jewish rest is, under the gospel, THE LORD'S DAY.

6.   One more indication must be noticed, which binds together all the preceding.   THE CLAIMS WHICH CHRIST ADVANCED DURING HIS MINISTRY OF LEGISLATING FOR THE SABBATH, AS ITS SOVEREIGN AND LORD, lays a probable ground for the alteration of the day of its observance, and even intimates that some such change would take place.   One of the most striking of these claims is in the passage which we formerly considered.[2]   Jesus there asserts first the grand moral end of the Sabbath—then cautions us against the perverse traditions which would render man a slave to the external forms of that institution—and lastly, draws this emphatic and oracular conclusion, "THEREFORE THE SON OF MAN IS LORD ALSO OF THE SABBATH," exalted as that appointment confessedly is, most ancient in time, first in dignity, most universal as to extent, most durable and permanent in point of continuance—he is Lord even of the Sabbath, to claim it as his own, to transfer the day of its celebration, to fix on it his own name, to sweep away human traditions, and re-establish it in all its original simplicity and compassionate aspect upon man.   Yes, Jesus is the "Lord of the Sabbath;"—"the heir of all things," "the first-born from the dead," the "head over all things to his church," "the prince of life," the "only begotten of the Father," the "Lord of all." He is not like Moses "a servant," but has power "in

---

[1] Lightfoot.   [2] Mark ii. 27, 28, Sermon III.

his own house," as a "Son," to dispose of the affairs of that house as he may please.[1]

With this high claim, accords another which he made on the very same occasion—the defence of his disciples when accused wrongfully of having violated the Sabbath. "BUT I SAY UNTO YOU, IN THIS PLACE IS ONE GREATER THAN THE TEMPLE,"[2] glorious as it is, surrounded with tokens of the divine majesty, the seat of religious ordinances, and the place of the immediate manifestations of the Deity. "There is one greater than the temple,"—which is a figure merely of my human nature, and derives all its dignity from the indwelling Deity. "There is one greater than the temple,"—and therefore one authorized to regulate the service of the temple, and fix the day of religious assemblies in his church.

Once more, when accused of the Jews, most probably before the Sanhedrim, on the very same subject—a supposed violation of the Sabbath—how sublime is his reply! " MY FATHER WORKETH HITHERTO, AND I WORK."[3] What a claim is implied in these words! The interruption, indeed, given by the Jews, upon his uttering this language of deity, leaves us in some uncertainty as to the precise import of the argument; but if it be considered as only an assumption of divine operations generally, it is still conclusive as to his power over the Sabbath and the Jewish corruptions of the law of it. But if we refer it, with Dr. Lightfoot, to his working like his Father, who ever acts by his providence, even upon the Sabbath, though he rested from the works of creation on that day, and blessed and sanctified it; the argument of our Lord is more direct to his immediate purpose. It then imports, 'As my Father, though he hath ceased from the act of creation, worketh still in all succeeding time, the Sabbath not excepted, in sustaining man, rescuing him from danger, recovering him from sickness, sending him rain from heaven and fruitful showers, causing his sun to rise

---

[1] Heb. iii. 5. 6.   [2] Matt. xii. 6.   [3] John v. 17.

upon him; so I, the Son of God, work also in carrying on my providential actings continually, and even on the Sabbath; fulfilling my divine mission, healing diseases when occasions present themselves, proving the truth of my doctrine by enabling an impotent man to bear away his couch before my assembled adversaries, vindicating the Sabbath from unauthorized impositions, claiming it as my proper institution, and fixing the day of its observance after my own pleasure.'

Here, then, are laid grounds for the alteration of the day. What more appropriate than the LORD's DAY, to mark the authority of " the Lord of the Sabbath?" " If one greater than the temple be here," what more becoming than that the worship of the New Testament temple should follow his resurrection? If as " the Father worketh hitherto, so he works," what more natural than that he should display his power in making the Sabbath his own, working on it his deeds of mercy and grace, and fixing it in his own kingdom as a trophy of his resurrection?'

Yes; these indications virtually prove the point in hand. We may now venture to profess and say, " The first day is the Sabbath of the Lord our Redeemer;" " The Lord Jesus hath blessed the first day and hallowed it:" even as the ancient church professed and said, " The Lord hath blessed the seventh day and hallowed it"—" The seventh day is the Sabbath of the Lord our God." In a word, the last declaration which our Saviour made in commissioning his apostles after his resurrection, includes an unlimited power over his church, and therefore the authority of changing the day of celebrating its weekly rest: " ALL POWER is given me in heaven and earth; go ye, therefore, and teach all nations— teaching them to observe all things, WHATSOEVER I COMMAND YOU."[1]

We proceed, then, to consider

II. THE MANNER in which the change of the Sab-

---

[1] Matt. xxviii. 18—20.

bath from the last to the first day of the week, WAS GRADUALLY INTRODUCED BY THE DIVINE AUTHORITY OF OUR LORD AND HIS APOSTLES.

After such preparatory indications of the transfer of the day of rest, and such arrangements, from the very beginning, to admit of it, much will not be necessary to show the divine authority of it, when actually introduced. For the change being in itself subordinate, and in no way touching the substance of the command, nay, being agreeable to the very wording of that command, we want nothing but sufficient intimations of the will of God, to warrant our compliance with the practice of the universal church from the days of the apostles. When an objector says, he requires an express injunction, in precise and formal terms, for the observation of the Lord's day, he speaks without consideration. If he requires an express injunction in precise and formal terms for the religious dedication of one day in seven to God, we have it in the institution in Paradise, and in the words of the fourth commandment. But if he requires such an express and formal injunction for a subordinate change in the day of the week when that Sabbath should be kept, we reply, that the case does not require it. If God had so made our faculties, that we were not capable of receiving intimations of his will, even in matters not affecting the substance of a commandment, in any other way than by a new and express injunction, there would be some reason to require one. But God hath given us such understandings, that we are capable of ascertaining his will in such cases, in another manner. If God deals with us, then, agreeably to our nature and in a way suitable to our capacities, it is enough : and he may expect our notice and observance, and does expect our notice and observance, in the same manner as if he had made known his will in express terms.[1] In a case, then, like the present, we want no direct precept. The perpetual moral obligation of giving one day to God,

---

[1] J. Edwards.

after every six days' labour, is confessed.   The institution has been preserved on this footing through every
dispensation.   It is honoured and left in all its force
by Christ and his apostles.   There is no room then
for a new precept, as for a duty unknown.   On a point
not in itself essential to the command, the tacit example of our Lord,—the time of the fulfilment of the
chief promise of the New Testament,—the doctrine and
conduct of the inspired apostles,—the events in providence which swept away the Jewish polity and Sabbath,
—the universal practice of the Christian church in the
primitive and all following ages,—and the uninterrupted
blessing of God resting from their time to the present
on the transferred day; — these constitute sufficient
intimations of the will of God.   We deduce the
divine authority of the change of the weekly rest from
the Jewish to the Lord's day, as certainly from such
intimations, as we deduce the divine authority of the
essential duty of a weekly rest itself, from the transactions in Paradise and the formal and express injunctions of the moral law.

1. Our Saviour, then, after his passion, BEGAN TO
INTRODUCE the actual change tacitly and gently, by
his own divine conduct.   The first day of the week is
the day of his resurrection.   In the eternal councils
of the Almighty was this, and no other, day fixed.
The whole arrangement of the institution of the passover had from the first a respect to his great fulfilment
of this typical sacrifice.   Accordingly it is repeatedly
and emphatically noted by the evangelists as the precise day of his conquest over the grave.   He foretold
it himself.   The Jews were aware of the expected fact,
and prepared, as they could, against it.   His appear-
ances after his resurrection, marked the day which was
to become the Lord's.   Having risen on that blessed morn, he manifested himself four times before its
close, to his disciples; and thus celebrated, or rather
constituted, the first Christian Sabbath, on its new day
of being observed, by his own presence.   All the evangelists seem to delight in marking that it was on the first

day of the week, and no other, that these transactions took place.. St. Matthew tells us that at the "very dawn of the first day," the two Marys had the early tidings of the resurrection of their Lord. St. Mark informs us, that "very early in the morning," that , glorious event occurred. St. Luke relates the same, with the same notification of its being on the first day of the week. St. John bears testimony, that " on the first day of the week cometh Mary, when it was yet dark, unto the sepulchre," and there witnesseth the first manifestation of her risen Redeemer. [1] The second appearance, to the three women, was vouchsafed the same day. [2] The journey to Emmaus, and the being " known in the breaking of bread," was the third visit. And the fourth closed the first Christian Sabbath. It was made to the assembled disciples, who were already convened on that day, ready to begin, as it were, that joyful season, the moment their Lord should appear, to open its solemnities. Accordingly, ''the same day, at evening, being the first day of the . week, when the doors were shut, where the disciples were assembled, for fear of the Jews, came Jesus and stood in the midst, and saith unto them, Peace be unto you. Then were the disciples glad when they saw the Lord."[3] Their joy in the resurrection of their Master now began the Lord's day; to mark out and separate which more distinctly, the intervening week is allowed to pass without any repetition of his visits. But lo, after six days' work, the day of rest returns, and the second Lord's day is honoured likewise with the presence of Christ; the evangelist especially noting the time of this manifestation, which is not done as to any other, by any of the evangelists. " And after eight days again,"[4] (the Jews including the portion of the days from which, and to which, they reckon) " his disciples were within, and Thomas with them ; then came Jesus, the doors

---

[1] John xx. 19.   [2] Matt. xxviii. 9—11.
[3] John xx. 19, 20.   [4] John xx. 26.

being shut, and stood in the midst." " This second meeting on the same day of the week," says Paley, " has all the appearance of an appointment, a design to meet on that particular day."

Nothing is said as to the time on which the following manifestations were made; nor do we want them. They would have introduced the new day, not so gently and gradually, as we shall see it was our Saviour's intention to introduce it. It now, as it were, insinuates itself by the very circumstances in which the apostles were placed. The Lord of the Sabbath was lying in the grave on the precise day of the Jewish rest. It would have been impossible for the mourning disciples to have celebrated the praises of the great Creator, of the Redeemer from Egyptian bondage, of the God who promised, and had given them, the Messiah and Saviour, whilst that Messiah and Saviour was in the tomb, and all the prospects of his kingdom were shrouded with the darkness of death. That last Jewish Sabbath was no Sabbath to them; but a day of sorrow, dejection, anguish, consternation. The spouse could not rejoice whilst the bridegroom lay buried in the grave. But when the Lord arose on the first day of the week, then, and not before, were " the disciples glad. " THEN DID THEIR SABBATH BEGIN; the necessity of the case changed the day of peaceful happy rest in the worship and praise of God, from the Jewish Sabbath to the Lord's day. The celebration was retarded, not forgotten. The old day was buried with Christ— the new arose with him. He had in the old creation rested (as being the author, one with the Father, of that six days' work) on the seventh day and sanctified it; but now, as the author of the new work of creation, being detained in the prison of the grave on the old seventh day, he takes another day to rest in, the following or first of the week, which thus becomes the Lord's day. Every thing essential in the command goes on as it did: the non-essential point of the precise time is changed, or rather delayed, a single day, to wait for its rising Master, and assume a new dignity, and be a memorial of the manifestations of a new and greater creation.

2. The first day, thus begun to be introduced, is next marked by THE GIFT OF THE GREAT PROMISE OF THE DISPENSATION which it was to characterize. This will demand only a moment's notice. The day of pentecost has been abundantly shown by learned men[1] to have fallen on the Lord's day. The disciples are assembled with one accord in one place—the usual place of prayer : " when suddenly there came a sound from heaven, as of a mighty rushing wind; and they were filled with the Holy Ghost."[2] By this gift the gospel church is first erected, and its heralds endued with power from on high. Thus the great distinguishing benefit of the New Testament being vouchsafed on the Lord's day, confirms the newly instituted season, which is to be henceforth known as the Christian Sabbath. The Holy Ghost descended upon it. The author of the " new creation" had already arisen upon the same day. We join then these topics of joy to the original praises due for the glories of the first creation; and our Lord's day is dedicated to our triune God and Saviour—it is dedicated to God the Father, as the day on which the praises of the most noble creatures for their first production are offered—it is dedicated to God the Son, whose resurrection this day was the new creation of the world—it is dedicated to God the Holy Ghost, who on this day descended visibly upon the apostles, as if he would proclaim aloud that he hallowed it unto himself.[3] The gift of the Holy Ghost on the day of pentecost, honours and marks out the Lord's day.

III. THE DOCTRINE AND CONDUCT OF THE APOSTLES will, in the next place, be found to bring in more decidedly, yet still tenderly and gradually, the new day of Sabbath.

They were endued with the Holy Spirit granted at

[1] Lightfoot, Dwight, &c.   [2] Acts ii. 2.
[3] Archbishop Bramhall.

this very season, on purpose to found the gospel dispensation, and settle its order and worship. The conduct of these holy men, who were commissioned and delegated as ambassadors for Christ, has a divine authority. They teach indeed by their writings, they teach by their sermons and instructions; but they teach also by their conduct and example. They had the infallible guidance of the Holy Spirit. They delivered nothing to be observed in the worship of God, but what has the same force as if delivered by Christ himself—it proceeds indeed from Christ himself. In a matter of subordinate regulation, when the substance of a command has been known from the creation of man, their intimations are abundantly sufficient; just as their devout and detailed instructions are indispensable on important and fundamental points of doctrine or practice. "If men will presume," says Baxter, "that apostles filled with the Spirit, appointed the Christian Sabbath without the Spirit, they may question any chapter or verse of the New Testament."

We have their testimony, then, for nearly sixty years recorded in the inspired pages; and this incidentally, and in a manner which supposes the change from the Jewish to the Christian Sabbath to be known and received in the churches. Thus, in two references made after an interval of nearly thirty years from the resurrection, the observance of the first day of the week was so far established even in the remotest places, that the sacred writers speak of it as a matter familiar and customary. "We came to Troas," saith St. Luke in the Acts, "where we abode seven days. And upon the first day of the week, when the disciples came together to break bread, Paul preached unto them, ready to depart on the morrow."[1] Here on the first day of the week is a meeting, not of a few friends, but of the whole body of the disciples, in a Christian church at a great distance from Jerusalem. It is spoken of as a practice already established and well

---

[1] Acts xx. 6, 7.

known—it is an accustomed meeting, not upon an ex-
traordinary summons.   Paul preaches to them being
thus assembled together.   The zealous apostle doubtless taught privately on other days : but it was on the
first day of the week, when the whole church was
accustomed to meet, according to their duty, for the
celebration of Christian ordinances, that he preached
solemnly and publicly to them.   It even seems that he
waited the arrival of the day—for he was ready to
depart, and did depart on the morrow of it—but he
would not proceed on his journey till after the first day
of the week, and the instruction and ordinances of that
sacred season, had taken place.   We thus learn that
already the same, or nearly the same, mode of celebrating the Sabbath was observed as in modern times
—public assemblies—the preaching of God's holy
word—the administration of the sacraments—with
public prayer and praise, and acts of charity to the
poor, constituted the Christian worship.

At the same, or nearly the same, period St. Paul,
in his Epistle to the Corinthian church, incidentally
mentions the observation of the Lord's day as a matter
of course, not to give directions about the day itself, but
in order to enjoin certain additional duties which were
to form an important part of the sanctification of it.
" Now concerning the collection for the saints, as I
have given order to the churches of Galatia, even so do
ye.   Upon the first day of the week let every one of
you lay by him in store, as God hath prospered him,
that there be no gatherings when I come." [1]   It hence
appears that the constant day of the church's assembling was fixed and well known—it was the first day.
The apostle, therefore, merely directs the discharge of
an especial duty upon it, in addition to the ordinary
ones of prayer, breaking of bread, and preaching the
gospel.   He directs them to charitable contributions ;
and he directs this in a manner which implies that it
should be done on the first day of the week and no

---

[1] 1 Cor. xvi. 1, 2.

other, as if no other time would do so well as that, or was so proper a season for such a work. He notices also, that he had given the same order to other churches, especially to the churches in Galatia, though divided by the sea, and lying at a great distance from Corinth. Thus the Lord's day was generally acknowledged. It was celebrated by Christians, we see, before the New Testament was written, and is referred to in the books of it as already established. Indeed the obedience to the gospel, and to its ordinances, began first upon the authority which the apostles received from Christ, and the plenary inspiration of the Holy Spirit. Thus the churches were formed, and the doctrine and sacraments admitted. And thus also the Lord's day was sanctified, as appears from the casual references made in the history and epistles of their founders.

But we go on. At the close of the first century, and after an interval of thirty or forty years from the time when the above passages were written, the words of our text were uttered by the beloved apostle—the father and sole survivor of the apostolic college, in his extreme old age, and when about to record the revelations made to him by the Spirit. This brings down the direct scriptural evidence to the close of the first century.[1] "I WAS IN THE SPIRIT ON THE LORD'S DAY," is the brief and pregnant expression. He merely denotes in this way the time when the revelations of the Spirit were made to him, by the mention of a day, the appellation of which was well known throughout the Christian churches. It is no new appellation, or he would not thus incidentally have introduced it. A new name would have created surprise, not communicated information. By the Lord's day was undoubtedly meant the first day of the week, for we find no footsteps of any distinction of days which could entitle any other to that appellation.[2] Now, if this be so; if sixty or seventy years after the resurrection, and when the destruction of Jerusalem had made way for

---

[1] About A. D. 96.   [2] Paley.

the full development of the gospel, the first day of the week is called THE LORD'S DAY, even as St. Paul calls the Eucharist THE LORD'S SUPPER—if the one be the memorial of the Lord's resurrection, as the other is of his death and passion,—then we have the most satisfactory evidence of the apostolic usage, and there-fore of the divine authority of the change of the Jewish into the Christian Sabbath.

4. But the EVENTS OF GOD'S WONDERFUL PROVI-DENCE, which swept away the Jewish polity and Sab-bath, completed the change which had thus gradually been introduced, and had spread so widely.   To avoid needlessly exasperating the prejudices of the Jewish converts, and the malice of the great body of that nation, the transfer of the day of the Sabbath was made for a long time silently and gradually.   Our Lord lays the foundation of the change in his example, and in the choice of the day for conferring the great gift of the New Testament.   The apostles follow his example; and, as we have seen, the practice had be-come general within thirty years from the crucifixion. But we have no express prohibition of the Jewish, nor injunction of the Christian Sabbath.   It was a matter subordinate, and was now to make its way by the force of circumstances and the tacit influence of the apos-tle's doctrine.   On the question of the Jewish cere-monies indeed controversy arose—circumcision and keep-ing the law of Moses were made the occasion of sup-planting the great doctrine of justification.   But where no dispute arose—where all observed one day in seven for religious rest—where no yoke was attempted to be imposed on the Gentiles, the apostles were "gentle as a nurse cherisheth her own children."   The Jewish converts were allowed to observe the Mosaic Sab-bath.   The Gentiles, who had previously cele-brated their pagan festivals, renounced these on their conversion, for the holy rest of the Lord's day. They spontaneously kept the Christian Sabbath as a natural duty, a branch of the moral law, an effect of that most general commandment, "Thou shalt love the Lord thy God with all thy heart"—and

an injunction ·expressly given in the fourth commandment. The Jewish converts still observed their own Sabbath; but then they yielded without objection to the apostolic example and authority, in joining the Gentile converts in celebrating the day of their Lord's resurrection. They were circumcised; but they were also willingly baptized. They celebrated the passover; but they willingly added the Lord's Supper. They worshipped in the temples and the synagogues; but they assembled also in the Christian churches. So long as the Jewish services were neither attacked nor neglected, they made no objection to that of the Christian church. Thus the new ordinances grew into use, veneration, habit. When the apostles declared in the Epistles to the Galatians and Hebrews, that the Jewish covenant was ready to vanish away, and that no reliance whatever upon its ceremonies was to interfere with a simple faith in Christ for justification, the minds of the Jewish believers were prepared to submit. Thus things continued for nearly forty years after the resurrection.

The destruction of Jerusalem takes place. The Jewish polity is dissolved. The temple is left without one stone upon another. The Jewish priesthood, altars, sacrifices, covenant, Sabbath, all disappear. The Lord's day becomes the day of religious rest. No controversy arises. The seventh-day Sabbath dies without a struggle, by the force of circumstances directed by an unfailing providence. What wisdom and consideration, then, appears in the conduct of the apostles! As the whole church of Jewish and Christian converts agreed in one grand moral duty, the consecration of a day of rest to God, and as the stream of events was about to carry away the whole Jewish economy, the apostles left matters to work. They laid down the general truth of the non-obligation of the Mosaical law—they consecrated by their example, the change of the day of the Sabbath; but they awakened no unnecessary prejudices. They cheerfully met the Jewish assemblies on the seventh day, for the purpose of preaching the gospel to them. They issued no public decree. A non-essential matter, they were assured, would find its level. How great would have been the consternation of the Jewish believers, if their Sabbath, their golden day, the first of their commandments, the badge of their nation, the glory of their state as a church, had been openly impugned! Nor could the apostles have abolished it, so far as it was a political ordinance, and interwoven with the civil policy of the Jewish people. They waited therefore. They left the Jewish Sabbath gradually to expire, and the Christian to succeed, without any express command, or any attempt at a violent and sudden transfer.

After the destruction of Jerusalem, the case became different. The time of concession was over. Moses had vanished away. The Jewish church was no longer the church of God. The dispersed Jews were under the judicial blindness which the · rejection of their Messiah had brought upon them. Their hatred of Christianity was infuriate. Christians then must now openly separate from the communion of a repudiated church. The Jewish Sabbath, the most visible character of their worship, must now openly give place to the Lord's day. The consecration of that day is now a necessary protest against Judaism, even as the Jewish Sabbath had been against idolatry. Christians unite the two. Their Lord's day is an open protest against atheism and idolatry on the one hand, and Judaism and superstition on the other. By it they publicly profess their belief in the three grand articles of the creed—"In God the Father Almighty, the maker of heaven and earth," who first instituted at the creation a weekly rest after six days' labour—"And in Jesus Christ his only Son our Lord," who rose on this day, and drew to it the season of sacred joy—and in "the Holy Ghost," who descended on the same day to found the church and to qualify the apostles, and who is its abiding comforter and guide.

And thus the Lord's day is gradually but firmly and completely established, by exactly that kind of evidence which the nature of the case demanded, and the wisdom of God saw to be best. Its authority is divine, because the example of the Lord of the Sabbath, and of his apostles, inspired to found his church, is a divine authority for any change; especially for one immaterial in itself, and entirely consistent with the fundamental law of the institution.

5. But it may naturally be asked, what say ECCLE-SIASTICAL HISTORIANS---what the apostolic Fathers? Do they bear witness to the observation of the first day of the week ? Do they ascribe to the command of Christ and the inspired founders of their churches, the transfer of the day of rest from the last to the first of the week ? To this we reply, that there is no one fact upon which all testimony more completely agrees than this. " I should hold it too long," says Bishop An-drews, to "cite them in particular; I avow it on my cre-dit, that there is not an ecclesiastical writer in whom it is not to be found."[1]

Ignatius, a companion of the apostle, says, " Let us no more sabbatize, but let us keep the Lord's day, on which our life arose,"

Justin Martyr, at the close of the first, and the begin-ning of the second century tells us, " On the day called Sunday is an assembly of all who live in the city or country, and the memoirs of the apostles and the writ-ings of the prophets are read."   And he adds, that " it was the day on which the creation of the world began, and on which Christ arose from the dead.'

Irenæus, a disciple of Polycarp, who had been the disciple of St. John himself, says, "On the Lord's day every one of us Christians keeps the Sabbath, meditat-ing on the law, and rejoicing in the works of God."

Tertullian, at the close of the second century, asserts it to be " the holy day of the Christian church assem-blies, and holy worship"---that " every eighth day is the Christian's festival "---" kept as a day of rejoic-ing."

---

[1] Bishop Andrews on the ten commandments---a work of in-comparable value---from which, and Baxter and Dwight, I col-lect my testimonies.

Dionysius, Bishop of Corinth, in the time of Irenæus, says, in his second letter to the church of Rome, "To-day we celebrate the Lord's day, when we read your epistle to us."

St. Ambrose observes, "the Lord's day was sacred or consecrated by the resurrection of Christ."

The council of Laodicea, about the year 363, forbad Christians to rest from labour on the seventh day, "for Christians ought not to rest on the Sabbath, that is, the seventh day, but preferring the Lord's day to rest as Christians, if indeed it is in their power."

St. Augustine tells us, that "the Lord's day was by the resurrection of Christ declared to Christians, and from that very time it began to be celebrated as the Christian's festival."

Epiphanius, in his sermon upon the day of Christ's resurrection, has this expression, "This is the day which God blessed and sanctified, because in it he ceased from all his labours which he had perfectly accomplished, the salvation both of those on earth, and those under the earth."

Athanasius says, "The Lord transferred the Sabbath to the Lord's day." The Emperor Constantine, as soon as he embraced the Christian faith, made a law to exempt the Lord's day from being Juridical.

And finally, Leo (A. D. 469) thus expresses the sentiments of the whole Christian church: "We ordain according to the true meaning of the Holy Ghost, and of the apostles thereby directed, that on the sacred day wherein our own integrity was restored, all do rest and cease from labour; that neither husbandmen nor other on that day, put their hand to forbidden work. For if the Jews did so much reverence their Sabbaths, which were but a shadow of ours, are not we which inhabit the light and truth of grace, bound to honour that day which the Lord himself hath honoured, and hath therein delivered us from dishonour and from death? Are we not bound to keep it singular and inviolable, well contenting ourselves with so liberal a grant of the rest, and not encroaching upon that one day which God hath chosen to his own honour? Were it not reckless neglect of religion to make that very day common, and to think we may do with it as with the rest?"[1]

Thus decisive is the testimony to the fact, that the Lord's day was considered by the primitive church to be appointed by the divine authority of the apostles, the especial delegates and ambassadors of Christ, armed with his commission, and inspired with his spirit.

It deserves remark, that the brief description which Pliny, in his celebrated letter to Trajan, gives of the Christian worship, entirely accords with our general testimony : "They are accustomed to meet on a stated day before light, and to sing amongst themselves hymns to Christ, as to a God." Indeed, the celebration of the Lord's day was so notorious even to the Heathens themselves, that it was ever a question of theirs to the martyrs, " Dominicum servasti?" " Do you keep Sunday?" And their answer was equally well known ; they all aver it : " I am a Christian ; I cannot omit it."

6. And why should I detain you longer? Why should I do more than notice THAT PERPETUAL BLESSING WHICH HAS ATTENDED THE CHRISTIAN SABBATH, and which attends it now? Why should I call to your memory all the conversions which have crowned the Lord's day during eighteen centuries, in every part of the world? The whole church has been built up upon this divinely transferred season—the whole church has been enlarged, comforted, sanctified on it. If the primitive Christians were mistaken in supposing the change from the seventh to the first day of the week to have been of apostolic authority, then God has permitted this mistake to be confirmed, and to take root, by his especial blessing, and the continued operations of his grace, during the whole period of the Christian church. But the idea is too absurd. For when we consider the comparative non-importance in itself, of the particular day in the week on which we keep the Sabbath, supposing the portion of time which the eternal rule of the fourth commandment requires, is preserved ; and when we reflect on all the preparatory circumstances which laid a probable ground for the

[1] Hooker.

change; and when to these we add the gradual but decisive manner in which that change was introduced, sustained by the events of God's awful providence in the destruction of the Jewish polity and Sabbath, and testified by the united voice of all ecclesiastical antiquity; we have a mass of evidence to the divine authority of our Christian Sabbath, sufficient to satisfy every candid mind. The blessing of God, therefore, which has actually attended, and is actually attending, in such large and perpetual operations of grace, the Lord's day, is in full accordance with every other species of proof, and crowns the whole argument.

The change, indeed, after all, amounts only to this. Under the patriarchal and Jewish dispensations, the Sabbath was considered as following the other days. Under the Christian it precedes. Under the former economies, creation and the redemption from Egypt were the greatest benefits conferred upon man. Under the Christian, the spiritual redemption---the resurrection of Christ—the new creation of the world. The Sabbath, therefore, waited a day for the triumph of its divine Lord, and then took the precedence, and led on the other days. In all these dispensations, the proportion of time dedicated to the immediate service of God, in which the substance of the command lay, remained the same, as well as the anticipation and pledge of that rest in heaven in which our Sabbaths are to terminate.

And thus all the obligations that can combine to enforce a moral command on man, have been found to unite in the case of the Christian Sabbath. The argument has gone on accumulating through each part of our progress. The objections have not only been overcome, but turned into additional confirmations. We have seen that from the creation to the rest of eternity, a day of weekly repose and religious worship has been appointed for man. We have seen the six days' work laid out, and the seventh day's refreshment enforced by the Almighty; first in his own example, and then by his

command. We have discovered the traces of this most
ancient of institutions during the patriarchal ages.
After the redemption from Egypt we perceived its re-
enactment before the law of ceremonies : and its insertion in the moral law, in common with the other primary duties of a responsible creature. It enters the
Mosaical economy, not as belonging to it, but as springing, with many other ordinances, from the patriarchal
church. As it preceded the existence of the ceremonial dispensation, so it survived its extinction. Even
during its passage through the parenthetical and temporary economy, we saw how it lifted up itself on high,
above all mere figures and ceremonies. The Saviour
appears and reverences, honours, distinguishes the
Sabbath by his doctrine and his miracles. The ten
commandments he recognizes without omission or alteration. As the Jews had fallen into various superstitions contrary to the true import of the law of the Sabbath, he sweeps away these austerities, and leaves it in
its genuine simplicity and grace—as being " made for
man, and not man for it." He intimates, also, a change
to be made in its observance, and claims to be its ruler,
sovereign, and lord. The particular day not being of the
essence of the law, it is silently introduced. The very
nature of the gospel as an universal religion might seem to
lead to it. The Lord of the Sabbath, he that was greater
than the temple, he that wrought in the works of the
new creation as Almighty God had in those of the old,
laid the grounds for the change before his passion.
After his resurrection he established the first day's rest
by his gracious appearance on that day, and his mission of the Holy Ghost. The apostles follow their
Master's example—they declare in their epistles the
Mosaical law abolished. They tolerate indeed, till the
destruction of Jerusalem, those who from prejudices
and misapprehensions kept the Jewish Sabbath, and
they attend the synagogues in order to meet the Jews
and proclaim the gospel, but they themselves honour
the Christian Sabbath ; and, after the abolition of the
Mosaical polity and state, they leave it as the badge of

our faith in Christ, as our protest against Judaism, as our season of Paradisaical and Patriarchal repose transferred to the day of the gospel ; as our pledge and anticipation of the rest and salvation of heaven—and they charge the universal church to celebrate on that day, not only the glories of creation, the blessings of redemption, and the hopes of a heavenly felicity, but the triumph of the Redeemer, in which they centre, and by which they are secured.

Let us then, in conclusion—I. ADORE in solemn acts of thanksgiving and praise, THE WISDOM AND GOODNESS OF THAT GOD, who, seeing the end from the beginning, thus laid out the bountiful provision for man's religious repose in his first creation, carried it through all the dispensations of his mercy, and revived it with so many advantages in the Christian church ! Yes ; we magnify thy counsels of grace, Thou only wise God ; we see something of that manifold and varied wisdom and prudence, with which thou hast abounded towards us. We glorify thy name, not only for the revelation of thy grace in Christ Jesus, and for all the dispensations of it since the world began, but for that attendant ordinance which gives us time to meditate upon them, and to repose in Thee our great and final end. We discern the footsteps of an infinite wisdom, in the magnitude and boldness of that record of the institution of a sabbath, which the six days' work exhibited ; and which is large and clear enough to catch every eye, to penetrate every conscience, to decide every honest doubt. We adore Thee yet more, for that regard to human infirmity, which led thee to insert this command in the moral law, and thus bind it upon the hearts of the whole human race, in common with their other most indispensable duties. And in thy gospel, thy wisdom still strikes our view with brighter splendour, in the gracious explications of thy law, uttered by the lips of our Redeemer, and in the gradual and silent introduction of the change of the day of its observance made by thy apostles. O, teach us to adore thee, in this thy appointment ! Let us believe, that every degree of evidence of the divine origin and permanent obligation of thy day, which is good for us in this imperfect state of trial, has been granted; that more evidence would probably have been unnecessary and injurious; and do thou cause us to acquiesce in thy mode of revealing this day of rest, in thy manner of transferring it to the day of the glorious resurrection of our Lord, and in the motives which thou hast accumulated, to urge us to sanctify it aright!

II. But let us notice as a further thought by way of application, that the changes in the circumstances of the law of the Sabbath HAVE SPRUNG UP FROM NEW BENEFITS CONFERRED ON MAN, and should increase his sense of obligation and gratitude. Every change is a fresh blessing. Every new dispensation is a new grace. Every alteration is an advance in the development of redemption on the one hand, and in the uses and importance of the institution on the other. The various modes in which the Sabbath has been presented to man, have not been isolated, much less arbitrary enactments, but economies of mercy, divisions in the grand progress of man's salvation by Jesus Christ, new pledges of "the rest remaining for the people of God." Every re-enactment, then, has brought with it new bonds, new obligations, new attractions, towards the spiritual observation of the sacred season. Creation poured its first benefits upon man, the offspring of his God, and bound upon him the day of rest, by all the ties of gratitude to an all-bountiful Lord. The separation of a particular family, to be the repository of truth, and the confessors of the one living God, amidst surrounding idolatry, brought with it new calls to duty, new reasons of religious worship and praise. The covenant of Abraham, the promise of "the seed in whom all the families of the earth should be blessed," the imputation of faith to him for righteousness, augmented the obligations of sacrifice, of circumcision, and especially of the Sabbath. The establishment of the Mosaic dispensation on the footing of the redemption of Egypt, and with the promise of the rest in Canaan, placed the Sabbath in yet a new and more inviting light, shed upon it richer grace, made it the commemoration of mightier blessings. The promulgation of the moral law, as connected with the dispensation of Moses, and subservient to the promises of grace typified in that dispensation, was an inconceivable favour to a wandering, and yet responsible creature, uncertain of his duties, surrounded with temptation, lost amidst the corruption and darkness of the world. Every hymn of the royal Psalmist, every prediction of the inspired prophets, augmented the materials of sabbath-praise and meditation, and increased the duty of making such a return of gratitude to God. At last, Messiah appears. Blessed Immanuel, we hail thy birth! Thou art the King, and Priest, and Prophet of an universal dispensation. Thy infinite benefits bind us to thyself. "Whether we eat, or drink, or whatever we do, we are to do every thing to thy glory." All thy mercies flow together into this thy day, which thou hast transferred to be the trophy of thy resurrection. This is the field where all thy blessings flourish; this the scene where all thy operations of grace are carried on; this the season when all thy praises are set forth.

Yes, my brethren, it is to this Saviour's love that we owe our Christian Sabbath; it is by this Saviour's death and passion, that its duties are bound upon us; it is by this Saviour's Spirit, that its consolations are poured into our hearts.

And mark, I entreat you, that in proportion as THE BENEFITS, AND LIBERTY, AND SPIRITUAL CHARACTER OF THE GOSPEL ARE MORE EXALTED, so should our hearts catch the intimations of our Lord's will with more alacrity, and fulfil them with warmer delight. He re-enacts not in direct terms his day of rest, because all the previous publications of it will act with a thousandfold more force upon the mind of his true people. He leaves it to be inferred from his own example and doctrine, and that of his apostles; because under his gospel, the love of his person, name, worship, will be a spontaneous and overflowing principle, dictated by his Spirit, bursting forth from every heart which is touched with the benefits of redemption, and constituting the very badge and characteristic of his kingdom.

Here then, we close the first division of our series of discourses—the Divine Authority and Obligation of a weekly day of rest in God, is under all dispensations the same; but under the gospel shines forth with the concentrated light of each preceding period; and is clothed with all the additional majesty, which infinite grace and love throw around it. Every thing illustrates the duty, and exalts the privilege of that institution, which before the fall was needful to man; but which, in his corrupted and sinful state, is the grand means of preserving religion in the world; the noblest rite of the Christian faith; the substratum and groundwork on which are erected all the means of grace, and all the hopes of glory.

And let it be remembered, that the objections raised against the several branches of our great argument, having been satisfactorily answered, they should no longer be allowed to harass our minds, or weaken our faith, or contract our obedience. THE FULL AUTHORITY OF THE DIVINE INSTITUTION should be admitted; and our efforts turned to those practical questions, which will be the subject of the remaining division of our discourses.

SERMON V.

THE PRACTICAL DUTIES OF THE CHRISTIAN SABBATH.

EZEKIEL xx. 12.

Moreover also, I gave them my Sabbaths, to be a sign between me and them, that they might know that I am the Lord that sanctify them.

THE divine authority and perpetual obligation of a day of holy rest and religious worship, have been abundantly proved. Every thing conspires to impress us with its supreme importance to man in all ages, and under all dispensations. Such is its antiquity, that it was instituted in Paradise. Such its essential moral nature, that it was inserted in the Ten Commandments. Its dignity is so great, that it lifts its head high above the ceremonies of Moses, whilst under that economy. Such is its spirituality, that the holy prophets and reformers insist upon it, as a point of fundamental duty, and as about to form a part of the gospel kingdom. Its perpetual force and native majesty, are so distinguished, that our Lord, after explaining what the comments of the Jewish doctors had obscured, leaves it in more than its original glory; transfers the day of its celebration to that of his resurrection, and erects it into a trophy of his victory. Such, in a word, is its paramount authority upon the human conscience, that the Christian church in every age, including the Apostolical, has confessed its claims, and made it the occasion of their delight and joy.

It is in truth, " a sign of the covenant" between God and man; a badge of our Christian profession; the acknowledgment we publicly make of the God who created, and the Saviour who redeemed us; a chief means of that dedication and sanctification of man to his Almighty Lord, which creation and redemption are designed to produce.

And this leads us to the second, and practical division of our whole subject. How is this holy day to be observed under the gospel?—What is the importance of observing it, and the evils of the opposite neglect?[1] What is the necessity of personal and national repentance for our violation of it?[2]—Grave questions these, and demanding all our attention. For why the accumulated proofs of the institution, stretching from the creation of man to the rest of heaven, but to enforce its practical duties? And what is the true source of almost all the objections to its divine authority, but the dislike which fallen man has to its spiritual worship, and holy demands? Let the rest be admitted to be external and civil merely—let the public duties of the worship of God be confined to a brief and cursory service —let the private hours of the Sabbath be spent in worldly, or intellectual, or festive indulgences—and all objections to its authority would cease. But if we maintain, that the great end of the appointment is to be a sign of God's covenant, and a means of sanctification—if we maintain the duties of it to extend to all classes of persons, and during the whole of the sacred day—if we maintain that the spirit in which these are to be performed is the filial temper of joy and delight in God— if we maintain that the mighty blessings which are to be especially commemorated are no other than creation, redemption, heaven—if, in a word, we show that the Sabbath, practically considered, is Christianity embodied—revelation set forth visibly in its simple and

---

[1] Sermon VI.   [2] Sermon VII.

majestic features—the sign and representation of the covenant of grace,---the means of sanctification exhibited and set before our eyes,---then the corrupt reason and perverted affections of man unite to invent objections to its authority, that they may escape its unwelcome bonds.

These, then, are the very points which in the present discourse we shall endeavour to illustrate : the GREAT END of the institution—its PUBLIC AND PRIVATE DUTIES—the SPIRIT AND TEMPER WHICH it cherishes ---the ESPECIAL BLESSINGS which it commemorates.

And here let two remarks be premised. We enforce not the duties of the Jewish, but of the Christian Sabbath. The ceremonial and civil appendages of the Mosaic law, the spirit of bondage, the terrors of Mount Sinai, are passed. It is the gospel in all its grace and loveliness which we maintain---that mild and merciful institution, cleared from the traditionary yoke of the Jewish masters, which our Lord confirmed as the boon and gift originally granted to man. Every thing in the Christian Sabbath is tender and considerate on the one hand, every thing is spiritual and elevated on the other ; and is, in both views, adapted and suited to the real state and exigencies of our nature, under the last and most perfect dispensation of religion.

But then the determination of what is really spiritual, of what is really for the welfare of man, of what are the real duties and employments of the day, must be taken from the Scriptures themselves, and not from the opinions, much less from the inclinations and fashions, of a corrupt world. We must rise to the standard of the Sabbath as set forth in the Bible, not sink the Bible to the level of our wayward passions. This is the second remark. The doctrine of the institution, like the counsel of a skilful physician, is designed to produce a cure of our moral maladies by wholesome medicines, not to foment the disease by cordials, or hide its worst symptoms by opiates and palliatives.

And do Thou, Almighty God and Father, who

G

madest the Sabbath for man, assist us to rise up to its true demands! May thy Spirit teach us what thy revelation really imports, and what the day which Thou callest thine own, is designed to become! That, knowing our own misery, and receiving with humble faith the redemption of thy Son, we may delight in the services of that season which is one chief means of communicating the blessings procured by it to our souls!

In considering, then, the practical duties of the Lord's day, we must,

I. Keep ever in view THE GREAT END OF THE INSTITUTION—which is to be a visible sign of the covenant between God and us, and a principal means of that sanctification which it is one object of that covenant to produce.

For it is not merely in the words of the text that this express end is assigned to it; almost a thousand years before, the Lord had declared by Moses, "Verily my Sabbaths ye shall keep; for it is a sign between me and you throughout your generations, that ye may know that I am the Lord that doth sanctify you."[1] Thus we learn that this is an essential design of the institution. It received, indeed, especial sanctions, and was connected with particular observances, during the continuance of the national covenant with the people of Israel. But, as in SANCTIFICATION the whole human race are interested, the Sabbath becomes a SIGN to every nation in every age, where Revelation with its weekly rest reaches. It is accordingly immediately connected in the passage above cited with the original appointment in paradise: "Six days may work be done; but on the seventh is the Sabbath of rest, holy to the Lord—for in six days the Lord made heaven and earth, and on the seventh day he rested, and was refreshed."[2] And so Moses, after reciting the decalogue, and the two commands which form the summary of it, pronounced in another place, "Thou shalt bind them for a SIGN upon thine hand."[3]

[1] Exodus xxxi. 13.   [2] ver. 15 & 17.   [3] Deut. vi. 8.

The holy day of rest is, then, to be regarded as the sign, badge, or profession of the God whom we serve, and of the covenant of his grace, of which we profess to be members. We testify our allegiance to the Lord who rose again from the dead " through the blood of the everlasting covenant." The Sabbath, interrupting our secular pursuits, and calling us off to the spiritual duties of religion, is a symbol whereby we declare what God it is we worship, acknowledge that the Lord revealed in the Bible is our God and no other; proclaim ourselves the vassals and servants of that only God who created the heavens and the earth in six days and rested the seventh, and commanded us to observe this suitable distribution of time as a badge and livery that we worship him alone.[1] And we keep it under the gospel on the Lord's day, to avow our belief that on the morning of that day, the first of the week, redemption, like a second creation, was accomplished, our Lord rose from the dead, and ceased from his work, and rested and was refreshed; and that we are the servants and worshippers of that adorable Saviour. Thus the covenant of grace in Christ Jesus is set forth in our Christian celebration of this festival. We are not Jews but Christians; and wherever the religion of Christ is established, the symbol and cognizance of the Resurrection comes with it.

. And this not for the mere avowal of our allegiance, or the manifestation of the attributes and glory of our Creator and Redeemer, but also for the purpose of promoting that SANCTIFICATION which it is the end of the covenant to produce. The expression of the text and of the similar passage just cited, is most remarkable, " Moreover, I gave them my Sabbaths to be a sign between me and them, that they might know that I am the Lord that SANCTIFY them." What an exalted end and design of the institution! Sanctification is the work of God's Holy Spirit by his secret but effectual influences upon the heart, separating man from

[1] J. Mede.

the love and service of sin, and turning him to God
and holiness. The idea is that of setting apart, separating, consecrating for certain holy purposes. Thus,
when applied to sacred persons, times, services, garments, buildings, it imports the separation of them from
profane uses, and the dedication of them to the honour
of God. So the Sabbath was in Paradise sanctified
by the Almighty, that is, separated from ordinary employments, and set apart for the service and worship of
God. And how important is the thought, that the
design of the Almighty in sanctifying and hallowing a
a day of Sabbath, was, that man, his moral and accountable creature, might be sanctified and dedicated
by means of it—that the external consecration of the
season ends in the internal consecration of the heart
of man to his Creator and Redeemer!

All the designs of the institution terminate here.
The Sabbath, was made, granted, vouchsafed to man,
as the principal season when all the means of sanctification should have their effect—when man's immortal
nature should be restored to its true elevation—when his
spiritual and accountable powers should be especially
exercised—when his relation to God, his dependance
upon him, his obligations, his gratitude and love, his
offerings of praise, his prayers and aspirations for future
blessings, should be declared and presented.

To rise up to the dignity of the Sabbath, and perform any of its duties aright, we must understand what
sanctification is, who the great God is to whose service
we are to be devoted, what that Creator and Redeemer
claims of us who on this day rose from the dead, what
are the terms of that covenant of which he is the Mediator and Lord.

Even before the fall, man in paradise, as we have
said, needed a Sabbath, a day of religion; and for the
like ends—to be a sign between God and him—to be
a means of exercising and carrying on that sanctification, the principles and habits of which he already
possessed. He was permitted to cease, he was commanded to cease, one day in seven from the gentle toil

of dressing the garden of Eden, that he might devote the time more immediately to his Almighty Creator—to his glory—to the meditation on his perfections and works—to the duties of holy worship and praise—that thus the sanctification of all his powers to his service might be confirmed and heightened.

How much more, then, must man since the fall need this holy day, both as a sign of the covenant and a means of sanctification. He has now not merely to carry on and strengthen habits of holiness, like his first parent, but to acquire them. The covenant, as it respects him, is not a covenant of creation, but of restoration; not of works, but of grace; not to show his obedience by observing a law to which his will is already conformed, but to obtain redemption by believing in the divine Mediator of a new and better covenant. Sanctification as to man since the fall, is the recovery of the soul to the lost image of God, the illumination of a darkened understanding, the giving a right direction to the will, the changing of the whole bias and course of his affections and conduct, the bringing him back to God, his great end, and the preparing him for the enjoyment of God, his ultimate felicity.

And this answers the objection which is sometimes absurdly or ignorantly made, "That under the gospel every day is a Sabbath—all we do is to be done to the glory of God—a spiritual and perfect dispensation claims all we have and are." And yet in paradise, where man walked before God in his original uprightness, he was called on to keep a Sabbath. How idle then is the plea, now that man is fallen. Those who urge it, know little of the nature of true sanctification, and of the difficulties under which it is attained in this world of conflict. Even if entire holiness could be reached in this imperfect state, a day of rest would be indispensable for the honour of God's name, for the more immediate duties of public and private devotion, and for the carrying out into full exercise the principles of holiness. But it is folly, it is presumption to talk thus, whilst man in his best attainments is full of defects and errors, full of corrupt tendencies—needs a day of sanctification to remind him of his dangers, to bring him out from the snares of life, to lift his heart more entirely towards heaven. Those who talk of every day being a Sabbath, mean in fact that no day should be such. Besides, the expression " keeping holy," as it applies to the ordinary days of the week, and as it fixes itself on the day of God, has a different force and application. To keep holy the six days of the week, means only that we intermingle family and private devotions with our lawful labour and work on those days—that we direct our secular calling to God's glory—that we implore his blessing upon all our occupations. But " to keep holy" the seventh day is to suspend those occupations, to forbear all our ordinary works, to renounce all our secular business, and to devote all the hours of the day to the immediate care of our souls, and the immediate worship of God. We are as much called to work the six days, as we are to rest on the seventh.

This is, then, the first practical duty of the Lord's day, to keep ever in view its great end. The sanctification of it begins, as to us, when our dedication to God begins. We hallow the Sabbath when we ourselves are hallowed to God. We awake to the true importance of the institution, when we feel our fallen and sinful state, when we receive the covenant of grace as proposed in the gospel, when we seek to be sanctified, body, soul and spirit, to be the Lord's. A divine life infused into the soul of man—a perception of the nature and excellency of spiritual things—a view of the glory and majesty of the great Redeemer—a reliance upon his death and resurrection— a dependance upon the influence of his Holy Spirit,—these bring the Sabbath and the human heart together. The Sabbath is born to man when he is born of God. Then it recalls, revives, strengthens, all the principles of sanctification. Then it not only gives him the time, and affords him the means, and calls him to the duties of sanctification;

but it leads him to employ all these to their proper end. And thus the Lord is pleased to sanctify man; thus the day is a sign between him and us; thus the final ends of all religion are advanced.

And here lies the fundamental defect in so many of our cases—we do not feel the unspeakable import-ance of holiness—we do not desire sanctification—we stop in the external and official parts of the sabbatical institution: we have lost the due sense of what consecra-tion of heart to God means, and therefore of what we should aim at on the day with which it is connected.

Consider, then, I entreat you, my dear brethren, the only manner in which you can enter on the practical duties of the Lord's day aright. Examine your state before God. Have you any desire to be made holy, to be pardoned, to be separated from sin, to be dedicated to God? Do you wish really to know the demands which Christianity makes upon you? Do you seek earnestly the way of salvation?—Behold, then, what you want. There is the day when all this is to be learned. There is the covenant of which that day is a sign. There is the sanctification which all the ordi-nances and exercises of that day are calculated to pro-duce. Implore, then, the grace of the Holy Spirit to affect your heart seriously with these truths, and thus will all the other directions we may offer fall into their due place. For sanctification being proposed as the great end of the Sabbath,

II. THE PUBLIC AND PRIVATE DUTIES OF IT will follow most naturally.

These will demand of us less time, because the main design being comprehended and felt, the details of particular rules will be easy; and yet we must not omit them. They relate to the public worship of the Almighty; the care of our family; our personal and private communion with God; a due attention to all dependant on us, extending even to our cattle; toge-ther with such necessary offices of charity as arise in the course of the sacred duties of the day.

1. The public exercises of God's worship, and the fellowship of Christians with each other in common acts of prayer and praise, are the leading business of this holy season. The rest from temporal employments is in order to perform the solemn services of the sanctuary in the first place. A holy convocation was a part of the sabbatical worship under the law. The psalmist, and the prophets after him, dwell much upon the public ordinances, the temple, the house of prayer, the courts of the Lord's house. The first mention of our Lord's conduct on the Sabbath, is that his custom was to attend the synagogue. He appeared to his disciples, also, more than once, on the first day of the week, after his resurrection, and changed the day of rest to honour this event. It was on the first day of the week, again, that the apostles met the Christian churches, and preached the gospel to them, and celebrated " the breaking of bread," as the Eucharist is sometimes called. The precept " not to forsake the assembling of themselves together," completes the proof and devolves the duty upon us. Man as a social creature, never glorifies God more, nor advances his own sanctification in a larger measure, than when he openly recognizes the Christian religion, and honours the resurrection of its divine Founder in public assemblies. There the Holy Spirit loves to dwell—there the people unite in the confession of sin to the glory of God's righteousness—there they implore in common the gift of pardon and receive its assurances—there they hear the word of God solemnly read—there the sacraments are administered—there they pour out their litanies at the throne of grace— there they hear the gospel preached and its truths applied to their hearts and consciences,—and there, finally, they sing the high praises of their Maker, Benefactor, Redeemer, and Sanctifier. Such worship resembles that of the angelic choirs of heaven. The six days' work and toil and temptation are forgotten—Christ himself is present—it is " none other than the house of God, it is the gate of heaven." Heaven is the place of the public uninterrupted worship

of God.   Angels and glorified spirits unceasingly cry
" Holy, holy, holy is the Lord of hosts." And in nothing
does the church on earth so nearly approach the church
above, as in the harmonious and devout exercises of
public worship.

An early attendance—a devout interest in all the
parts of the service—an application to our own case
of the prayers, lessons, sermons—fervent gratitude in
the offerings of praise—an edifying posture and de-
meanor—a candid and docile consideration of the doctrine delivered—audible and solemn responses—these
are the indications of the true worshipper ; who confines not his public duties to one attendance, but rejoices twice to appear in those " courts " where his heart
wishes to " dwell."

2. THE CARE OF OUR FAMILIES must not, however,
be neglected, whilst we first discharge our public duties.
We must not leave our children and servants to do as
they please, but we must stop all the secular work which
might tempt them to violate the holy day, dispose of
our concerns with the best management, so as to admit
of our household devoting themselves to their religious
offices, and encourage them to perform those offices
both public and private, by every suitable means. And
therefore the fourth commandment is A FAMILY COM-
MANDMENT.   The heads of families are made answer-
able for all who are under their roof.   " Six days are
we to labour, and do," not the greatest part, but " all
our work."   There is no exception for the idle, the
busy, or the sick. But lest any should feign a plea, the
commandment goes on and prohibits us expressly
from doing any work.   " In it thou shalt not do any
work."   And that a depraved heart, fertile in evasions,
may not be able to suggest that children, servants, and
cattle, are not included, each class is enumerated :
" In it thou shalt not do any work, thou, nor thy son,
nor thy daughter, nor thy man-servant, nor thy maid-
servant, nor the stranger that is within thy gates ;" and
the merciful reason is adjoined in the recapitulation of

G 5

the law, " that thy man-servant and thy maid-servant may rest as well as thou." The discharge of them from all ordinary and servile work is indispensable. If they serve us the six days, we are to take care that they serve God on the seventh. The boon and grant of one day's rest extends to the whole human race; and we must see that in our household the gift is not lost. It is our business to complete on the Saturday, or postpone to the Monday, what would intrench on the sabbath-rest. It is easy, it is delightful for the master of the family to do this. He will provide time for all his household to attend once, and if possible twice, the public worship. His domestic prayers will on that sacred day be extended. The more solemn reading and explaining of God's word, with prayers for a suitable state of mind for public services, will be the employ of the Sunday morning; and in the afternoon, or evening, as the case may be, he will catechise the young and give familiar and more detailed instruction to his servants. The head of every family has a charge of souls, as it were, committed to him; he is a priest in his own house. He has to promote the sanctification of all under his roof. His order, his piety, his appearance, in public church and in his house, surrounded with his children and dependants, is an acknowledgment and badge of the God whom he worships. He must not, like Eli, yield, from cowardice and a false indulgence, to the bad habits and inclinations of those around him; but like Abraham, "command his children and his household after him;" and, like Joshua, resolve, " As for me and my house we will serve the Lord."

3. THE PRIVATE AND PERSONAL DUTIES must prepare for, and succeed the public and domestic. For the Sabbath is for the sanctification of each individual. It is a barrier thrown in upon the current of worldly things, behind which, each one is to collect himself and stem the tide, and work himself back again to his God. More depends on the INTERVALS between

the social and public exercises of the Lord's day, than we may at first imagine. Fill them up with vain conversations, idle visits, worldly reading, carelessness, indolence, sloth, and all the fruit of public and domestic worship is destroyed—the taste for them is lost—and the form of them will not be long persevered in. But let these interstices be duly occupied with earnest prayer, examination of the heart, communion with God, meditation, intercession for children, family, friends, reflections on the public instruction we have received,—and all will assume another complexion. In these secret musings, the heart is visited with grace, the sermons and lessons sink deep into the habit, the mind is calmed and tranquillized, some additional power of interior devotion is acquired. And it is for these private duties, as well as for the more public, that the rest of the Sabbath is given. They are the cement, as it were, which binds together the separate materials of the sacred festival, which without it, fall to pieces, sink into decay, and lose all their plastic energy and force. How can we expect any breathings of grace, any communion with the Father of spirits, any quickening and elevation of the heart, if we draw nigh to God merely in the outward form, and mock him with a pretence of service, the affections being left behind? A heart unprepared by private duties, is not likely to be benefited by public : and, on the other hand, instructions and exercises in the house of God, not followed by secret meditation ;and prayer, are not likely to abide in the memory or influence the conduct.

4. But besides our immediate family, the duties of the Christian Sabbath extend to OUR DEPENDANTS—to "the stranger within our gates"— to all over whom we have any natural influence—and even to the irrational creatures who subserve our comfort, and whose repose is commanded both for their own sakes and to render more completely practical the duty of religious rest enjoined upon man, their lord. These provisions

breathe all the mercy of the divine law : the terms are remarkable—" That thy man-servant and thy maid-servant may rest as well as thou"—" Remember that thou wast a servant in the land of Egypt."—" Thou knowest the heart of a stranger."

How lamentably the spirit of these injunctions is violated, is but too manifest. The shops and ware-houses of too many witness against them. The count-ing-houses and offices and counsel-rooms of too many are the destruction of souls. The negligence of mas-ters as to the morals of the young, and their religious observance of the Sunday, merely on the plea that they are not domestics, will be no adequate defence at the tri-bunal of God. The workmen in manufactories are committed to the care of the persons whom they serve. Contrivance, management, order, are required of them. Influence is a talent for which an account must be ren-dered another day. All nature is to be hushed into repose on the blessed, hallowed season of rest—all the confusion of the world to cease—all the pursuits of even lawful gain to be suspended—all the hurry of life to be calmed—not only the master and parent with his family, but the principals and conductors of pro-fessional or commercial concerns—the statesman in his cabinet—the magistrate on the bench—the merchant in his house of affairs—the traveller on his journey—the lawyer in his office—the scholar in his study—all must be interrupted and called aside, to honour the day which is the sign of the Christian covenant, and the means of Christian sanctification—man and beast are to recreate their wasted powers, the beast in the repose of which it is capable, man in the dignified and rational refreshment, for which God has peculiarly qualified him.

Works of real necessity and mercy may, indeed, be done on the sacred day, such as our Lord by his ex-ample authorised, and as the great moral ends of the institution persuade. We relieve the sick from present suffering, we satisfy the demands of hunger, we pull an ox or an ass from a pit, we give food to our cattle, we use the gentle labour of our domestic animals,[1] so far as may be necessary for conveying us and our families to the public worship of God, when sickness or unavoidable distance compels. But we may not give a wider, or more lax construction to the fourth commandment, than what the intention of the great Legislator imports, and our Lord has determined. Such explanation, in opposition to the decrees of the Jewish doctors, as he judged necessary, he gave; but in all other respects, left the law just as he found it. Works of necessity and charity must not be multiplied without just cause; much less must works of vanity, sloth, carelessness, be performed under the cloke of them. No rule can be laid down for others. Conscience, and a sincere desire to glorify God, must determine. Let the main design of the day, our sanctification, and the practical duties of it, as it respects public and private, domestic and personal devotion, be performed in subserviency thereto, and WORKS OF NECESSARY CHARITY, (for such is the more accurate bearing of our Lord's example,[2]) will not be unduly undertaken.

And need I stop here to refute the mere evasion, which would allow the obligation of the Lord's day as to public worship, and deny it as to the remaining duties of the institution? What! is it enough merely to worship God for one meagre hour or two, and then resign ourselves to the world and its cares? What! can public worship be celebrated with any spirituality of mind, without preparatory and subsequent meditation and prayer? What! are the family devotions of other days to be discontinued on the day when they ought to be enlarged and multiplied? What! is it

[1] The Shunammite, when her child died begged of her husband to send her "one of his young men and one of the asses," that she might go to the man of God. The reply shows that the devoutest Jews made use of these animals on the Sabbath, for the purpose of attending the worship of God. "And he said, Wherefore wilt thou go to him to-day? It is neither new moon nor sabbath?" 2 Kings iv, 22, 23.
[2] Dr. Humphrey's Essays, p. 43.

the Sabbath MORNING that we are to sanctify, or the
Sabbath EVENING only, and not the SABBATH-DAY,—
the whole period from the close of the last working
day till the dawn of the next?   Yes ; the whole day
is not too long for God, for Christ, for the soul : if the
entire command is not complied with, none is.

Or need I stop to enumerate those various secular
works, which are unlawful on this day of the Lord?
Need I expose the miserable sophistry, which substi-
tutes a mere change of worldly engagements for the
holy duties of divine prayer and praise?—What, if I close
my office or my shop, and open my drawer of accounts,
and write letters of affairs, am I sanctifying the Sabbath ?   What, if I withdraw from the exchange, or the
courts of law, into the chamber of consultation, or the
secret room of settlements and bargains, is this keeping
the Lord's day?   What! 1 employ not my labourers
on Sunday, but I pay them their wages, and almost
oblige them to make their purchases on that sacred
day; and is this to keep it holy?   Or, I quit the hurry
of the city or town, for the mere sensual indulgence
of the suburban retreat—I " eat, and drink, and am
merry;" I collect around me friends as thoughtless as
myself—I employ my servants in the unnecessary toil
of preparing luxurious meals—I go from the church to
the ride, the garden, the park, the pleasure-ground,
the river.   I walk over my farm or my lands, I arrange
for the business of the following week, I plunge into
literary or scientific reading, I lose my devotional feelings in the abominations of a Sunday-newspaper—and
this I call religion—this I designate as the sanctification of the Lord's day !

But indeed, Christian brethren, the duties of this
holy season are so spiritual, so opposite to the carnal
and earthly tendencies of human nature, so surrounded by temptations and suggestions on all hands,
that there is not one of us but may discern much
to be amended, improved, omitted, supplied.   Our
order of engagements is incomplete, our care of our
family wanting in vigilance, our forethought drowsy

and treacherous, our interruptions of religious exercises too frequent and too long.   There is much that
admits of alteration.   Let us look well into our family
rules, family habits, family hours, family religion,
family attendance on the public worship of God, and
we shall discern lamentable marks of decay and lukewarmness—we shall discern many things, which, if
not dishonourable to the Sabbath, are at least not so
honourable to it as they might be.   But this leads me
to consider,

III. That in order to keep holy the Lord's day, we
must carry THE TRUE SPIRIT OF THE CHRISTIAN DIS-
PENSATION INTO THESE DUTIES.   We must not celebrate a Jewish, but a Christian festival.   We must
imbibe that spirit of rest and delight in God, that
sense of refreshment and repose, in his more immediate service, which the liberty of the gospel breathes,
and without some degree of which we can never discharge these duties aright.
The general habit of mind cannot be better described
than in the words of the psalmist : " How amiable are
thy tabernacles, O Lord of Hosts; my soul longeth,
yea, even fainteth for the courts of the Lord ; my heart
and my flesh crieth out for the living God—a day in
thy courts is better than a thousand ; I had rather be a
door-keeper in the house of my God, than to dwell in
the tents of wickedness."[1]   Or again, " One thing
have I desired of the Lord, that will I seek after, that
I may dwell in the house of the Lord all the days of
my life, to behold the fair beauty of the Lord, and inquire in his temple."[2]   Or again, " My soul shall be
satisfied as with marrow and fatness, and my mouth
shall praise thee with joyful lips."[3]
This is the language of delight, of repose of soul in
the duties of religion.   Join to this the particular dis-
coveries of the New Testament, as to the way of access
in the blood of Christ, and by the influences of the

[1] Ps. lxxxiv. 1, 2, 10.   [2] Ps. xxvii. 4.   [3] Ps. lxiii. 5.

Spirit, and we have the complete description of the devotional temper.

Iu like manner, the Holy prophets—" Blessed is the man that doeth this, and the son of man that layeth hold of it—that chooseth the things that please me—that join themselves to the Lord, to serve him, and to love the name of the Lord—even them will I bring to my holy mountain, and make them joyful in my house of prayer." [1] Love, choice of God, joy in the house of prayer, stand in complete contrast with a yoke, a burden, a mere task, as too many represent the duties of religion to be.

. But the most ample account of the spirit which should pervade the sabbatical duties, is in a passage which, in common with the preceding, we have formerly quoted for another purpose; " If thou turn away thy foot from the Sabbath, from doing thy pleasure on my holy day; and call the Sabbath a delight, the holy of the Lord, honourable; and shalt honour him, not doing thine own ways, nor finding thine own pleasure, nor speaking thine own words; then shalt thou delight thyself in the Lord." [2] Here, the spirit of the right observance of the Lord's day is expressed in a most striking phrase—" if thou call the Sabbath A DELIGHT, THE HOLY OF THE LORD, HONOURABLE, AND SHALT HONOUR HIM." We are to esteem it honourable, above all other days; we are peculiarly to honour Him, whose bounty created us, whose long-suffering has preserved us, and whose unsearchable goodness has provided for us a way of eternal redemption. Then joy will fill our hearts. The glory of our divine Lord, his majesty, his sovereignty over us, his infinite excellency, his continued benefits, his omnipotent, never-failing providence, will possess our minds ; and we shall feel, as the Sabbath-morn returns, that we are going to the palace of the great King, that we are approaching the abode of a heavenly Father, that we are going up to God, to " God our exceeding joy." From this temper

1 Isa. lvi. 2. 7.   2 Isa. lviii. 13, 14.

will flow the appropriate dispositions which should
govern the details of the day.   The chief of these is,
spiritual repose of heart in God, in opposition to earthly,
sensual, intellectual pleasure—" If thou turn away thy
foot from the Sabbath, from doing THY PLEASURE,
on my holy day."   Here is the main difficulty: so long
as sensual repose, instead of spiritual; intellectual
effort, instead of devotional; the pleasure of the mere
appetites, instead of the pleasure of the soul in God, is
the governing principle in our religion, the Sabbath
will never be kept aright.   A change in our taste and
estimate of things, must first touch the main springs of
happiness.   Then we shall cease from " doing our
pleasure;" and shall willingly aim at doing the pleasure of God.   Amusement, recreation, pastimes, indolent repose, satisfaction in worldly company, worldly
society, worldly banquets, will cease; and new pleasures will be sought for in the pleasures of devotion, of faith, of hope, of communion with God.
Then will the Sabbath be a " delight, the holy of the
Lord, honourable;" and we shall HONOUR GOD in it.
And thus will our pleasure, ways, words, works, be
newly directed.   Instead of " doing our own ways," we
shall choose the ways that God commands, and occupy
the Sabbath with its appropriate duties.   Instead of
" finding our own pleasure," we shall find God's, or
rather, shall perceive a new and more elevated pleasure
in his service; instead of " speaking our own words,"
we shall order our conversation to the glory of God,
and the edification of our neighbour.   Perhaps there
are few sins more common, and more insidious than
that to which these last words refer, " speaking our
own words," that is, secular conversation on the Sunday
—news, inquiries, discussions on matters literary, political, philosophical.   Thus all impression of spiritual
things fades from the mind; the seed of the word is
lost; the ordinary associations and habits of the six
days' labour are insensibly resumed, and the Holy
Spirit is quenched and grieved.
   I need not add here, that the reading of Sunday

newspapers is directly in contradiction to the whole spirit which should be cultivated on that blessed day. It encourages the most flagrant violation of the Sabbath, in those who print, who sell, who circulate these monstrous productions—too commonly filled with matter of the most licentious and sceptical tendency; and more injurious and contaminating, from the day on which they are disseminated. They totally unfit the mind for the religious duties before it; or rather, they make those duties impracticable.

But how delightful is the Sabbath, when occupied as it should be! Can any picture be more inviting, than that of a family, a neighbourhood, a parish, honouring the day of God with cheerful and grateful hearts—meditating on that sanctification which is the great design of the day of rest—filling up its hours with the various and important exercises of public and private devotion—and imbuing every act of duty with the Christian temper, with the filial spirit—the spirit not "of bondage again to fear, but the spirit of adoption, crying, Abba, Father?"[1] Howquickly would difficulties be overcome, if once we found our pleasure in the exercises of religion! See how men contrive, labour, surmount obstacles, for the enjoyment of what they love! Observe how eagerly they hasten on the hour, when the pleasure returns. Mark how they endeavour to lengthen the period of its continuance—then contrast with this the weariness they feel in the duties of the Sabbath—how they abridge the heavy employ—how they encroach insensibly on its prescribed limits—how they contrive pleas of necessity for escaping from some of its services—how tame and formal they are in the discharge of them—how late in their arrival at the house of God! What irreverence in their manner! How insensible to the sympathies of devotion! How awake to every slight inconvenience, every occasional prolongation of the prayers or sermon—every pressure of heat or cold—every defect in the manner or voice of

---

[1] Rom. viii. 15.

the minister! What does all this betray, but the inward dissatisfaction, the want of harmony of feeling in the services! Let the spirit of the Christian dispensation imbue their minds, and all would change its appearance. Pleasure, delight, would beam in the countenance, and all would be in keeping with the designs of the Almighty, in the institution of the day.

But we hasten to complete our review of the manner in which the Christian Sabbath should be observed, by suggesting, that in addition to what we have noted, we must

IV. Especially glorify God for THOSE MIGHTY BLESSINGS WHICH ARE APPOINTED TO BE COMMEMORATED ON THE LORD'S DAY—Creation, Redemption, Heaven.

These are the express topics in the divine praise, for which the Sabbath was constituted. We must join the commemoration of these to the other duties of sanctification, of public and private devotion, and of a temper of filial repose and joy in God. I conceive we are often lamentably deficient in those direct acts of adoration and gratitude, for the peculiar and stupendous blessings of providence and grace, which the Sabbath is designed to celebrate. We enter perhaps into the other branches of our duty with some feeling; but our minds are too exclusively occupied with ourselves, and our own immediate circle of trials and duties—we are selfish and contracted in our gratitude—we do not rise up to God in the magnificence of his benefits—we forget that songs ever new should be chanted to him who doeth such great things for us.

Call to mind how expressly CREATION is assigned as a reason for the appointment of the sacred day—"For in six days the Lord made heaven and earth, the sea, and all things that are therein,"—not merely at the institution in paradise, but in the Mosaic law, in the various recapitulations of it, and even in the epistle to the Hebrews, where the subject is merely referred to.   Yes, the Sabbath is the celebration of God's glory in nature.   We confess ourselves the worshippers of the one living and true God.   We separate ourselves from atheists, unbelievers, sceptics, profane contemners of God, now ; just as the patriarchs and Israelites of old separated themselves from heathens, from idolaters, from the pagan worshippers of the nations around them.   We should every Sabbath, when we rehearse our articles of faith in the temple of the Lord, or when the sacred histories, and psalms which relate to the creation, are read, as well as in our own private and domestic devotions, glorify expressly the great God of heaven and earth, adore the wonders of his hand, meditate on his wisdom, goodness, and power, and ascribe to him the praise of creation, preservation, continual deliverance.   A Chrstian is the only true philosopher.   He sees God in every thing. He acknowledges the traces of his matchless skill on every side.   He discovers a father's love in all the order of the universe.   He imitates the song by which the first Sabbath was celebrated at the creation of man, when " the morning stars sang together, and all the sons of God shouted for joy."   The Sabbath is to him a sign, a badge, a cognizance of his allegiance to his glorious Creator, the "King eternal, immortal, invisible, the only wise God."   He " in whose hands our breath is, and whose are all our ways."

2. But REDEMPTION is a yet higher note in the choir of praise, which on the Sabbath surrounds our heavenly King.   At the deliverance from Egypt this song was begun ; but at the great deliverance from the spiritual Egypt, it was amplified and exalted.   This temporal redemption was prefixed to the promulgation of the whole decalogue, from the Mount of Sinai : " I am the Lord thy God which brought thee out of the land of Egypt, out of the house of bondage ;"   and it was attached especially to the fourth commandment, in the last recapitulation of it by Moses : " And remember that thou wast a stranger in the land of Egypt, and

that the Lord thy God brought thee out hence, through a mighty hand, and by a stretched out arm; therefore the Lord thy God commanded thee to keep the Sabbath-day." And the spiritual redemption was the reason of that change of the day of celebration, which from the temporal, transferred it to the eternal blessing. Yes; on the first day of the week we adore a triumphant Saviour, we meditate on his ceasing and resting and being refreshed from the work of the new creation; even as Almighty God ceased from his. No Sabbath should pass without the praises of our rising, ascending, interceding Redeemer being sounded in the church. It is his own day, the day of his glory, the day of his resting from his labours, the day of his "opening the kingdom of heaven to all believers." The song is already prepared to our hands : "Thou hast ascended up on high ; thou hast led captivity captive, thou hast received gifts for men, yea for the rebellious also, that the Lord God might dwell among them."[1] We must add to the other especial duties of the Sabbath, this record of our faith in Christ. We must subjoin to our praises to God the Father who created us, the adoration of God the Son who redeemed us. We must make our public confession of Christ Jesus our Lord. The Lord's day is the badge of the covenant of grace. " He that offereth praise glorifieth me," saith the Lord by the psalmist, " and to him that ordereth his conversation aright, will I show the salvation of God."[2]

3. Nor should the praise of the Holy Ghost be omitted amongst the especial blessings celebrated on the Sabbath. THE REST OF HEAVEN is, by his grace and the anticipations he vouchsafes, sealed to our hopes. This is that eternal repose in God which from the record of the first institution in paradise, to the latest argument of St. Paul, has been presented as the final object of the day of rest. It typifies, sets forth, assures to every sincere believer the ultimate happiness at which he aims. " There remaineth " this last refreshment and salvation " for the people of God."

[1] Psalm lxviii. 18.   [2] Psalm l. 23.

Let us look up towards it, dear brethren, in our meditations and hopes. Let every Sabbath prepare us for its appropriate employment. Let the Holy Ghost, who on this day was vouchsafed to the church, to be the comforter, teacher, guide, sanctifier, and great Author of all grace under the New Testament, be adored and glorified. Let us implore of him the power to realise the promises of redemption, to view with gratitude the wonders of creation and providence, and to unite all with the prospects of the rest of heaven. St. Augustine considers the Sabbath as peculiarly the law of the Holy Ghost. The first two commandments he looks upon as relating to the honour of God the Father; the third, as especially referring to God the Son, the eternal word, whose name is not to be taken in vain, nor to be reduced to the rank of a mere creature; and the fourth, or sabbatical precept, he refers to the praise of the Holy Ghost, who, as the author of rest and peace in his church, is peculiarly honoured on the day which agrees so entirely with his own office.[1] We enter not into a defence critically of the sentiment of the holy Father. We seize the thought; and glorify God the Spirit on the day which is to raise us by his inspiration to the foretaste and pledge of our heavenly rest!

And now from these considerations on the practical duties of the Christian Sabbath, let us, in applying the discourse,

I. Remark THE CONVICTION WHICH SUCH A DISCUSSION SHOULD FIX IN THE MINDS OF THE IRRELIGIOUS AND UNCONVERTED. At what a distance are they from the true spirit and temper of the servants of God! They dispute against the divine authority of the Lord's day. They complain of the various duties we enjoin. They declare the impossibility of rising up to such a tone of piety. They invent excuses for absence and omission. But what do they in fact admit in all this, but their want of religious taste and feeling? What do they avow, but the want of spiritual judgment,

[1] British Review, viii. 483.

pleasures, pursuits?   The more they argue against the
Sabbath, the more they condemn themselves.   The
further they recede from devotional habits and delights,
the greater distance do they place between themselves
and God.

Yes, let such be induced to consider their own ways
and turn to the Lord.   Let them weigh the authority,
and remember the duties of God's blessed day; and
let them seek that fundamental change of heart which
will render the devotions of the day a pleasure, its
duties a choice, its proper exercises the spontaneous
overflowing of gratitude and love.   Then would these
Sabbaths be the NUNDINÆ SPIRITUALES, the spiritual
market-days (to speak with Bishop Andrews) to their
souls;   then would they be as anxious to carry away
COMMEATUM ANIMÆ, provision for the mind, for re-
forming the will, for regulating the affection, for illuminating the understanding, as they are careful to
carry away provision for the body from the markets
whither they resort.

But what can we say as to the spiritual state of those
multitudes, who still continue to have little or no conscience about hallowing God's blessed day?   Where
shall we place them?   Under what class are they to be
arranged?   Where is the indolent and sensual Sab-
bath-keeper, or rather Sabbath-violator to be placed,
who rests only as his ox, or his ass, or his cattle?
Where is the pleasure-taking Sabbath-breaker to be
arranged?   Where the gluttonous and wine-bibbing?
Where the busy, mercantile, or professional Sabbath-breaker, who thinks that the hurries of his concerns excuse him from the worship of God?   Where
is the formalist's Sabbath, whose heart remains behind,
when his person and his lips seem to approach his
Maker and Redeemer?   And what shall we say to the
infidel's Sabbath, the scoffer's Sabbath, the debauchee's
Sabbath?   Alas! the heart turns sick at the fearful
guilt of the numbers, who, with knowledge, and opportunities, and means of sanctifying the day of grace,

abuse, neglect, despise, violate it.[1]   Let such awake,
ere it be too late, to their immense loss, as well as to
their heavy criminality before Almighty God.

Shall God, my fellow sinners, have consecrated a
day from the creation of man, and wilt thou stand out
against his gracious command?   Shall God have republished his will in the fourth commandment of the
decalogue—shall he have enforced it by all the motives
of his righteous authority---shall he have poured around
it all the milder glories of the new covenant, as well as
the tremendous judgments of the old, and wilt thou
not give God his due?   Wilt thou not yield him the
just rent which he demands upon the gift of thy time,
thy health, thy property, thy six days' labour?   Wilt
thou remain insensible to thine eternal interest, thy
present and future happiness, the preparation thou
needest for death and judgment?   O, consider thy
ways, seek thy Saviour's forgiveness, be ashamed and
confounded for thy past neglect.   Begin a new life.
Enter upon a new course.   Seek that holy taste and
divine principle of life which will make the Christian
Sabbath natural, interesting, pleasant, delightful, necessary.

Take at least the preparatory steps.   If you cannot
enter into all the engagements of the Sabbath, enter into
some of them.   By degrees new and better habits will
be formed.   By degrees the whole compass of sabbatical duties will become easy.   Only begin in the strength
of God, and relying on the operations of his grace.
Take a view first of the great end of the institution,
the sanctification of the soul.   Then follow out the
different classes of duties which spring from it, as
branches from the parent stock.   Next seek for something of the spiritual taste which forms the Christian
temper.   And lastly, let the grand blessings of crea-

[1] Bishop Andrews speaks wittily of the Sabbatum as inorum---
Sabbatum aurei vituli---Sabbatum Satanæ—Sabbatum Tyri;
---the Sabbath of Asses---of the Golden Calf---of Satan---of the
men of Tyre.

tion and redemption, and the hope of heaven, be in some degree the topics of your praise.

II. But may we not, all of us, Christian brethren, disco-cover TOPICS ENOUGH OF HUMILIATION in the discussion which has taken place? Which of us discharges the duties of the holy day of God as we should? In fact, the Sabbath is so closely connected with Christianity itself, that as our Christianity rises or falls, so will our obser-vation of the sacred season be elevated, or decline. Nothing is more difficult, considering our corrup-tion and the snares of Satan, than a holy, wise and kind, and yet resolute government of ourselves and families on the Lord's day. All possible hindrances arise to oppose this duty. Especially in the management of our children and household, we meet continual ob-stacles to our best purposes. One remark, however, may be offered on the other side. We must pre-serve the amiable spirit of our Saviour, and the gentle temper of his religion in our domestic arrangements. Few things are more important than to make the Sun-day agreeable, in a proper sense of the term, to young persons and servants. If any thing morose and rigid is apparent in our manner, to those placed under our care, it will inevitably create disgust and aversion. And yet remissness, negligence, cowardice, must not creep in. The wise balancing of these things, then, will require much consideration and prayer. Variety may be thrown into the duties, so as to interest the young mind, without lessening in the least their general effect. The read-ing of the Scripture—the writing or finding texts upon a given subject—the learning of hymns—catechising—the family devotions of the morning and evening—the public worship of God afford sufficient diversity, to ex-cite attention and dissipate lassitude. Much wisdom must, however, be employed, kindness of manner, con-sideration of age, health, circumstances. There should ever be a due admixture of firmness with benignity—all supported by an uniform example, and accompanied with fervent prayer.

H

Indeed prayer, especially for larger measures of the Holy Spirit, is indispensable to the right discharge of these important duties.   If we can do nothing aright without prayer, much less can we sustain a course of obedience, with love and delight, in the consecration of the Sabbath, without the continual supplies of grace and strength.   But these supplies will not be refused to us.   Our defects will be forgiven us through the blood of Christ, our infirmities succoured by the power of the Holy Ghost.   Thus will our Sabbaths pour into our hearts the consolation of the promises, and will at length terminate in God himself who first instituted the day and is its highest consummation and end.

SERMON VI.

THE UNSPEAKABLE IMPORTANCE OF THE RIGHT OBSERVATION OF THE SABBATH, WITH THE EVILS OF THE OPPOSITE ABUSE.

ISAIAH lviii. 1, 2.

Cry aloud, spare not, lift up thy voice like a trumpet, and shew my people their transgressions, and the house of Jacob their sins. Yet they seek me daily, and delight to know my ways, as a nation that did righteously and forsook not the ordinances of their God; they ask of me the ordinances of justice, they take delight in approaching to God.

DOCTRINE is not enough, precept is not enough, on such a subject as that which we have been treating. We must address the conscience; we must be bold in our appeals to the heart of man—we must assert all the authority and majesty of truth. The minister of religion must not shrink from his task on such a question; he must "cry aloud, and spare not; he must show" the people of God "their transgressions, and the house of Jacob," the professed church of Christ, "their sins." He must penetrate the thin disguises which a false religion assumes, and tear off the mask which a pretence of "seeking God and of delighting in his ways" may present: and must declare that the external advan-

H 2

tages and opportunities of religion only increase the guilt of the nation which tramples on that very day, when all these benefits would have their best effect.

We proceed, therefore, to set before you THE UN-SPEAKABLE IMPORTANCE OF A RIGHT OBSERVATION OF THE LORD'S DAY, WITH THE EVILS OF THE OP-POSITE ABUSE—a subject difficult to treat from its very magnitude, from the multitude of topics which it embraces, and from the little perception men in general have of the sin of neglecting and dishonouring God's most ancient institution.

For this may be premised; that the corruption of man, which resists generally all the great doctrines and duties of Christianity, may be expected to press with peculiar violence against a barrier, which, like the Lord's day, is raised against the whole current of that corruption.

Nor is it unimportant to add, that an institution like this, which takes men off from their ordinary pursuits and gives them an interval for religious rest and public worship of Almighty God, must, if abused, become, from the very nature of the case, a source of unnumbered vices and disorders; must draw into itself torrents of those particular evils, which are ever ready to accumulate, as in a common receptacle, where space is given.   There is no middle state here—the influence of the Sabbath for good or for evil upon nations, churches, families, individuals, is incalculable.   It is meant to be the best and holiest day of the week; but, if perverted, it becomes the worst and most destructive.

But how shall we impress you most deeply with this subject? Shall we show you that a due regard to the institution by a Christian nation is of the nature of a sacred compact? That it is essential to man's temporal and spiritual welfare, as a fallen but accountable creature? That it includes all the application of the Christian religion, and, in fact, its preservation in the world? That it binds together all the links and obligations of civil society? That it immediately respects the authority and honour of Almighty God, and his favour and blessing upon a people?—And that, of course, the opposite abuse overturns every one of these things, and brings on the contrary evils?

May God assist us by the influences of his Spirit; that, having no end in view but his glory, and depending for success on no power but his own; we may direct our inquiries with simplicity, and obey the dictates of truth with unreserved courage and joy!

I. For what, in fact, is the observation of the Christian Sabbath, but A MOST SACRED COMPACT; and what the abuse of it but the violation of that compact? It is obvious, that it can only be by the very general and almost universal agreements of a nation, that secular affairs can be suspended, business stopped, public recreation and amusements forbidden, offices and establishments closed, the ministers of religion furnished with protection in the discharge of their duties, the interruptions of open profligacy prevented, Christian assemblies authorized, churches erected for their use—in short, the whole frame-work of the public worship of God set up and continued. Laws are the expression of public opinion—and go a certain length, both negatively in the repression of open insults on Christianity, and positively in sustaining and supporting the ministers and officers of the sanctuary. But all the real operation and success of such a system rests upon the compact and covenant of a Christian people one with another, and with their gracious God and Saviour.

The scattered converts of the first Christian churches could only celebrate their Sabbaths in early darkness, or the unobserved hours of the night: persecution hung over their meetings—they were happy if they were not dragged to the idol's temple and urged to join in the idol worship. This is one reason probably, why the apostles less frequently dwell upon the express duties of the Lord's day in the New Testament; leaving it rather to the consciences of their converts and the universal conviction that a Sabbath was of perpetual

moral obligation, to fill up the detail.   The condition of
domestic slavery, in which most of the Gentile converts
were, would tend to increase the apostles' tenderness on
the point.   Still the first Christians kept holy the
Lord's day, the badge of their redemption, to the utmost of their power.   When Christianity triumphed
over emperors and kings and statesmen and magistrates
by the mild influence of the truth, things were changed.
The holy day of weekly rest succeeded the festivals of
the heathen worship.   When England was converted in
the course of the divine mercy, her Heathen rites, her
Druidical orgies, her savage customs, her brutal and
idolatrous sacrifices, were cast away—and the love of
God, the preaching of the blessed gospel, the singing
praises to Christ, the celebration of the mysteries of
his death, and the observation of the hallowed day on
which all these were to be performed, succeeded to
them.   Christian legislators in our own, as in other
countries, arose to do what they could in guarding the
new institutions.   They continued thus to act.   But
still upon the consciences of individuals has ever rested,
and must rest, the real and effectual obligation.   The
inhabitants of the nation, having submitted to the
yoke of the gospel, assumed its profession in the celebration of one day of religious joy.   The covenant
was signed and sealed, as it were, in this visible acknowledgment of the Christian faith ; but the spirit
and conduct of individuals and families fill up the
conditions of it.   Thus it is a compact.   If devout
care of children and servants, abstinence from ordinary duties and cheerful attendance upon the public and private offices of religion, mark the households
of our towns and cities, the compact is fulfilled.   If
carelessness, indifference, non-attendance, creep in
upon the general body, the compact is violated.   It
may remain, indeed, in its form—the external law may
be unabrogated—the churches may stand as before—the
ministers of religion may retain their office,—but the
compact is made void.   The Christian obligation is

virtually abjured.   If the evil goes on, every outward order and regulation will be by degrees weakened, evaded, contemned, and the Sabbath will be no more.

I ask, then, whether, in this view, the importance of the due observance of the Lord's day is not immense? It is the fulfilment of a compact.   Every act of violation tends to undermine the whole frame-work.   Every wilful breach has the guilt of breaking down the universal consent, of beginning a destructive habit, of infecting the entire community.   The good example, the influence, the devout conduct of each family, each person, goes to sustain the general duty, to make the covenant valid, to enable others to consecrate the day.

The place, then, which each separate action fills, is like a stone in an arch, important, not only as to its isolated magnitude, but from its position, its coherence with the other parts, its necessity to the firmness and solidity of the whole structure.

Look in this view at all the separate acts of all the careless, the profane, the covetous, the unbelieving amongst our population—see their Sabbaths—estimate the evil done, not by the independent acts, but by the fearful influence, by the covenant broken, the stipulation trodden under foot, the engagements rendered difficult to others, impossible to themselves.   Let no one say, " I am but an individual,"—for the nation is made up of individuals.   Let no one say, " A single act can be of small evil,"—for the observance of a national Sabbath is composed of single acts.   Let no one pretend, " The stream and current of religious duty cannot be stopped by my particular resistance;" for the whole tide is constituted and impelled by the aggregation of unnumbered minute elements; and every obstacle retards the flow.

II. But estimate, in the next place, if you can, the importance of the universal observation of the Christian Sabbath, from its bearings upon man's TEMPORAL AND SPIRITUAL WELFARE, AS A FALLEN BUT ACCOUNTABLE CREATURE.   For is man, or is he not, an

immortal being ? Has he, or has he not, a soul allied
to God, capable of knowing, destined to serve him,
and utterly void of real happiness, till it be found in
him ? Has he, or has he not, received a revelation from
Almighty God, according to which he will be judged
at the last day? Then, what is man's truest interest,
what his essential duty, what his first and noblest object ? And what is the great hindrance to his real
welfare—to his attention to his religious convictions ?
Is it not the pressure of earthly things, the undue magnitude and importance which, from their proximity,
they assume? Is it not the want of leisure for reflection, the want of a realising apprehension of the truth
of unseen objects? Then the Sabbath gives all this
leisure, calls man off from all this turmoil, interposes a
day of repose, of recollection, of distinct time for
the care of his soul and the worship of God.   The
Sabbath raises the standard of his moral feelings,
brings him to act upon his higher nature, his mind, his
rational part, his responsibility to an eternal Judge.
The necessities of the body chiefly occupy the six days ;
the immortal destiny of man and his ultimate vocation
by the gospel, claim the seventh.   Nothing more tends
to improve all the faculties, to quicken the practical
judgment, to mature and invigorate the powers of the
mind, to enlarge the sphere and multiply the sources
of intellectual pleasure, to open the widest avenues to
happiness, to unite man with his true end, than the
care of the soul and the celebration of the divine worship.

What a sight for angels is the assembly of all the
inhabitants of a nation, in its various subdivisions, before the Almighty God—confessing their sins, acknowledging his goodness, celebrating his praises, hearing
his word, partaking of his mysteries. Creation, redemption, heaven brought, after an interval of six
days' toil and secularity, full before their view, and
elevating and attracting the heart of a wayward, perverse, but noble race !

It is to be further borne in mind, that man is fallen,

corrupted, propense to the external objects which surround him—that the Lord's day is not merely the day
of religious duty and rest, but the restoring, the awakening day—the day of recovery and reformation. It tends
to bring man back to recollection, to seriousness, to penitence, to prayer. If the Sabbath be desecrated,
his original disease gains ground, his convalescence,
only incipient and doubtful, is suspended, and his whole
spiritual prosperity and existence are endangered. It
is not of Adam uncorrupted that we speak, but of
Adam's race, sunk in selfishness and flesh, with only
faint remains of moral feeling, and far from God and
godliness. Nor is it of the devout and fervent part
of the professed Christian world, or of the Protestant
Christian world in any form, that we exclusively speak;
it is for the family of man scattered over the face of
the earth, lost in heathenism and infidelity, that we
would reserve the Sabbath; it is for Pagans and
Mahometans, for the members of the Roman Catho-
lic and Greek churches, that we plead. We would
exhibit to them the holy Sabbath in the example of the
purer Christian bodies, to draw their attention, to mark
the reality of our religion, to provide them information
upon its nature and duties. How is a wandering,
fallen, and depraved world to be recalled to God, without that day which celebrates the works and word and
grace of God—that day which recognizes his authority
over man—that day which proclaims his intellectual
and accountable nature, his future, his eternal hopes?
The Sabbath interposes a space between total irreligion and the conscience of man; it puts in the claims
of God upon the human heart.

Nor is the temporal welfare of mankind less concerned than their spiritual, in the observation of the
Lord's day. Man was created for six days' work, not
for seven: his faculties cannot bear an unremitted
strain. Children, and servants, and the labouring
classes of mankind, (by far the more numerous, and
the most liable to be oppressed,) require what this institution gives—a day of repose, of refreshment, of re-

ligious recollection and peace. The whole world rests and is still, that God may speak, that conscience may resume her sway, that the exhausted body and mind may recruit their powers, and be fitted for a more vigorous effort. The utmost productive labour of man, is in the proportion of rest and exertion, ordained by his merciful Creator. The best prevention of disease is in the same provision. The prolongation of human life depends on the like alternation of toil and repose. The springs of pleasure are thus augmented and purified. The satiety, the sameness, the weariness, the uniformity of human life is broken; and a blessed, hallowed period for religion is interposed. The interval between these seasons is neither so distant as to be ineffectual to its end, nor so near as to injure the real interests of our worldly callings—but, like every thing else in God's revelation, unites the prosperity of the soul with the highest welfare of the body and concerns of man.

How great, then, is the importance of every one's falling in with the designs of this institution! Can any one estimate adequately the soul, eternity, heaven and hell, God, Christ, salvation, pardon, hope, happiness—the whole intellectual, moral, and religious welfare of man, formed after his Creator's image, fallen from it by sin, called to the renovation of it by the blessings and duties of the Christian Sabbath!

Look at the evils of the contrary abuse. See man sunk from his real honours into the rank of the brute; see him lost in appetite, vice, lust, pride, carelessness; with nothing to redeem, nothing to call him back, nothing to restore; the Spirit of God departed from him; a reprobate sense possessing and weighing down his soul. The main difference between heathen and Christian nations is the recurrence of a Sabbath, and of what follows upon it. The violation of this day in Christian countries, is the brand upon the forehead of nominal religion. See the Sabbath-breaker opening his shop, writing his letters, preparing his accounts: see him entering his office; see him imposing upon his servants, his clerks, his dependants, the yoke of unpermitted and unholy labour. Observe him in languid carelessness, idling away the morning hours, and disgracing, by excess and worldly company, the evening. Notice the effect upon his own mind and habits. He boasts of his liberty, his freedom from superstitious fears, his superiority to ordinary prejudices. But he is the slave of covetousness, of pride, of appetite. The violation of the Sabbath draws with it the neglect of all other religious duties—prayer, family religion, reading of the Scriptures. Misery follows in the train. In vain he blusters, and protests and affects independence : the moral judgments of the Almighty overtake him—the selfish, earthly creature, vegetating rather than living, is lost in shifting speculations ; diffuses mischief all around ; neglects and corrupts his children and servants ; has no corrective to his jealous and irritated temper, no cordial to his drooping spirits, no prospects to enliven the future, no friend, no Saviour to relieve him as to the past. The Sunday journal, the Sunday festival, the Sunday amusements, fail to please. He sinks into lifeless despondency, or frets with infuriated malice—all his noble capacities perverted, because his God has been contemned, and the day of religion abused.

And mark his inhumanity and want of sympathy, with the feelings and miseries of his dependants, the poor, the weak, the depressed. He robs the human family of the best boon of heaven ; he compels them to work when God allowed them to repose ; he chains down in vice and ignorance three-fourths of mankind ; he raises a barrier against the entrance of light, purity, salvation ; he tends by his example to abolish Christianity, to deny his God, to erect the vain idol of an imaginary deity, and to sink at last into a practical Atheism.

III. But we proceed to show, that the due observation of the Lord's day includes ALL THE APPLICATION OF THE CHRISTIAN RELIGION, and in fact, its preservation in the world ; whilst the violation of it goes to the ex-

actly contrary effect. For what is the Christian religion, without its means of instruction and grace?
What is Christianity, without the Bible, without the
ministry of God's word, without meditation and prayer,
without the education of children, without the familiar
communication of truth to the poor and ignorant?
And when and how are these means to be put into effect, if the day appointed for that very purpose is desecrated, dishonoured, lost? And what is the application of Christianity by all these methods, but the
grand point, the main end of that divine revelation?
It was given to be made known, to be applied to the
conscience of every human being. It was given to be
an universal religion. It was given, not to be a theory
in the schools of philosophy, but to be a grand practical blessing to the hearts and lives of men. In this
view, it stands distinct from the Levitical dispensation,
and in contrast with all the idolatries of the heathen
superstitions. It is not a limited design of separating
a single family or nation; but it extends itself to the
whole world—the partition-wall broken down—the distinctions of tongue, and clime, and people, abolished—
the ceremonial observances swept away—and all mankind the common objects of religious care. Much less
is it the confused and groundless theory of a superstitious idolatry, ignorant of all the principles of truth,
wasting itself in interminable controversies, confined to
the schools of learning, as to its real tenets, and leaving the multitude in the gloom of a cruel and debasing
bondage. No; Christianity flows from the Father of
lights; it brings plain, interesting, all-important truth
to man. It reveals a scheme of infinite love for the
recovery of apostate, sinful creatures, in the death of
the eternal Son of God. It promises the divine and
effectual grace of the Holy Spirit. It constitutes a
system of means, in which man is to wait upon God,
and where God has promised to communicate himself
to man. These means, simple, unostentatious, easy to
be employed, are the great medium between the infinite God and his feeble creature. As the substratum

of these methods of instruction is laid the HOLY SAB-
BATH—this gives the time, the space, the monitory
call, the privilege, the motive for the employment of
them.

There stands Christianity—it speaks in the Bible,
the inspired book of God, "able to make man wise
unto salvation," which every one is bound to read, to
search, to meditate upon. But when? On the day of
the Bible, the day which the very first history in its
pages institutes and hallows. Blot out the Sabbath ;
you make the regular and deliberate study of the
Scriptures impossible to the vast body of mankind.

Christianity stands forth---she designates an order of
men to preach her blessed tidings---she institutes the
ministry of the word---she bids the faithful pastor,
evangelist, and ambassador of grace, go into all the
world, preach the fall and recovery of man, take out
truth from the written volume and apply it to the conscience, open it to the understanding, press it upon the
heart of man. There stands the minister of Christ,
" as the voice of one crying in the wilderness, Prepare
ye the way of the Lord." He vindicates truth, he
clears it from the subterfuges of human folly, he sets
forth its genuine importance. Then he convokes the
assemblies of men, he calls them to repentance and
faith, he forms them into churches; he meets them for
the purposes of edification, exhortation, comfort. But
when is all this to be done? Who is to form the agree-
ment for the time and place of meeting? What is to
oblige, invite, persuade men? Who is to suspend the
ordinary business of life, and make it possible for the
great body of mankind to assist at religious convoca-
tions? The HOLY CHRISTIAN SABBATH. Without the
Sabbath, all is confusion, distraction, defeat. You
have no regular public ministry, no time for calm attention to the preaching of the word, no place for the
grand instrument of awakening souls, and building up
the Christian temple.

But public and private supplication, confession,
giving of thanks, intercession, are essential to the ap-

plication of Christianity. What is religion without prayer? Where is the profession of the faith of Christ, without holy supplication, in assembled bodies, to seek the divine favour, to honour the divine majesty, to avow our dependance on the divine grace? How are the blessings of revelation to be obtained, without that humble suit and united petition, to which God has been pleased to attach them? The Sabbath abolished, neglected, dishonoured; prayer is blotted out from the earth; Christianity is paralysed; the humility of heart which distinguishes the faith of the Bible from all other creeds, is no more. For it is the day of rest which gives time for prayer, which calls to public and private and domestic devotion, which shuts out the world, and brings man before the presence of his God.

And when, again, are the blessed sacraments of Christ's religion to be administered, if the Christian Sabbath be obliterated, which is destined for the celebration of them, and without which they can never be decently and devoutly attended? These are the external symbols and pledges of the redeeming blood and sanctifying Spirit of our Lord. They are the peculiar channels and means of grace. They follow the Bible, the ministry of the word, prayer. They are the bond of communion between Christians and their divine Head. They constitute a grand branch of the profession of the Christian religion. But they stand upon the platform of the Sabbath, and expire with its fall.

And what will become of the education of children, and the familiar communication of truth to the vast body of the poor and ignorant, without a time and space for those duties, banked in from the wild waste of worldly cares? Look at your Sunday schools, your infant schools, your adult schools, your catechetical lectures, your books and tracts for the young and the poorer classes. Look at the open spot left by the Sabbath for the erection of this spiritual machinery, and its easy operation and blessed fruits. Abolish the Lord's day, and you abolish the education of the population, the inculcation of primary truth, the diffusion of religious knowledge, the amelioration and safe elevation in the scale of intellectual and moral being, of the very classes for whom the Saviour came, to whom he declared his gospel to be best adapted, and whose welfare, temporal and spiritual, he especially consulted.

Consider, then, the unspeakable obligation of the Sabbath. On the means enumerated no one will dispute that the application of Christianity depends—to those means God promises his blessing—in and by these means the Holy Spirit works. We do not speak too strongly when we assert that the efficacy of our divine religion—its holy influences—its transforming, renovating power, very much depends on this one single point, the sanctification of the Christian Sabbath. Every act of profanation of its holy duties, every argument levelled against its authority, every example of a careless, irreligious family, neglecting its claims, goes to undo or prevent the healing virtues of Christianity—it goes to turn religion from a practical, holy, blessed principle, into a form, a name, a pretence.

And this it becomes, as the abuse of the day of God prevails. The ground on which we press the immense importance of the Sabbath, is from the evils which the violation of it occasions. Sabbath-breaking not only annuls the sacred compact of Christian nations, not only opposes the temporal and spiritual welfare of man, as a feeble but accountable being; but prevents all the application of Christianity in its blessings to the human heart. The separate instances of infringing the law of the Sabbath, may appear of little moment. We see not the interior process of the evil—the outward garb of decent morals is not at once thrown off. But look at the sure result. What is the Sabbath-breaker about? Is he reading his Bible?—He never opens that book which condemns his sin. Does he attend the ministry of God's word?—He dislikes more and more its admonitions, its calls to repentance. As his violation of the Sabbath increases, his disposition to attend the public preaching of the gospel lessens, his resolutions of returning to it become weaker, his regard for Christianity itself gradually expires.   Does he join in public or domestic prayer?—Alas! he has left off the devout practice since the Sabbath has been broken.   When he began the occasional neglect, first of a part, and then of the whole of that sacred day, prayer was not altogether forgotten.   Some private devotions lingered amongst his habits—education and conscience had not wholly lost their force.   But the evil acquired strength.   The Sunday was first wearisome, then disgusting, then perverted to occasional, and lastly to continued, indulgences of a secular kind— and with this, prayer was renounced, forgotten.   And what has the Sabbath-breaker to do with the sacrament, or with the religious education of the young, and the poor and ignorant?   He may promote the pride of intellectual knowledge, he may diffuse a literature tinged with infidelity, he may nourish the daring spirit of inquiry which a false philosophy proclaims; but the solid, religious, useful education of the young and ignorant in their immortal destinies, in their accountableness to God, in their duties to their Creator, Redeemer, Sanctifier, he utterly neglects and opposes. In short, if the real want of religious character in the violator of God's holy day could be estimated, it would be found to be just in the proportion as that institution was forsaken.

Nor is it too much to say, startling as it may sound in some ears, that the existence of Christianity in the world depends upon the observation of the Sabbath. Let this visible pledge of allegiance be withdrawn, let this sacred time be filled up by the cares and follies of the world, let public prayer and sacraments, public preaching of God's word and instruction of the ignorant be neglected and virtually renounced—and where is Christianity, where its hold upon man, where its means of operation, where its healing influence, where its application to the heart?   Yes; God has bound every thing together. In appointing a Sabbath, he has not instituted a useless, secondary, non-essential rite. The SABBATH WAS MADE FOR MAN—for such a creature as he is—in such a system of means, and with such a revelation as Christianity proposes to him. The same God that knew what was in that Revelation, and what was also in man, ordained the holy Sabbath as the accompanying means of the whole scheme of redemption—as the field in which all its blessings might be sown—as the scaffolding, by the aid of which all the building might be erected. The institution is nothing indeed if left in theory, nothing if abused to wrong ends, nothing if relied on with pride, or frittered away by superstition ; but every thing if used for its proper purposes, every thing if practically employed, every thing if animated and blessed with the presence and power of God. But this is not all.

IV. So important is the Lord's day, that it connects and holds together ALL THE LINKS AND OBLIGATIONS OF HUMAN SOCIETY, which the violation of it tends to destroy. Government cannot subsist without religion. The institution which sustains Christianity, sustains those duties and habits, those virtues of the heart, that mildness and humanity, that regard to truth and the sanctity of an oath, that sense of conscience and prospect of the tribunal of Christ, which strengthens human authority, preserves the peace of communities and nations, and is the bond of human society. The Sabbath recalls all these great principles, impresses them anew when effaced, urges them when neglected, deepens them more and more, and preserves them in activity upon the heart. If the Sabbath be lost, man is selfish, proud, discontented, disloyal, turbulent. His conscience becomes hardened, his passions restless, his submission to human authority reluctant. If the Sabbath be duly observed, God governs the moral and intellectual being, the law of God sustains the just rule of man, the grace and mercy of God in Jesus Christ attract the weary sinner, the obligations of conscience are vigorous and effectual, peace reigns within the breast, and willing subjection to authority as the ordinance of God, follows. Civil society is contained and held together by the Sabbath: which gives firmness and consistency to all the intercourse of man with man, to all the engagements which cement honourable commerce and the affairs of a peaceful agriculture, to all the current opinions and feelings which form the standard of morals.

The law of the Sabbath also unites all the classes of men one with another, by teaching them their common origin, their common guilt, their common mercies, their common duties. It places them before an Almighty Judge, and shrivels into insignificance the petty distinctions of rank and wealth, in the view of the eternal and all-glorious Potentate. To meet in one common temple, before one common Saviour, to supplicate one and the same salvation, sheds a humanizing, softening influence, gives a common sympathy, excites the feelings of brotherhood and intercommunity.

The Sabbath tends to humble man, and thus dispose him to all the duties of social and public life. The obstacles it removes. The pride and self-sufficiency of man it abates. It lays the foundation of lowliness, suavity of temper, forgiveness of injuries. It promotes a courteous, obliging carriage. "The rich and the poor meet together, the Lord is the maker of them all." The Sabbath annihilates human vanity, teaches that God is no respecter of persons, exalts those of low degree. The Sabbath humanizes man by the very neatness and cleanliness and frugality which it diffuses. Its good order, decency, and comfort, elevate the moral character. Its mildness and calmness of devotion engender self-respect, in a proper sense of the word. Its doctrines and duties and sacraments and prayers subdue the ruder feelings, awaken the humane and tender associations, expel the ruffian-passions, relieve the servant, the child, the dependant, from the oppression of the austere master, and compose and mollify the intercourse of the world.

Take the opposite abuses, and tell me what vices

and outrages are not committed upon the Sabbath, when it is dishonoured and violated. Of those who are executed as victims to the infraction of the laws of their country, the greater part date their ruin from the flagrant breaches of this sacred day. Of the hideous and fearful sins of impurity and licentiousness, the Sabbath is the season. Of the degrading habits of drunkenness, the Sabbath is the period, the spot, the occasion. Schemes of rapine and dishonesty, are almost all planned in the abused hours of the Lord's day. The first steps are perhaps not discernible. An occasional neglect of the ordinances of religion brings no instant profligacy of principle. Society is secure. But the tendency soon appears. The moral sense is loosened. The fear of God, like a barrier, being removed, the torrent of passion and concupiscence pours out of itself. The danger is augmented from the concealed labyrinths of the process. Should a loose companion say to a sober, religious youth, on the morning of the Christian Sabbath, "Go with me to-day, ruin your health, destroy your reputation, lose your money, kill your aged parents with grief, be a companion of prostitutes, rob your master, break the laws of your country, scorn God, be executed as a criminal, and plunge in the lake which burneth with fire and brimstone"—certainly the undebauched youth would tremble and flee. But the tempter conceals all this; he only says, " Do not go to church to-day, spend the day with me;"—all the rest follows of course :—" the companion of fools shall be destroyed." The Sabbath-breaker is in truth prepared for every enormity, and every crime. He is a bold transgressor; he practically denies God's right to be worshipped, honoured, reverenced, obeyed. He says, God is not an object of admiration, fear, gratitude, love. He that thus contemns God, has no regard for man. Society is not safe with him. He may be restrained from crime by selfish motives : he is not restrained by conscience and religious ones.

Cast an eye on any one Lord's day in our great towns, and especially in our metropolis. Follow the Sabbath-breakers through the day. Class them. Tell me who they are. Count up their actions during the course of the sacred hours. Penetrate their secret chamber. See the influence of their doings on the subsequent week. Society totters under their crimes. Observe the families, the establishments for merchandize, the offices, the posts of public responsibility which they fill—and trace the crimes, the outrages, the neglects, the falsehoods, the subterfuges, the nefarious and dark designs which the profanation of the Lord's day has engendered or matured—Yes, you have VICE in all its forms and enormities, in the one sin of Sabbath-breaking.

But the consideration is too painful. I hasten to point out, in the last place,

V. That the observation of the Sabbath immediately HONOURS ALMIGHTY GOD, AND BRINGS HIS FAVOUR AND BLESSING upon a people; whilst the profanation of it provokes his highest displeasure.

For the Sabbath is God's day; it is the Lord's tribute; it is the acknowledgment which he requires for all his blessings, temporal and spiritual; it is the mark of regard and reverence which he demands from man. What, then, can so immediately touch his honour as the wilful profanation of this institution? It precisely demonstrates man's contempt and ingratitude, his pride and secularity, his secret enmity against the government, and dislike of the worship of his God.

The easier the observance of it is, the more grievous insult to the Majesty of heaven is its violation. The greater the benefit which it is calculated to confer upon man, both in body and soul, the more perverse and unreasonable is his disobedience.

The clearer, again, the light of that dispensation of the gospel under which he lives, the deeper becomes that moral criminality which the sin against so much light brings with it. The more free from false doctrines our creed, and the more favourable our position for a distinct view of our duty, the higher presumption is involved in our neglect of it.

It is not possible for the mind of man to measure the dimensions of that guilt, which the deliberate profanation of the Lord's day under the gospel dispensation, in a free protestant country, involves.

To admit the truth of a divine revelation, and then reject the first and most remarkable feature which distinguishes that religion from every other—the only institution which includes all the worship, all the adoration, all the prayer, all the spiritual duties of that religion—is an inconsistency in itself, as well as an affront put upon our Almighty benefactor, which no words can adequately express. And this, when our country acknowledges a Sabbath, when the laws protect us in some measure in the observation of it, when the habits and usages of commerce are suspended, when some ingenuity must be employed and some force done to our feelings, and some loss of reputation hazarded, in violating the command !

A command which, were there no religious obligation, man would be glad enough to fulfil—which, if he could choose it for himself, and employ it to his own ends, and separate it from the authority of the Almighty, he would rejoice to celebrate—which his bodily powers demand, which his fatigue persuades, which his satiety with the uniformity of worldly pursuits invites,[1]—but which, because God requires it, because religion fixes her eye upon it, because his highest spiritual duties concur with his temporal interest in enjoining it, he spurns and contemns ; thus demonstrating the bitter root of enmity against God, from which his rebellion springs.

[1] During the excesses of the French Revolution, at the close of the last century, Christianity and its Sabbath were abolished—but the mere necessities of man's nature compelled that infidel and atheistic government to institute a day of rest of their own, what they called A DECADE, occurring every tenth day. A confession this of the reasonableness of the divine command !

And yet men in Christian countries expect God to bless them ; they affect to be his worshippers, they call themselves by his name, they profess a general reliance upon his providence, they allow that the affairs of empires, nations, families, individuals, only prosper by his favour and mercy. But how can they reasonably look for this favour and this mercy, if they profane the day which is the seal and pledge of both ? Can a people thus insulting God in the institution which must immediately affect his honour, really believe that he will bless and prosper them ? No, my brethren ; let us first reverence his name, let us first " turn away our foot " from trampling upon his holy day, let us first put away from us " the accursed thing," which, like Achan, infects our camp ; and then, and not before, may we hope for the abiding goodness of God to repose upon us, and for the Lord to delight himself in us.

But what are the excuses which men assign for the desecration of the Sabbath—a sin against which such mighty reasons lie, and the guilt of which is of so aggravated a hue ? Let us, in conclusion, strengthen our argument by exposing the weakness of the opposing excuses : let us then resolve on no half measures, but to enter without delay on the full performance of our duty ; let us lastly notice, the additional bonds we are under to consecrate the Sabbath, from the immense honour which God has put upon it by the blessings of his grace and providence in every age.

I. For what are THE EXCUSES which men allege in extenuation of a neglect of the day of God ?

1. Do they say that " every day under the gospel is to be kept holy"? They say truly ; but each in its own manner. The working day is kept holy, as we have already shown, by performing diligently the duties of our callings, and interweaving religious feelings and exercises therein ; the Sabbath, by celebrating devoutly the express worship of God. The six days, if given up to religious acts, would be idleness, superstition, and

tempting of God ; the seventh, if not dedicated to them, is impiety, pride, and contempt of the Almighty. Nor does he who pretends the universal sanctity to which the Christian is called, as a palliation of Sunday violations, ever serve God at all. If he knew anything of that delightful employment, all his affections would centre on that privileged day which God has given him for communion with himself, and for public and private acts of solemn devotion.

2. But you charge the due observation of the Sabbath with pharisaical strictness ; you say " the demand is enthusiastic, precise, puritanical, intolerable." But you forget then all the benignity of the blessed Saviour, which swept away the inventions of man, and recalled the institution from the austerities of the scribes to its primitive simplicity ; and you feign a severity which does not exist, except you consider piety as a task, the love of your Saviour a yoke, the praises of redemption gloomy, the offices of prayer and supplication a weariness. And this is what you really mean—your thin disguises conceal not your dislike to religion and the name of Christ. We understand you. You are at home in the world of sin and folly, but religious repose is unwelcome. You are at ease in secular employs; spiritual are strange. You show then, that all is to begin in the business of your salvation—enter heartily upon that, and the Sabbath will be honoured as it ought.

3. I make a similar reply to the plea of the EXCES-SIVE HURRY OF AFFAIRS, of the "impossibility of finding time to give a whole day to religion : besides, you only violate the Sunday occasionally, and as you affirm, reluctantly !" The plain meaning of all which is, that worldly things are so important, and eternal so trivial, that six days are too few for the first, and one too long for the second. The more lawful business any Christian has, the more is the necessity of a thorough religious interval on the Sabbath increased. Every man must find time to die, and ought to find time for devoting to God that day which prepares for death.

Nor does worldly business ever proceed so prosperously, as when subordinated to religion.

4. And why should I pause to refute the miserable excuse, " that you see not that persons who go so much to church are BETTER THAN OTHERS"—which is false in fact. Those who attend the house of God with any sincerity, are better than others ; and those who do not, yet are acquiring habits of public reverence to the Almighty, and are kept out of a thousand temptations, which the breaking of the Sabbath would present. And if all attended the worship of God aright, all would become, not better than others would then be, but better than they now are—all would be true servants of God, and heirs of heaven.

5. You have still pleas in reserve---" the immediate sacrifice of your temporal interests, the rivalry of neighbours, the general example of persons of your trade or profession, THE NECESSITY OF THE CASE,—unwilling as you are to violate the Sabbath, and ready to agree to close your shops, your counting-houses, your offices, if others would do the same ; the inutility of one in a circle acting without the concurrence of all"—excuses which would overturn all morals and religion, and make every man a judge of his measure of obedience to God. If on the ground of an alleged necessity, or of waiting for the concert of others, we may violate an express command of God, where are we to stop ? what commandment will retain its force? Why not break the second as well as the fourth ? Why not plead against the sixth or eighth in the same strain ? The very foundation of Christian faith is to obey God rather than man. Six days' work with the divine blessing, is infinitely better than seven without. The excuse is cowardice, the fear of man, unbelief. Venture, and God will bless you. You shall be recompensed a hundred-fold in this life, and " in the world to come shall have life everlasting."

6. But I am interrupted by another class of objectors, persons of better education as they consider themselves,

and higher advantages of station in society, who allege " that public worship is for the poor and uninstructed—but that for themselves THEY HAVE LESS NEED OF IT—they have little to learn—it is enough that they venerate the Deity at home." Vain and miserable pretexts! Who have so much need of the Sabbath as those, who from pride of intellect and luxurious indulgences and vicious example, are ordinarily further from God and practical religion than any other class? They have little to learn! when they prove, by the very excuse, that they " know nothing yet as they ought to know." And is not the Lord's day designed to honour God, to acknowledge his benefits, to celebrate his praises, to implore his grace, to enjoy communion of spirit with him, to prepare for meeting him at the throne of judgment? And are not these obligations strong in proportion to the divine benefits in providence, to our dangers and temptations, and the influence which our example might have upon others? Yes, the rich and great are most of all bound to the sanctification of the day of God.

II. Let us, then, cease from such wretched pleas, which cannot deceive ourselves, much less others, and which strengthen the argument they in vain attempt to evade; and let us ENTER FULLY AND DETERMINATELY ON THE RELIGIOUS DUTY OF HONOURING GOD. Half measures never succeed in moral questions, and least of all on the Sabbath; where the casuist is a man's own passions, and temptation perverts the judge who has to decide. So long as half-measures are taken, Satan and the world push their victory—the will remains entangled—new pleas of interruption are framed—every Sunday the pressure of business or the solicitations of pleasure are strengthened—whilst the disposition to serve God is weakened. Make at once a bold stand, and the duty will become easy. The enemy will yield. Satan will be discomfited. Your worldly companions will cease to molest. You will begin to find a pleasure in religion. God

I

will hear your prayers.   Conscience will be at peace.
The only happy man in this world is he that "follows
God fully."

III. Let the IMMENSE HONOUR WHICH GOD ON
HIS PART HAS BEEN PLEASED TO PUT UPON the
Sabbath, and the blessings of his grace and providence
which he has vouchsafed on it, conclude the subject,
and impress every heart with an additional conviction
of the incalculable importance of a right observation
of the Lord's day.   We have alluded to this more than
once.   And well we may.   For what an honour has
God put upon this institution throughout the whole
dispensation of the gospel?   Who can trace out its
history!   Who can number the souls converted, the
graces of Christians quickened, the sorrows of the
afflicted consoled, the influence of the Holy Spirit
granted, the assurances of the Saviour's presence
vouchsafed, the sermons and prayers and sacraments
rendered effectual?   Figure to yourselves what has
been transacted on all the Sabbaths throughout all the
world, since the promulgation of the Christian faith.
You find that almost all the glory of Christianity has
shone upon the Sabbath.   You find that God has
wrought most of his works of grace upon the Sabbath.
You find that the blessed Saviour has been most glorified upon the Sabbath.   You find that the Holy Spirit
has exerted his agency most upon the Sabbath.   What
confessions of sins, what enlargements of heart, what
consolations of prayer, what gifts of pardon, what
tokens of acceptance, what anticipations of heaven!
The testimony of God to his own day, on any one recurrence of it, confirms all our arguments for its inestimable value.   Yes, blessed Sabbath, we go forth to
meet thee as thou revisitest man; [1] we hail thee as the
court day of our Sovereign and Lord ; we rejoice in
thy return as the open throne presented to us for ap-

[1] The ancient wise men used to gather their scholars together,
and to say, Come, let us go meet king Sabbath."—*Lightfoot,*
iii. 56.

proaching our Heavenly Father; we behold thee as testifying of our Redeemer's resurrection—we honour thee as the peculiar province of the Holy Spirit ; we behold thee uniting all that can interest and bless man—creation with all its natural benefits—redemption with all its remedial grace—heaven with all its consummating glories!

SERMON VII.

THE GUILT WHICH IS CONTRACTED BY CHRISTIAN
NATIONS, IN PROPORTION AS THE LORD'S DAY IS
OPENLY PROFANED.

NEHEMIAH XIII. 17 & 18.

*Then I contended with the nobles of Judah, and said
unto them, What evil is this that ye do, and profane the
Sabbath-day ?   Did not your fathers thus, and did not
our God bring all this evil upon us and upon this city?
Yet ye bring more wrath upon Israel by profaning the
Sabbath.*

THERE remains yet another branch of the subject.
We must appeal to the nation at large. We must
prefer against it the charge of public connivance at
the violation of the Sabbath.   We must call on every
one, by his faith as a Christian, by the reverence he
feels for his Creator and Redeemer, by his love to his
country, by his regard to the happiness of his neighbours and family, by his concern for his own eternal salvation, to do all in his power to awaken the public conscience, and arouse it to do its duty.   We must declare
the anger of the Lord for this great national sin, and
solemnly charge all classes of men to repent and turn
unto the Lord.
It is true the evil is gigantic, it spreads through all
orders of persons, it fixes itself firmly in the corruption
of the human heart.   It stands, as the uncircumcised

champion of old, and defies the armies of the living
God.   But we must rely, like David, on another power
than that of man.   We must take the word of truth.
We must go forth with our sling and our stone, as it
were, in the name of the Lord God of Israel, and
must humbly believe that the enormous evil, as
another Goliath, shall fall before us.

Do Thou, O Lord God Almighty, be pleased to aid
us and all thy servants, who at this time are pleading
thy righteous cause!   Do thou enable us so to imitate
thy holy servant Nehemiah of old, that we may set
forth thy truth in all simplicity and fervour, that we
may not fear the face of man, and that, accompanied
and aided by thine effectual grace, we may witness a
revival of the observation of thy holy day, and of the
religious blessings which attend it, in our own land
and throughout all the nations of Christendom !

First, then, we must substantiate the charge, that
our nation is guilty in conniving at the violation of the
Lord's day.

We must next show the divine judgments that may
be justly dreaded in consequence.

We must lastly point out the practical measures
which each one may take towards a national repentance
and return to God.

I. In SUBSTANTIATING THE CHARGE ITSELF against
the British nation, we are aware of the caution necessary.   Having now no inspired prophets or apostles to
apply authoritatively the language of Scripture, we
can only form the best judgment we are able, from its
evident scope, and the similar bearing of our privileges
on the one hand, and of our conduct on the other.   We
must avoid all presumption, haste, self-confidence, personality.   We must proceed on the general and un-
doubted grounds of revealed truth, as applicable to
nations and individuals ; and only claim attention as
we are evidently supported by that truth, and the plain
facts of the case.

What, then, constitutes, in a scriptural sense, national guilt? Is it not the prevalence of any open, flagrant violation of the law of God, committed by large classes of men? Is it not the continued invention of new modes of committing it, and additions to the numbers amongst whom it spreads? Is it not the countenance which the example of the nobles and princes of the land give to it? Is it not the connivance at those enormities by legislators, ministers of state, magistrates, clergy? Is it not the general coldness and indifference, and even scorn, with which measures of prevention or of remedy are received?

And does not the violation of the Christian Sabbath in this country comprehend every one of these particulars?

1. Does it not prevail AMONGST LARGE CLASSES OF MEN? If the divine authority of that day be what we have shown; if the right manner of observing it be as we have described it; if the immense importance of a due sanctification of it be commensurate with Christianity itself; then what is the national guilt accumulated every day amongst us? Go through the different orders of society in our country, and, after making every allowance of the kindliest charity, estimate the sins committed every Sabbath as it returns, by each class before the face of the Almighty.

Begin with the HUMBLER ORDERS—the artizans, the labourers, the agricultural workmen, the smaller tradespeople. How widely is Sabbath-breaking diffused! Accounts settled, shops opened, markets frequented, workmen paid, business transacted,—calmly, systematically, almost avowedly.

Consider the numbers engaged in furnishing entertainment to the violators of the Lord's day, as well as the violators-themselves. The hotels, the inns, the tea-gardens, the public-houses, the shops and stalls for fruit and confectionary, the domestics and waiters occupied, beyond any plea of necessity, or any permission of the law.

Look at the environs of London generally—the thousands poured out every Sunday into the fields and villages, for idleness, for pastimes, for intoxication, in open profanation of the Sabbath.[1]   Enter the unnumbered abodes for retailing spirituous liquors; see the formerly decent ale-houses converted into spirit shops, with doors ever open to attract the careless youth.

I admit that these evils are not universal amongst the poor—I admit that very many are still under the influence of religion, and I bless God for it—but how few are there, compared with our increasing population! How vast the number who never regularly attend the worship of God! How lamentable the state of our crowded cities!

Next examine the MIDDLE CLASSES of our nation. How do multitudes of the tradesmen, the merchants, the soldiers, the lawyers, the physicians and medical-practitioners, the private gentlemen, the retired merchants and traders, spend the Lord's day? After a reluctant attendance in the house of God, where are they, and what are they engaged in for the remainder of the Sabbath?—I mean, what are too many of them engaged in; I am speaking of large numbers in each class, not of every individual—there is still a goodly remnant that serve and fear God. But as to the great mass, is it not the day of indulgence, the day of banqueting, the day of pleasurable parties as they are termed? What are the servants of the household occupied about? Is it not in preparing entertainments? Is not their labor tenfold that which the necessity of the Sabbath demands, or its repose allows?

You ascend to the GENTRY AND NOBILITY of our land. These have, alas, too generally "broken the yoke and burst the bonds." The law of the Sabbath is void to them. The day is the same as other days except as increased festivity dishonours and abuses it —the same irreligion, the same pride, the same neglect

[1] Two thousand five hundred persons were counted by a public officer one Sunday evening last summer, in one tea-garden—the White Conduit House, Islington---each having paid 6d. at entering, besides what he might expend afterwards. Consider the tax this is upon the poor.

of God. In too many cases, large festivals are given, crowded parties assembled, an open infraction of decency committed. How many are there in public stations, where example is most widely diffused, who have regularly Sunday dinners during a certain portion of the year! I ask if the aggregation of these enormities do not outstrip mere personal criminality, and form a distinct branch of national guilt?

2. Then consider the continual INVENTION OF NEW MODES OF SABBATH VIOLATION and of additional temptations extended to new classes of persons. This marks national guilt. The evil is on the increase. The SUNDAY NEWSPAPER is of late invention: a few years since it was almost unknown—now it enlarges its fatal snares every year. Forty thousand copies are said to be circulated every Sabbath. Not content with leaving it in the hands of the open infidel and enemy of civil and religious order, it has been seized by some of the avowed and clamourous friends of church and state, and made a channel of private calumny and public ridicule of all eminent virtue and piety. SUNDAY STAGES are a second invention of a novel kind. They were some years back uniformly suspended on the Lord's day, that "our cattle and our servants might rest as well as we;" now they openly violate the decencies of public worship—they pass our churches during divine service—they detain the innkeeper from the house of God—they tempt our people to venture on Sunday journeys. VESSELS OF PLEASURE impelled by steam, have just been added to the inventions of the Sabbath-breaker, and thousands are conveyed on the Lord's-day, during the months of summer, to the various spots on our coast, where pleasure and dissipation may drown conscience and the remains of a pious education. Commercial speculations for MORE EXPEDITIOUS TRAVELLING, by means of the same process, are also calculated upon the supposition of regularly and systematically profaning and tempt-

[1] The labours of the Rev. Herbert Smith, near Winchester, deserve great praise in his endeavours to check this great evil.

ing others to profane the Sabbath.   Our HOUSES OF
COMMERCE, again, have been deserted of late years on
the Lord's day by their masters, and are left to the
discretion of clerks and shopmen, to violate the Sabbath without restraint or controul.

New classes of our people are thus pushed into the
fatal vortex of Sunday dissipation.   Each humbler
order imitates the vices of the rank immediately above
it.   The example infects the very remotest classes. All
are learning by degrees to encroach upon the sanctity
of the holy day of God. " Hand joins in hand." One
encourages another.   Religious repose and rest in
God as a distinct duty of Christians, is more and more
discredited; and the false notion that the Sabbath
was ordained for what is termed innocent amusement,
as well as for the worship of Almighty God, is more
and more avowed.

3. Then inquire we next into THE COUNTENANCE
which the nobles and princes of our land give to this
Sunday-violation.   Much of the character of national
sins arises from the conduct of the great, from the open
avowal or disavowal of God, which they are found upon
the whole to make. I ask, then,—with grief and shame I
ask,—does not the prevalent example of the great go to
encourage, to create, to render necessary in large circles
of dependants, the open breach of the day of God ? Do
not they often profess that public worship is chiefly needful to restrain the common people ? Do not they avow,
that religion is little more than a state-engine ? Does
not their too general conduct authorize and embolden
the neglect of the Lord's day, the omission of public
worship, the frivolous engagements of the after division of the Sabbath, the enormous evils of Sunday
dinners, Sunday visits, Sunday music-parties, Sunday
diversions ? Do we not read on every Monday, the ca-
talogue of the festivals, conversaziones, assemblies for
music—sacred music, as it is profanely termed—which
desecrated the preceding day ? And do not these evils
begin with those of the highest rank---with nobles, ministers of state, princes ? And does not the eye of God

I 5

behold all this, and mark the aggravations of its guilt? Do not the gentry and nobility form a prominent and influential part of a nation in its collective capacity? Is not their example the standard by which thousands form their notions of morals and of Sunday obligation?

4. But may we not, ought we not, to go farther than this? It is not merely countenance afforded by the great, but it is A SINFUL CONNIVANCE on the part of legislators, ministers of state, magistrates, clergy, persons in authority, and with natural influence entrusted to them, which constitutes the real amount of national crime on this subject. If the gentry, clergy, and magistracy, have used such moral power as God and the laws and usages of their country have committed to them, for the honour of the Sabbath—and which power they are employing daily on a thousand trifling topics which interest them—then there is no national guilt incurred in this respect. But what is the fact? Let conscience speak. It is to the eternal God we appeal, who is the searcher of every heart. Have not legislators, and magistrates, both in their private and their collective capacity, connived, and do they not connive, at the violation of the holy law of the Sabbath? Do they not mock too often at its divine authority? Do they not shrink from avowing their reverence for religion as a spiritual subjection of man to the obedience of his Maker? Alas! it is too well known, that little of their attention can be obtained on these subjects—that occasions are perpetually lost for diminishing the evils of Sabbath-breaking—that the miserable limits of the three or four hours of public services are considered sufficient, in the framing of acts of parliament, for the Sabbath; and all the other hours are resigned without scruple to the world and folly—that the too frequent excuse of magistrates and individual members of either House, is that the temper of the times will not endure religious measures to be brought forward. Thus the influence of persons in authority is on the whole decidedly unfavourable; they dis-

countenance spiritual religion ; they refuse to put into
execution the laws actually in force, and they decline
preparing new ones—they frown on active individuals
who would call on them to maintain the honor of the
day of God.   How was the proposal of Sunday drill-
ing, for instance, during the late war, welcomed and admitted for a course of years ; though the voice of
bold remonstrance afterwards prevailed for its repeal ?
How were the petitions and remonstrances early made
against Sunday newspapers, rejected; and the later
ones scorned and contemned?   What attention has
been paid to the denial of the Sunday to the colonial
slave, and to the atrocious evils of his Sunday market?
How, again, do individual ministers of state, and individual magistrates, receive the applications made for the
suppression of Sabbath-breaking ! What encourage-
ment does the conscientious clergyman, or minister, or
parochial officer, receive from the magistrates, in his
attempts to check the evil ? Where is there the individual in either chamber of parliament, now ready to
take up the question concerning the law of the Sabbath, reduce the existing statutes to a consistent code,
and strengthen them with such new enactments as the
change of circumstances, since the time of the second
Charles, may require ? [1]

[1] Eclec. Rev. 1830.—And here the author cannot but mention
his own melancholy disappointment, when he attempted, a year
or two since, to lessen the profanation which the Monday morning
(or rather Sunday afternoon) cattle market at Smithfield, produces
in his own parish.   A bill was before Parliament which went to
alter the market-days from Monday and Friday, to Monday and
Thursday.   He used every exertion slightly to change the plan,
that the Monday market might be transferred to Tuesday, leaving
the days Tuesday and Friday.   His parishioners and the parochial authorities seconded him. The bishop of the diocese warmly
espoused the cause.   It was all in vain.   A total apathy as to the
profanation of the Lord's day manifested itself---the wishes of the
butchers were sufficient for the City authorities---the government declined taking any step---individual members of Parliament were tardy---the attempt was defeated---and at this moment a thousand men are engaged, take the whole neighbourhood
of London together, on the Sunday, all the year round, in pre-

5. And next allow me, as a minister of religion, to
join in the confession of the share which I, together
with my brethren, have borne in the guilt which we are
now considering. Too many of us, THE CLERGY, have
not sufficiently enforced the duty of the observation of
the Sabbath : we have not expounded the doctrine—we
have not urged the authority—we have not protested
as we should against the violation—we have not sustained by a firm example, the honour of this holy and
most ancient of institutions—we have been cowardly,
tame, silent, indifferent. Some of us have connived sinfully at the enormous mischief—have shrunk
from measures of energy and courage—have rather
" followed the multitude to do evil," than struggled
manfully, and at all hazards, against the current.

The religious public also—who reverence and observe to a certain extent the Sabbath—have shared
and are sharing the guilt. They listen to objections.
They read the works which plausibly sap the divine
obligations of the Lord's day. Their minds are poison-
ed. They lose that firm standing on which they formerly planted their feet. Their family habits are unfavourable. Their own example is in some things du-
bious. The estimate which their children and households form of the Sabbath, low. They do not contend
boldly, in public and private, against the sin of dishonouring the day, as their fathers did. Compare the
last generation of evangelical and pious Christian
households with the present—the decay is manifest—
that is, the national guilt is augmented.

6. For in truth it amounts to this—let God be
judge—THERE IS A TOO GENERAL INDIFFERENCE,
COLDNESS, AND EVEN SCORN, amongst large numbers, to the sanctification of the Lord's day, and to remedial measures for retaining its honourable obser-

paring for the Monday cattle-market. His own parishioners can
seldom go to church, without being terrified and molested by
droves of oxen encroaching on the foot-path on their way, whilst
the brutal drovers show the indifference that might be expected.

vance—which stamps the broad mark of public connivance on the sin of Sabbath-breaking. Thank God,
we are not so deeply sunk in this evil, as many of the
continental nations—thank God, much honour is still
put upon the holy appointment—thank God, a remnant of devoted Christians continues to hallow it
aright---thank God, " a pillar is raised, as it were,
on the border of the land unto the Lord." Thank
God, our iniquities, as we trust, are not yet full ; and
a revival of deep concern for religion, and for the day
of religion, is, as we hope, going on. But we must still
look the facts full in the face. Our real repentance and
reformation will depend on our conviction of our actual
delinquency. Have we, then, or have we not, as a people, including the classes professing the peculiar grace
of Christ, departed from the Lord, in conniving and
sitting calmly by, when his name was polluted and the
Sabbath profaned ? Is not a portion of the indifference
and scorn poured upon this institution chargeable upon
us---us the ministers of religion—us the people of God ?
Would the names of reproach cast upon the religious
observation of the day and upon those who sustain it,
be so keen, so opprobrious, so extended, if the standard of general sentiment had been nearer that of the
Scriptures ?

Yes, brethren, as the various classes in the Jewish
nation at the time of Nehemiah, had departed from
their God, and had joined in polluting the Sabbath ; so
have too many in all classes, in our own country, departed from their Saviour, and united, unconsciously in
some cases and imperceptibly, in conniving at the violation of the Christian Sabbath.

It is time for us to return to the Lord. Steps have
been lately taken by persons high in authority, which
encourage hope of improvement. Let us, then, in
order to this,

II. Consider THE NATIONAL JUDGMENTS which
we may too certainly dread, if we repent not.

For nations rise and fall. A retributive justice is

going through the world. No nation, however powerful, however wise, however free, however prosperous, can resist the divine arm. Where is the empire of the Babylonians, of the Medo-Persians, of the Grecians, of the Romans? Where is the power and grandeur of Alexander, Cæsar, Charlemagne? Look over the map of Europe during the last half century: what nations have not been overthrown, shaken to their centre, visited with the most frightful calamities? Except our favoured country, there was hardly another which escaped the actual sword of war. And in our own previous annals, what scenes of bloodshed, what overthrows of royal houses, what civil contests, what changes, do not appear!

I open the Bible and I see that this fall of empires is connected with the guilt of the different nations, and especially of those which were the most eminently privileged. " You only have I known of all the nations of the earth, therefore will I punish you for your iniquity;"[1] such is the divine rule of proceeding. " For judgment must begin at the house of God, and if it first begins with us, what shall the end be of them that obey not the gospel of God?"[2] There is the spot where judgments first alight. " But in the fourth generation they shall come again, for the iniquity of the Amorite is not yet full;"[3] the measure is rising---the augmented mass is noted by the divine eye---iniquity, according to the prophetic vision, is seated within the ephah; the vessel fills; it is accomplished; the talent of lead is sealed upon its mouth, and it is transported from its place to the scene of visitation.[4]

Do I want specific examples? I look to Sodom and Gomorrha and the cities of the plain, " suffering the vengeance of eternal fire."[5] I behold the old world " filled with violence and having corrupted its ways, till the flood came and destroyed them all."[6] I look on the nations of Canaan, " that are sinners before the Lord exceedingly, and the land cannot contain them."[7]

[1] Amos iii. 2.   [2] 1 Pet. iv. 17.   [3] Gen. xv. 16.
    [4] Zechariah v. 6---11.   [5] Jude 7.
        [6] Gen. vi. 12.   [7] Numb. xxxv. 33.

But mark, above all, the history of the favoured people—the inheritance, the peculiar treasure of the Lord, the kingdom of priests. And what is that history? The Assyrian king is sent against them when hypocritical and degenerate---" he meaneth not so, neither doth his heart think so"—but he is " the axe" in the hand of the divine workman, to execute his holy will against the guilty people.   And what was the captivity and dispersion of the ten tribes, and what the seventy years' bondage of the two in Babylon, but punishments for national guilt?

And why should England presume? Why should her capital, her commerce, her armies, her fleets, her power and influence, elate her with pride? What are all these but talents entrusted to her for certain ends? What is the weight of responsibility which presses upon her in consequence? What is the aggravation which all these blessings add to her sins against God? For wherefore has God given her these distinctions, but that she may diffuse the divine glory, exhibit the conduct of a righteous nation, uphold the honour of pure Christianity, vindicate the majesty of the Lord's day, educate her population in sound religion, and propagate the gospel at home and abroad? If she neglect all these high ends and be filled with vanity and contempt of God, what judgment may she not expect? What is she more than Nineveh, Tyre, Babylon? Her naval power is perhaps not greater, in proportion to the existing state of the world, her commerce is not more extended, her riches are not more abundant, her prosperity is not more elevated, than the ships, and commerce, and glory, and prosperity of Tyre were in her day?

Consider, then, the judgment which England may reasonably dread, in proportion to the duty which she violates—in proportion to her knowledge of the Bible—in proportion to her pure Protestant form of Christianity—in proportion to the strength of the arguments on which the divine authority and perpetual obligation of the Lord's day repose—in proportion to her

means of estimating these arguments, and detecting the
contrary error. Reflect how every such consideration
should aggravate the fear which penetrates us, of the
awful displeasure of God for our pollution of the Sabbath.[1]

Then what, England, is thy guilt before thy God?
A sin like this, against a command so authoritative, so
easy of performance, so beneficial, marks thy temper as
a nation as it respects God. The sins committed against
thy fellow-creatures are of another character. The
duties of property and life, the duties concerning common truth and honesty, are bound upon thee by thy
immediate secular interests—society cannot hold together for a moment without them. But the duties of the
Sabbath are a test of the real measure of thy faith and
reverence towards Almighty God. They show how far
thou carriest thy religion into practice. They prove
whether or not thy admissions of the authority of God
are sincere. Estimate, then, the guilt which all thy
Sabbaths, England, have been heaping upon thine
head.[2] Estimate the contempt, the neglect of God,
the declension of heart from his fear, the hardy
and obstinate resistance to his will, the slight put upon
his immediate majesty and honour, which thy conduct
involves. The closing denunciations against the apoca-
lyptic churches, will be applicable to thee, if thou con-
tinuest to imitate those declining bodies. Fear the
removal of thy candlestick, the silencing of thy preachers, the dispersion of thy assemblies, the obscuring of
thy peace, the loosening of the frame of society—counsels bewildered—commerce paralysed—union broken

[1] Let no one say he doubts the force of some of these grounds
of authority. Be it so. Take away any one of these grounds,
and the remainder binds the conscience of the inquirer. Nay,
it is observable, that no one Divine has yet written or spoken,
(except those who are really not, properly speaking, Christians)
that does not acknowledge the obligation of sanctifying the Lord's
day. A few writers may place its authority on the New Testament examples only---1 agree not with these writers---but their
admission is all I now want---for they all consent in admitting
the duty of a day of religious rest.

[2] Every twenty years, more than a thousand Sundays pass.

—disorder and contention sown—tumult and insur-
rection bursting forth—thy king, thy princes, thy
nobles given up to infatuation—thy enemies made
to triumph—thy name and place a proverb amongst
the nations. Consider, these are but the beginning of
sorrows. Where is Sardis, and Pergamos, and Thya-
tira, and Ephesus, and Laodicea? Swept with the
besom of destruction—effaced from the memory of the
church—exhibited as monuments of divine indignation. And why? "They left their first and fervent
love; they did not their first works; they had a name
to live, but were dead; they were neither cold nor
hot; they defiled their garments." And what art
thou doing in thy levity, thy profanation of the Lord's
day, thy contempt of religion, but imitating those very
sins, which brought down these exterminating judgments?

And how soon these chastisements may fall, God
only knows. We dive not into his secret counsels; we
venture not to penetrate his purposes. But thou hast
every reason to fear. Around the profanation and contempt of the Sabbath, are gathered all the accompanying sins of neglect of the gospel, self-righteousness,
cruelty and inhumanity to the colonial slave, an infidel and sceptical temper—the Bible contemned,
Christianity dishonoured. The violation of God's
day is the symptom, not the disease. It is an indication of the inward pride, impurity, vanity, self-
confidence, provocations of the Almighty, which are
filling up the measure of thine iniquities. Thou art
again warned. The voice of mercy and of expostulation is lifted up. Listen, then, ere it be too late. Attend, ye princes, and nobles, and bishops, and clergy,
and magistrates, and gentry. Listen, governors and legislators of the land. Receive the divine call. Repentance is not now too late. Punishments may be averted
or mitigated. "The Lord's voice crieth in the city, and
the man of wisdom will hear thy voice; know ye the
rod, and who hath appointed it."[1]

[1] Micah vi. 9.

And this brings us to point out,

III. THE PRACTICAL MEASURES, WHICH EACH ONE MAY ADOPT, TO PROMOTE A NATIONAL REPENTANCE AND RETURN TO GOD.

For this is the question after all. What is to be done? Whither are we to direct our steps? How can we fully return unto the Lord?—By inquiring, how other nations expressed their penitence; how the reformations took place in the time of Samuel, and Hezekiah, and Jehoshaphat; how the revivals were effected under Augustine in the fourth century, Claudius of Turin in the ninth, Peter Waldo in the twelfth, and Wickliffe in the century which followed: how the glorious Reformation from Popery in the sixteenth century was begun and established?—Each individual Christian reformed himself: fervent prayer was offered for the Holy Spirit; bold, decisive appeals were made to the consciences of the people; princes and magistrates were led to listen to the counsel of devoted and enlightened ministers; shame and persecution were cheerfully endured for the cause of Christ; an unflinching protest was entered against the sins which remained; humiliation of soul under past transgressions, and hope in the divine mercy for future deliverance and ·ultimate triumph, were exercised. Let such, then, be our course now.

1. Let EACH ONE REFORM HIMSELF, HIS FAMILY, HIS OWN CIRCLE. This is the first step. Here we are sure our efforts will be successful: we begin at home. The ministers of the sanctuary should lead the way. The holy Sabbath has much to complain of in us. Reverence it more, ye preachers and stewards of Christ, sanctify it more. Study its authority more. Watch against unfavourable habits more. Let your own conduct, and that of your families, give a more decided testimony to the Lord, and to his blessed day. Heads of families, begin each one for yourselves: the Almighty Redeemer demands it of you. Look on your present course ; correct, amend, what is amiss. Be not ashamed of confessing past error. Magistrates,

propose a better example; execute the laws of which you are the guardians. Awake to your first duties, the worshipping and glorifying of your God. Merchants, " buy the truth, and sell it not;" close your offices and counting-houses on the Sabbath; refuse the unholy gain which Satan offers. Tradesmen, farmers, artizans, consecrate your labours to " the Lord of the whole earth." Servants, clerks, dependants, honour the Saviour on the days which he allows you as the period of rest, peace, composure. Too long have you obeyed the world, the flesh, and Satan; now God calls you to repentance and consideration. Each individual reformation will go to form the national return to duty which we are pressing upon you. This is the first measure. Let every one into whose hands these pages may fall, examine and reform himself.

2. And let FERVENT PRAYER for the grace of the Holy Spirit be offered up. God alone can effectually do the work. All doctrine is vain, without the operations of his Spirit. The fundamental truths of the gospel, the glorious perfections and excellencies of God, the value of the soul, the inestimable worth of redemption, the necessity of a spiritual and heartfelt religion, of separation from the world, and communion with the Father of spirits, are unknown, till the Spirit touch and quicken the heart. If we rely on our arguments and proofs merely, we shall never succeed. What are demonstrations of the authority and obligation of the Christian Sabbath, to him who is dead in sin, careless upon the subject of his salvation, and wedded to his worldly companions? The heart of man has reasons against all persuasions of theology; the reasons of evil inclination, previous choice, corrupt habit, perverted associations of thought. Prayer, then, for the mercy of God, is essential to success. Then Babel is deserted; then the walls of Jericho fall flat; then Dagon is overthrown before the ark; then Babylon opens her gates of brass: then the human heart yields to truth. And when the new and divine life begins in the soul, the Sabbath becomes the natural, the important privilege

of the new-born Christian. He rejoices in the interval from the duties of this lower world: his food, his joy, his restoration are in the ordinances of God. Let the gracious Spirit be granted to fervent, united prayer, and things will soon revive—the desert will burst out with new bloom—the wills of men will be swayed—the Sabbath will re-appear in its mild dignity—the young will reverence, the old rejoice in the day of God. The ministers of Christ will see unwonted audiences thronging around them—fresh and deeper-toned devotion will preside. National penitence for misused Sabbaths will appear in the very cry for mercy which will ascend to heaven—and from the sanctification of them in future, every temporal and spiritual blessing will germinate.

3. As this proceeds, and in order to advance it, BOLD AND DECISIVE APPEALS must be addressed to the consciences of the people. The adversary must not be allowed to sow tares unmolested. Plain and popular statements, adapted to the comprehension of the different classes of men, must be made—addresses from the pulpit, from the press—addresses in the form of argument, and in the way of appeal and persuasion—short treatises must be widely diffused—the heart must be touched. Thus the circle of truth must be widened. The efforts of a false and spurious religion must be defeated, and God honoured amongst the people. A national feeling in favour of the Lord's day, can only be expected from a revival, distinct and uncompromising, of the national conscience. Each one must use the talents entrusted to him by the great Householder. The artful sophistry which assails the divine authority of the Sabbath, must be detected; the false reasonings exposed. Truth must be manifested and sustained—not indeed with affected eloquence, not with artificial ornaments of speech, not with an overstrained or scrupulous pertinacity of debate; but in simplicity, in openness of heart; neither relaxing the spiritual demands of the Sabbath, nor overrating the relative magnitude of this particular branch of the public guilt.

Thus will God bless our nation ; thus will the holy day be re-established in its authority and grace.

4. PRINCES AND MAGISTRATES will not be long before they listen to the voice of faithful and enlightened ministers. Legislators, and statesmen, and nobles, will hear the voice of truth. In the progress of a general revival, this has been God's method. He has raised up persons of authority, and guided their minds by the wisdom and counsels of well-informed and devoted ministers of Christ, in the affairs relating to the worship of God, and the souls of men. Instead of false teachers, corrupt ecclesiastics, proud and worldly-minded priests—-men who have domineered, or fawned, as their interests and power permitted ; and, surrounding princes and magistrates, have flattered them to their ruin ; God blesses his servants with pious and simple hearted bishops and ministers, who understand the Scriptures, who know the value of the Sabbath, who distinguish the true welfare of government, who discern and admit the claims of God upon princes and rulers. With such aids, the secular magistrates will decree righteous statutes, the parliament will be swayed by sound religion, the measures needful for protecting the worship of God will be taken, the oppression and insults of the profane will be redressed, the open and national violation of God's Sabbaths will be prohibited, the decent and devout order of a Christian land will be preserved. These aids from without, conspiring with the influence of grace within the church, will produce the desired result. The nation will return to the Lord. The Sabbath will be again " the sign of God's covenant, that he is the Lord that doth sanctify us ;" and all other Christian virtues and habits will follow.

5. But this cannot be expected to be brought about, in a world like ours, without much of THAT PREVIOUS REPROACH AND CONTUMELY, which have always attended the progress of a really spiritual reformation. Nothing disturbs and offends the world so much as the Lord's day strongly urged. The leaders must be con-

tent to receive the treatment which their Lord and
Saviour received before them. And this deters the
merely well-disposed part of mankind : they shrink
from decisive steps, for fear of shame and names of
contempt. The term Lollard, at one period, of Wick-
liffite, Lutheran, Puritan, Methodist, Calvinist, at
others, have been a successful instrument in Satan's
hands, of alarming the timid, and securing his hold of
the worldly. Against such opposition, (even if it were to
rise to persecution,) the Christian minister and hero
must be ready to stand. He must disregard the honour
of men, that he may obtain the favour of God: he
must be proof against these assaults : he must be
willing to risk his name, his character, his reputation, for his Saviour. The holy Sabbath must be
dedicated, consecrated, reverenced, under whatever
reproaches he may have to labour, who asserts its
claims. As national reformation advances, these very
men, once cast out and scorned, will become the objects of veneration, their counsels be prized, and their
persons loved and esteemed.

6. Still much will remain unredressed, amidst the
wrongs of the Sabbath—at least, for a considerable
period—many great evils may be expected to survive
and struggle—the spiritual church, if it gain, by the
mercy of God, much, must reckon upon being discomfited in certain respects. She must, then, PROTEST
BOLDLY AND FEARLESSLY AGAINST THE SINS WHICH
ARE PERSISTED IN. Nothing honours God more than
the confession of his truth, which his faithful servants
make, when they are unable to succeed fully in their
honest endeavours. A body of devoted followers of
Christ, allowed to preach his truth in the world, and
entering their open protest against flagrant evils, is a
token for good in a country, of the most hopeful character.
God never gives up a nation to his desolating judgments, when there is a considerable number of worshippers, thus averring their allegiance, and crying out
aloud against the dishonour done unto his name and
Sabbaths.

7. Lastly, HUMILIATION FOR PAST TRANSGRESSIONS, AND HOPE IN THE DIVINE MERCY FOR FUTURE DELIVERANCE AND ULTIMATE TRIUMPH, are the dispositions of heart which we should most cultivate. After we have done all, we shall leave much, very much to be humbled and abased for before our God; and our hope must be reposed, not in man, but in his power, mercy, and grace. The holy Sabbath, which, as a nation and as individuals, we have abused in times past, the dishonour we have done to him and to God thereby, the loss to our own souls which has followed, the injury to the spiritual welfare of others which has been occasioned, the slight put upon the blessed Spirit of grace, are topics of deep sorrow and penitential confession before God. To humble ourselves under his awful majesty, to deprecate his wrath, to accept the punishment of our iniquity; this is the way to obtain mercy; this will bring back our people as the heart of one man, to the Lord: this will prepare us for all the holy duties of our Sundays, and all the communion with God which they bring with them.

Thus our hope will be placed in the unmerited grace of God, for deliverance and triumph; we shall wait his holy will; we shall expect and look for his powerful succour, we shall despair of nothing under his mighty protection; we shall rejoice in the sanctification of his day, the conversion of souls, the consolation and edification of his faithful servants, the pledge and anticipation of heaven.

Having now completed our original design in these sermons; having established the divine obligation of a weekly Sabbath in the first four, and the practical duties arising from it in the last three of the series;

Let us in conclusion of the whole, remark,

I. That it is not for the Sabbath in itself that we have been pleading in the course of this work, but THE SABBATH AS A MEANS TO CERTAIN ENDS, as the channel and conveyance of the waters of life, as the standing institution for the declaration of God's glory, of the Saviour's resurrection, the rest of heaven; as the moment of calm granted for rational and irrational creatures to breathe from toil, and recruit their exhausted powers; as the needful interval of repose and cessation to a feeble creature like man; as the appointed period for the instruction and salvation of souls; as the most visible representation of our faith in our Maker and Benefactor, and the grand peculiarity of revealed religion.

Let then this thought ever be present with us. It is for no inferior matter we have pleaded; it is for no external and formal point; no ceremony; no superstition—we teach not that " man was made for the Sabbath"—we should never be contented with any observation of it which was merely decorous, constrained, reluctant. We plead for the simplest and noblest institution of the religion of the Bible, which includes and embraces within its range every other. We plead for the most important means of grace and instruction, which is the platform upon which every other is erected. We plead for the highest testimony man can bear to the glory of God; in which the praise of creation, of redemption, of eternal happiness is united. We plead for the most merciful of all the divine appointments, which suspends the struggle of nature, and bids all creation repose, and refresh itself from its labour and toil.

Let us not, then, undervalue, or misunderstand the subject we have been treating. We have not been drivelling about a questionable, an indifferent, a secondary duty. We have pleaded the cause of God, the interests of man, the peace of the world, the instruction of the poor, the knowledge of Christ, the doctrine of salvation, the hope of heaven. We have treated the greatest question in all the compass of practical theology, because it provides for every other duty, lies at the foundation of every other duty, gives space and time for every other duty, derives the divine blessing upon every other duty.

II. We have been pleading, in the next place, for these

and ends of the Christian Sabbath, because of THE
UNSPEAKABLE VALUE OF THE SOUL OF MAN.   For
what is the gist of all we have argued?—that the soul
of man is so noble, so precious, so inestimable in the
eyes of God, so endless in its future state of happiness
or misery, that a seventh portion of all man's time is
taken out from ordinary employments to be dedicated
to this his immortal part.   Yes, the Sabbath proclaims
the responsibility of man, the unfathomable and inex-
pressible value of his soul, the price put upon it by the
Father of spirits, the dignity and capacities which it
possesses.   The Sabbath unites man with spiritual
objects, connects him with his invisible Creator, Redeemer, Friend; teaches him what he is, and whither
he is going.   It is for the soul, then, that we have been
pleading, that it may be blessed with the salutary
knowledge of its fall and its recovery, of its sin and its
remedy, of its guilt and condemnation in the first
Adam, and its pardon and acceptance in the second.

Let the importance of our subject be measured by this
standard.   Let all the souls of all the race of men
be brought before our view, and let all the unutterable
happiness of each of those souls be weighed and
balanced; and then let the value of that DAY be estimated, when the means of the repose, consolation, guidance, illumination, pardon, holiness, salvation, of all
these immortal minds are congregated and concentered
—when all the love of God our heavenly Father, all
the grace of God the Son, and all the operations of
God the Holy Ghost, are poured forth and brought into
effect.   It is this sublime thought which elevates the
topic we have been considering.   The violation of the
Sabbath sinks, degrades, materializes, destroys the
soul of man; the observation of it raises, honours, spi-
ritualizes, saves it.   If the Lord's day be annihilated,
religion fades away, secular pursuits bewilder man,
the bodily appetites prevail, the knowledge of salvation
is lost, the soul wanders wretched and ignorant, wayward and distressed, without a teacher, without a hope,
without a refuge.   The holy day sheds its gentle rays

K

upon the lost traveller, sends religion to his succour, interrupts the din of false alarms, recalls him from the clamour of passion to the soft voice of conscience, gives him the knowledge of salvation, satisfies all his doubts, soothes his distresses, becomes his comforter and guide to a heavenly and eternal rest.

III. But we have pleaded, further, for the Christian Sabbath—thus valuable from its combination of means bearing upon the welfare of the soul of man—because it APPEALS PLAINLY AND FULLY TO THE HUMAN CONSCIENCE, and puts in its claims upon every reasonable and accountable being, on the footing of its own divine institution and authority.

Truth cannot be trifled with. Men may turn away from any statement of it. They may cavil. They may object to this or that particular argument. They may set up the) sophisms of controversialists. But conscience cannot be thus silenced. The broad undeniable truth is, that a day of weekly rest has ever accompanied revealed religion under every dispensation of it. A Sabbath was celebrated even before the fall. A Sabbath forms a part of God's moral law. A Sabbath is insisted upon by the prophets. A Sabbath was observed by our Lord and his apostles. A Sabbath has been kept in every church, in every part of the world, in every age since. To cavil, then, at minute omissions in the history of it, or petty difficulties in the details of its progress, is worse than folly; it is dishonesty to truth. Nor can we escape the responsibility which attaches to knowledge proffered and set before us. There stands the institution. Great efforts have been made to impress its obligation upon the public mind. Discussions, sermons, treatises, tracts, have been circulated. Public meetings have been convened, and resolutions passed to enforce the better observance of the day. The public conscience has been aroused. God has given us a call, a special call to repent. If we refuse the call, " if we turn away from him that speaketh from heaven," if we " stop our ears," if " we harden our hearts," what can we expect but to be given up to a reprobate mind, and left to our own folly and presumption? With conscience, then, is the case left —to this inward vicegerent of the Almighty is our appeal. At its tribunal stands our cause to be adjudged. Let every one, then, yield to its sentence. Let every one bow to the voice and decree of this witness, judge, avenger. Let conscience stimulate us to hallow the Christian Sabbath, that coming within the sphere of the means of grace, we may actually learn the value of our souls, and the way of salvation for ourselves.

IV. But, lastly, we have pleaded for the Sabbath, because it is an indispensable preparation for THE HEAVENLY BLESSEDNESS. Its appeal to the human conscience terminates here. Heaven or hell is at stake. We all profess to look for a heavenly rest. There are few, perhaps none, who do not desire and expect to pass to a happy eternity when they die. Their ideas of its nature may be obscure, their preparations for it may be most defective. Still a vague hope of it, as opposed to eternal misery, and under the idea of a state of repose and felicity, occupies most minds. But let us consider the strict connexion which subsists between the employments and delights of the Sabbath upon earth, and those of that endless and beatific Sabbath which " remains for the people of God " at last. Do we recollect the descriptions given in the Bible, of the company, the praises, the spiritual and unceasing employs of that exalted place? Is it a carnal repose which it offers? Is it bodily indulgence? Is it mere cessation from toil and sorrow? Is it not the eternal presence, the eternal enjoyment, the eternal praises of our God, and the Redeemer? Open the heavenly gates. You see the worshippers. You hear their hymns. What do they chaunt? The praises of " the Lamb that was slain;" " the love of him who died for them;" the majesty, and wisdom, and power, and glory, of their Father and Lord. And what is the temper of mind, what the habits, the notions of happiness, what the moral condition which can derive felicity from such an employ? It is an employ of continual holiness, ceaseless adoration, perpetual activity in the service of God. The loose ideas formed of heaven, as an exemption from suffering merely, as standing only in opposition to fatigue and weariness, as being contrasted with misery and condemnation—are most delusive. It is holiness—it is the love of God—it is the worship of the Lamb that was slain—it is the resting not day nor night in the praises of the Almighty—it is felicity derived from the completion of the divine faculties and habits acquired in this world.

Observe, then, the connexion of the Sabbath-duties here on earth, with these ultimate and consummated duties of the eternal Sabbath above. The employments of the day here are holiness, the adoration of God in Christ, the praises of creating, redeeming love. The Sabbath is the day of God, of Christ, of the Holy Spirit: that is, it is the very same in essence with the heavenly Sabbath; has the same objects, the same joys, the same praises, the same gratitude, the same sources of happiness.

He that would prepare for heaven, must honour the Sabbath upon earth. He that would hope for the spiritual joys there, must acquire a taste and aptitude for them here.

All is connected in the divine plan. The Sabbath of the church militant is the pledge and foretaste of the Sabbath of the church triumphant. Were we in heaven without a new nature, a change of heart, a delight in the worship of God, an earnest longing after Christ, an acquiescence in holiness—we should neither derive happiness from it, nor be capable of its employments. They who argue against our feeble, preparatory Sabbaths; they who object, cavil, contemn; they who prefer every other employment to the worship of God; they who complain of weariness and satiety in the services of Christ—have an evidence in their own breasts of their unfitness for a heavenly world—they are condemned out of their own mouths. The louder they exclaim

against our Lord's day and its duties, the more decidedly do they exclude themselves from the Christian
character and the Christian hope.

Let us, then, awake to the truth of the case. The
day of Sabbath made and constituted for man, is essential to all his moral duties and hopes—it seals his
evidence for a heavenly world—it prepares him for its
joys and its employments—it forms its harbinger and
foretaste.

The Sabbath will, therefore, never cease till it be
fulfilled in the kingdom of God. As other figures
and emblems terminated not till the substance of
them came; so will not this grand type and foretaste
of the ultimate repose of eternity, be determined, till
earth gives place to heaven.

Let it again be remembered that we disclaim every
thing harsh, uncommanded, ceremonial—we disclaim
the Jewish, and much more the Pharasaical observances
—we say with our Saviour, " not man for the Sabbath;"
we follow also with delight the change of the day of
celebration, authorized by " the Lord of the Sabbath."
But all this only leaves the grand, fundamental principle
more strong and clear.—" The Sabbath was made for
man," to give him repose and religious peace, to give
him time for the worship and adoration of God on earth;
to be the solemn guarantee and type of his last rest; and
to prepare and introduce him to the joy and ceaseless
adorations of that glorious state. The Sabbath is
man's privilege, interest, duty. The Sabbath is the
glory of his religion, the highest exercise of his rational
nature, the bond and link which connects him with
all that is spiritual, all that is holy, all that is divine
on earth; and which then transmits him to that exalted
scene of eternal, and perfect, and uninterrupted spirituality, holiness, and blessedness in heaven, for which
he was created—and to which, may God be pleased
to bring the writer and every reader of these pages
through his infinite mercy in Jesus Christ our Lord!

APPENDIX.

THE DOCTRINE OF THE CHURCH OF ENGLAND CON-
CERNING THE DIVINE AUTHORITY AND PERPETUAL
OBLIGATION OF THE LORD'S DAY.

IN the course of the preceding sermons I have ab-
stained from alleging, except by an occasional allusion, the authority of our National Church, that I
might leave the duty on its highest and firmest and
only immoveable footing, the divine command as issued
in paradise, republished in the moral law, enforced by
the prophets, recognized and vindicated by the "Lord
of the Sabbath" and his apostles, and received and acknowledged in the primitive, and every succeeding
ages of the church.

But it will be important now, in an appendix, to ad-
duce its express testimony as an additional motive
with those of us who really reverence our Protestant reformed church, and more especially with
the clergy who have professed in the most solemn
manner that they were "moved by the Holy Ghost"
to take upon them the ministration of the gospel
therein—and who have signed her Articles, and
avowed their consent to the Liturgy and Book of

Homilies in which those articles are more fully explained.

And, first of all, concerning the perpetual obligation of the ten commandments, her Articles thus determine: "Although the law given from God by Moses, as touching ceremonies and rites, do not bind Christians now, nor the civil precepts thereof ought of necessity to be received in any commonwealth; yet, notwithstanding no Christian man whatever is free from the obedience of the commandments which are called moral."[1] This of course includes the fourth as well as any other of the ten.

Accordingly, in the catechism all the ten are directed to be taught our children as "God's holy will and commandments," by which they are to "serve him truly all the days of their life."

Every one of them also is read by the minister to the people continually in the church, as a part of God's perpetual law, and the congregations constantly ask God's mercy for their transgressions of the fourth commandment as well as of the other nine, and grace to keep the same for the time to come. And at the conclusion pray, without exception or difference, "Lord, have mercy upon us, and write ALL these thy laws in our hearts we beseech thee."

And these very commandments, the fourth as well as the rest, are written in broad characters, to be seen and read of the people, on the walls of the sacred building where they assemble, and usually over the very altar where the mysteries of Christianity are celebrated.

But in the following passages from "the Homily of the place and time of prayer," the doctrine of the preceding discourses, both in the first division concerning the perpetual obligation of the Lord's day, and in the second on its practical duties, is fully and most energetically established.

"Although we ought at all times, and in all places, to have in remembrance, and to be thankful to our gracious Lord—according as it is written (Psalm ciii.

[1] Art. vii.

22), 'I will magnify the Lord at all times:' and again, 'Wheresoever the Lord beareth rule, O my soul, praise the Lord'—yet it appeareth to be God's good will and pleasure, that we should at special times, and in special places, gather ourselves together, to the intent his name might be renowned, and his glory set forth in the congregation and assembly of his saints.

"As concerning the time, which Almighty God hath appointed his people to assemble together solemnly, it doth appear by the fourth commandment of God : 'Remember,' saith God, 'that thou keep holy the Sabbath-day.' Upon the which day, as is plain in the Acts of the Apostles (Acts xiii. 1), the people accustomably resorted together, and heard diligently the law and the prophets read among them. And albeit this commandment of God doth not bind Christian people so straitly to observe and keep the utter ceremonies of the Sabbath-day, as it was given unto the Jews, as touching the forbearing of work and labour in time of great necessity, and as touching the precise keeping of the seventh day, after the manner of the Jews;—for we keep now the first day, which is our Sunday, and make that our Sabbath, that is, our day of rest, in the honour of our Saviour Christ, who, as upon that day, rose from death, conquering the same most triumphantly;—yet, notwithstanding, whatsoever is found in the commandment appertaining to the law of nature, as a thing most godly, most just, and needful for the setting forth of God's glory, it ought to be retained and kept of all good Christian people. And therefore, by this commandment, we ought to have a time, as one day in the week, wherein we ought to rest, yea, from our lawful and needful works. For, like as it appeareth by this commandment, that no man in the six days ought to be slothful or idle, but diligently to labour in that state wherein God hath set him : even so, God hath given express charge to all men, that upon the Sabbath-day, which is now our Sunday, they should cease from all weekly and workday labour, to the intent, that, like as God himself

wrought six days, and rested the seventh, and blessed
and sanctified it, and consecrated it to quietness and
rest from labour; even so God's obedient people should
use the Sunday holily, and rest from their common
and daily business, and also give themselves wholly to
heavenly exercises of God's true religion and service.
So that God doth not only command the observation
of this holy day, but also by his own example doth
stir and provoke us to the diligent keeping of the same.
Good natural children will not only become obedient
to the commandment of their parents, but also have a
diligent eye to their doings, and gladly follow the same.
So if we will be the children of our heavenly Father,
we must be careful to keep the Christian Sabbath-day
—which is the Sunday—not only for that it is God's
express commandment, but also to declare ourselves to
be loving children, in following the example of our
gracious Lord and Father.

" Thus it may plainly appear, that God's will and
commandment was to have a solemn time and standing
day in the week, wherein the people should come together, and have in remembrance his wonderful benefits, and to render him thanks for them, as appertain-
eth to loving, kind, and obedient people.

" This example and commandment of God, the godly
Christian people began to follow, immediately after
the ascension of our Lord Christ, and began to choose
them a standing day of the week to come together in ;
yet not the seventh day—which the Jews kept—but
the Lord's day, the day of the Lord's resurrection, the
day after the seventh day, which is the first day of the
week. Of the which day mention is made by St.
Paul on this wise : ' In the first day of the Sabbath,
let every man lay up what he thinketh good ;' (1 Cor.
xvi.); meaning for the poor. By the first day of the
Sabbath is meant our Sunday ; which is the first day
after the Jews' seventh day. And in the Apocalypse
it is more plain, whereas St. John saith, ' I was in the
Spirit upon the Lord's day." (Rev. i. 10.) Sithence
which time God's people hath always, in all ages,

without any gainsaying, used to come together upon
the Sunday; to celebrate and honour the Lord's
blessed name, and carefully to keep that day in holy
rest and quietness, both man, woman, child, servant,
and stranger. For the transgression and breach of
which day, God hath declared himself much to be
grieved; as it may appear by him, who, for gathering
sticks on the Sabbath-day, was stoned to death."
(Numb. xv. 32.)

Here the fourth commandment is expressly acknowledged—the Jewish ceremonies and rites attached to it
and the precise seventh day in the week are, indeed, no
longer binding, but the Lord's day is declared to be our
Christian day of rest—the stress of the commandment
is said to lie in the proportion of time—it is considered essentially a law of nature or morals—the institution in paradise, and the command there given are
recognized—and the change from the seventh to the
first day is placed on the example and authority of
Christ and his apostles.

Nor is the judgment of the Church as to the holy
observation of the Christian Sabbath less remarkable—
thus it speaks. "But, alas! all these notwithstanding, it is lamentable to see the wicked boldness
of those that will be counted God's people, who pass
nothing at all of keeping and hallowing the Sunday.
And these people are of two sorts. The one sort, if
they have any business to do, though there be no extreme need, they must not spare for the Sunday; they
must ride and journey on the Sunday; they must drive
and carry on the Sunday; they must row and ferry on
the Sunday; they must buy and sell on the Sunday;
they must keep markets and fairs on the Sunday:
finally, they use all days alike; work-days and holy-
days all are one.
"The other sort is worse. For although they will
not travel nor labour on the Sunday as they do on the
week-day; yet they will not rest in holiness, as God

commandeth; but they rest in ungodliness and filthiness, prancing in their pride, pranking and pricking, pointing and painting themselves, to be gorgeous and gay: they rest in excess and superfluity, in gluttony and drunkenness, like rats and swine: they rest in brawling and railing, in quarrelling and fighting: they rest in wantonness, in toyish talking, in filthy fleshliness: so that it doth too evidently appear that God is more dishonoured, and the devil better served, on the Sunday, than upon all the days in the week besides. And I assure you, the beasts, which are commanded to rest on the Sunday, honour God better than this kind of people: for they offend not God, they break not their holy-day.

"Wherefore, O ye people of God, lay your hands upon your hearts; repent and amend this grievous and dangerous wickedness; stand in awe of the commandment of God; gladly follow the example of God himself; be not disobedient to the godly order of Christ's church, used and kept from the apostles' time until this day. Fear the displeasure and just plagues of Almighty God, if ye be negligent and forbear not labouring and travelling on the Sabbath-day, or Sunday, and do not resort together to celebrate and magnify God's blessed name, in quiet holiness and godly reverence."

I cannot forbear contrasting with this language of the church, the opinions which are now inconsistently, and in my mind irreverently and flippantly propagated. "Some persons, who do not really believe the Mosaic law relative to the Sabbath to be binding on Christians, yet think it right to encourage or tacitly connive at, that belief, from views of expediency, for fear of unsettling the minds of the common people." "The fourth commandment is evidently not a moral, but a *positive* precept, (it being a thing in itself indifferent, antecedent to any command, whether the seventh-day, or the sixth, or the eighth, be observed.)" "The dogma of the 'Assembly of Divines at Westminster,'—

(in their 'confession of faith,' chap. xxi. § 7)—that
the observance of the Sabbath is part of the moral law
—is to me utterly unintelligible." " In saying that
there is no mention of the Lord's day in the Mosaic
Law, I mean, that there is not only no mention of that
specific festival which Christians observe, on the *first*
day of the week, in memory of our Lord's resurrection
on the morning following the Jewish Sabbath, but
there is not (as has sometimes been incautiously stated)
any injunction to sanctify one day in seven." "It is
not merely that the apostles left us no command per-
petuating the observance of the Sabbath, and transferring the day from the seventh to the first; such a
change certainly would have been authorized by their
express injunction, and by nothing short of that; since
an express divine command can be abrogated or altered
only by the same power, and by the same distinct revelation by which it was delivered." " There is not even
any *tradition* of their having made such a change;
nay, more, it is even abundantly plain that they made
no such change." " And if we come down to later
ages of the church, we not only find no allusion to any
such tradition, but we find the contrary distinctly implied both in the writings of the early fathers, and in
those of the most eminent of the founders of our reformation ; *e. g.* in Cranmer's Catechism, published in
1548, viz. the first year of Edward VI. we find the following passage :—' And here note, good children, that
the Jewes in the Old Testament were commanded to
keep the Sabbath-day, and they observed it every
seventh-day, called the Sabbat or Satterday. But we
Christian men in the New Testament are not bound to
such commandments of Moses' law concerning differences of times, days, and meats, but have liberty
and freedom to use other days for our Sabbath-dayes,
therein to hear the word of God, and keep an holy
rest. And, therefore, that this Christian liberty may
be kept and maintained, we now keep no more the
Sabbath on Saturday as the Jews do ; but we observe
the Sundays and certain other days, as the magistrates

do judge convenient, whom in this thing we ought to obey.'"[1] " The greater part of what I have said will apply to the opinion of those also, who rest the observance of the Lord's day, not indeed on the Mosaic law, but on a *supposed* command to Adam, (for none is *recorded,*) implied in the declaration that the Lord hallowed the seventh day, because in that, he rested from the work of creation. But to these persons I would suggest, in addition to what has been urged, that it is not said in Genesis, that the Lord hallowed the seventh day at *that time,* but, *for that reason ;* and as Moses was writing for the Israelites, who were charged to keep the Sabbath, it was natural that, when recording the creation in six days, he should advert to the day which *they* observed in commemoration of it. This, I say, he would naturally have done, even had there never been any such observance till the delivery of the law from Sinai: just as any writer now, who should notice, in a summary of gospel-history, the ' Annunciation' to the Virgin Mary, might naturally remark that this is the event which Christians annually celebrate under the title of ' our Lady's Day ;' without at all meaning to imply that the festival was instituted at this or that period."

Let me entreat the younger clergy, so far as I may hope this little volume will reach their hands, to be on their guard against the tone and bearing of such language. The lengths to which an hypothesis may carry a man, is seen in the above quotations. But the warning is rendered more portentous by the fact,

---

[1] .To this most unfair quotation, it may be proper to oppose the Bishop of London's better knowledge of Cranmer's real sentiments. " The short instruction, translated from the German, and set forth by Archbishop Cranmer, in 1548, says that the Sabbath is profaned when ' we do not hear with great diligence and reverence, sermons and the most fruitful word of God, when we do not give our minds to prayer, and other godly works, but to idleness, eating, drinking, banqueting, dancing, lechery, dicing, carding, backbiting, · slandering, and other ungodly works.'"—*Letter on Lord's Day, p.* 35.

L

that the author is compelled to deny the authority of
the ten commandments—to abrogate the decalogue.[1]
For, in order to support his scheme, he thus writes
in the last citation which I shall make :—"These views,
though I cannot coincide in them, are not, it is
plain, at all at variance with what has been said in
the fifth essay. But the opinion, that Christians
are bound to the hallowing of the Lord's day, in
obedience to the fourth commandment, goes to nullify
all that I have here urged; since it implies that there
is a *part*, at least, of the Mosaic law binding on Christians ; I should say, the *whole*."[2]

And thus the Sabbath, the fourth commandment,
and the decalogue of which it is a part, are virtually
abrogated and denied, by a clergyman, high in station, notwithstanding the articles, liturgy, and homilies, of his church. Thank God, these FIXED FORMULARIES remain to reproach him with his defection,
and I trust, to recover him from it. · It is the first time
that any divine of the Church of England has attempted to sweep away the ten commandments—I
hope, and believe, it will be the last.

[1] It is no reparation of this portentous doctrine, that the author allows the authority of the Sabbath as appointed by the church ; for this is adding Popery to Neologism.
[2] " Thoughts on the Sabbath." Fellowes, London, 1830.
pp. 6, 8, 10, 11, 12, 14, 16.

THE END.

LONDON:

IBOTSON AND PALMER, PRINTERS, SAVOY STREET, STRAND.

Check Out More Titles From HardPress Classics Series In this collection we are offering thousands of classic and hard to find books. This series spans a vast array of subjects – so you are bound to find something of interest to enjoy reading and learning about.

Subjects:
Architecture
Art
Biography & Autobiography
Body, Mind &Spirit
Children & Young Adult
Dramas
Education
Fiction
History
Language Arts & Disciplines
Law
Literary Collections
Music
Poetry
Psychology
Science
…and many more.

Visit us at www.hardpress.net

CPSIA information can be obtained
at www.ICGtesting.com
Printed in the USA
BVHW061336120819

555665BV00017B/2098/P